OF BROTHER SUN

Praise be to Thee, my Lord, for
   Brother Wind,
And for the air and the cloud of fair
   and all weather
Through which Thou givest susten-
   ance to Thy creatures.

Praise be, my Lord, for Sister Water,
Who is most useful, humble, precious
   and chaste.

Praise be, my Lord, for Brother Fire,
By whom Thou lightest up the night:
He is beautiful, merry, robust and strong.

Praise be, my Lord, for our sister,
   Mother Earth,
Who sustains and governs us
And brings forth diverse fruits with
   many-hued flowers and grass.

THE PEACE OF ST. FRANCIS

THE PEAC

)F ST. FRANCIS

by MARIA STICCO

Translated from the Italian by *SALVATOR ATTANASIO*

With an Introduction by *AGOSTINO GEMELLI, O.F.M.*

AWTHORN BOOKS, INC.

blishers   *New York*

FIRST EDITION, *March, 1962*

NIHIL OBSTAT

James F. Rigney, S.T.D.

Censor Librorum

IMPRIMATUR

✠ Francis Cardinal Spellman
Archbishop of New York

New York, December 1, 1961

The nihil obstat and imprimatur are official declarations that a book or pamphlet is free of doctrinal or moral error. No implication is contained herein that those who have granted the nihil obstat and imprimatur agree with the contents, opinions or statements expressed.

CONTENTS

ILLUSTRATIONS

INTRODUCTION

THERE ARE MANY ways of writing the life of a saint and of presenting it.

There is the way of the historian who immerses himself in the study of documents. After completing a minute examination of the sources, he reconstructs the figure of the saint in the framework of the age to which he belonged. Undoubtedly this method has the advantage of giving the presentation of the saint a vividness which derives from contact with the reality of facts.

There is the way of the man of letters who gathers certain aspects and themes in the life of the saint and ties them together with the particular esthetic vividness which the writer, if he is an artist, has of the man and his work. This method has the advantage of making the saint be loved and known by many who find it difficult to accept saints, because to them the paths of sanctity seem too common or too exceptional.

And there is also the pious writer whose concern is to make of the saint's life a model to be imitated. His aim is to set more than a life before the reader, namely a manual of sanctity. Books of this kind undoubtedly are useful as a nourishing food for many souls to whom they afford comfort and assistance in the spiritual life.

Numerous lives of St. Francis fall into each of these three fundamental categories. But then there are others which do not fit any of these categories. In fact there are writers who have fashioned a St. Francis according to their own views, sometimes odd, and they have presented the saint as the true and ancient St. Francis newly discovered.

Thus there are lives of St. Francis for all tastes and some of them are good and useful.

It cannot really be said that this book by Maria Sticco fills the usual gap, but it has its characteristic feature: it teaches us to love in the Saint of Assisi the Franciscan conception of life.

In fact among the many books that speak of St. Francis this book, in my view, draws the features of the saint with greater fidelity. I am not saying that it is the best life of St. Francis; but I do say that it is the book which satisfies religious souls. It is a book which draws one to it because it is a life of St. Francis written by a soul who not only loves the saint, but who translates his teaching of the supernatural life into our life of everyday.

This has been the author's intention. From the episode, studied directly at the sources, she tries through meditation to arrive at such a penetration of the supernaturalness of St. Francis as to succeed in grasping his personality in an intimate fusion of its human and supernatural elements. Thereby to present him in a way so vivid and fresh as to arouse in the reader an immediate understanding of the significance of the saint's activity. In my view the author has completely succeeded in realizing her intention, an intention rendered arduous by the fact that while dealing with the episode she did not intend to halt at the episode itself, but to induce the reader spontaneously to find the echo of the eternal problems of the conscience therein, so that he might feel himself moved to re-live the highest forms of Christian life in meditation. Thus this book presents two aspects: it is profoundly religious, but it is also frankly artistic. And I think I am not in error to conclude that this essay represents a highly successful fusion of the religious element and the artistic element, thanks to which it becomes possible for literature to exercise a religious influence. The artistic expression does not suffocate the supernatural, but sets it in relief, so that it may become an efficacious instrument of religious education.

AGOSTINO GEMELLI, O.F.M.

THE PEACE OF ST. FRANCIS

I

the historical setting

SEVEN CENTURIES AGO there was no longer a Holy Roman Empire: there was a Holy Roman Emperor, but he was not always holy because the Pope frequently excommunicated him; nor was he Roman, because he was of German birth and background. But it was from Rome that he took his imperial right, law and insignia. This insignia, the eagle that had guided the Roman legions to the edges of the world, recalled such greatness that it seemed to be a bird of God, for the Germans as well as the Italians, although the latter had felt its claws.

The Holy Roman Emperor, Frederick Barbarossa of the house of Hohenstaufen, came from a remote castle in northern Swabia. He was of fair complexion, like most Germans, with curly red hair, and a happy face that seemed always ready to laugh, revealing a set of flashing white teeth. Frederick also had very beautiful hands, but his heart was as hard as steel.

In a little more than thirty years, from 1154 to 1185, Frederick Barbarossa descended on Italy six times to subjugate rebellious territories. The first time he burned three castles near Milan: Rosate, Trecate and Galliate. Then he put Chieri and Asti to the torch, and seized Tortona. The second time he assaulted Brescia, sacked Cremona, and laid siege to Milan for a whole year. He reduced the city to starvation, conquered it and razed it to the ground in six days, showing no mercy to its

11

citizens. The defeated Milanese, ranging from those of the noblest lineage to those of humblest origin, went in penitential procession to his camp at Lodi. They wore sackcloth, the ropes of which were tied around their necks; carried crucifixes, and their heads were sprinkled with ashes. Prostrating themselves before him, they surrendered the keys of the city, and spread the thirty-six standards of the commune at the emperor's feet. They even folded up the banner of the *Carroccio*, the ceremonial vehicle of church and commune, as an act of total submission. But the emperor gazed at it all, unyielding. At his orders, the three hundred towers of the city walls came crashing down and all that remained of the once beautiful and powerful city was a field of ruins.

On his third descent on Italy, Frederick tried to wage a war against the league of Verona, Vicenza, Padua and Treviso, but he did not prosecute it. The fourth time, he contented himself with the capture of Ancona. The fifth time he was overwhelmingly defeated at Legnano by the Lombard League. So overwhelming was this defeat that he himself was believed dead. When he appeared in Pavia, a few days later, he looked like a corpse risen from the grave. The Lombards had taught him a lesson. For the sixth time he entered Italy, it was only to attend a wedding. His son Henry was getting married in Milan to Constance d'Altavilla, the last female descendant of the Normans. And as a dowry she was bringing him the right of inheritance to the Sicilian throne.

Hard-hearted Frederick Barbarossa of necessity was an enemy of the freedom of the Italian communes. But the Italians respected him because of their love of the eagle. Not only were there some who celebrated his feats in hexameters, but the most renowned jurists of Bologna, summoned to the Diet of Roncaglia to study the legitimacy of his claims, pronounced a decision supporting them. He was the heir of the Caesars, so read their decision; he was the representative of the universal Roman Empire. Therefore his rights were inseparable from those of the empire. When, after he had left for the Third Crusade in 1188, it was learned that he had died like a tramp while bathing in a stream in Cilicia, a feeling of discouragement gripped the people, as if the inglorious end of such a great emperor presaged misfortunes for the West.

Five years before, while festivities were being prepared in Milan for the wedding of his son Henry to Constance of the Normans, the people had protested that the Antichrist would be born from such a marriage. The bridegroom was only twenty and of fierce disposition, and his bride was fifty. She was forcibly taken from the convent where she had been living, and, for political reasons, much against her will and against all the canons of decorum, was being forced to marry the emperor's son, the second one to come from Swabia, or Swavia as it was then called. But Henry VII, the husband, passed on like the wind, leaving behind a child who was named Frederick, after his grandfather, and who became the ward of the Pope.

This child, Frederick II, was born in Jesi, Italy, near Ravenna, and educated in Italy. He heard the vulgar tongue of the Marches and the Umbria regions before he ever heard a word of German. And he probably studied the Latin of the jurists and the glossarists; the French brought by the Normans to his mother's beautiful island, sung with such grace by the ancient troubadors; the Arabic of the Moslem savants in Palermo, and that Italian spoken by the common people which the poets were just beginning to celebrate in song at his court, much more than he ever studied German. He studied every-thing and interested himself in everything with the agile acumen of the Italian mind. He studied the physical sciences, then regarded as witchcraft, and philosophy. And, with the Arab thinkers of his court, he discussed the origin of the world, its Creator and the reason for its creation, as well as laws, hunt-ing, falconry, poetry, politics and the art of war.

His grandfather had come to Italy almost exclusively to fight, and had never ventured beyond Rome. Frederick II established himself in southern Italy and made Palermo and his castles in Puglia into royal residences. He was a noble emperor in every sense of the word, a model of courtesy in speech and manners, a keen judge of men of ability. Thus, people from all over the world came to his court, resplendent with genius, wealth, and the elegance of East and West: musicians, troubadors, artists, jousters, scientists. All men who had a record of extraordinary achievement in the arts and sciences were made welcome. And Frederick II rewarded them.

Seemingly, a Roman eagle, he was really a German eagle in everything. In philosophy, he cut himself off from the Latin tradition to follow the theories of the Arabs and of those who believed that the soul dies with the body. In politics, he fought against the freedom of the Italian communes, as his forebears had. He too waged wars of subjection in the Po Valley, as well as elsewhere in northern and central Italy, wars from which he emerged only as the apparent victor. He promised successive Popes that he would fight in the Crusades, but he did not keep his word. Or when he did set out for the Holy Land, he neglected the main task, the conquest of the Holy Sepulchre. Therefore the Popes excommunicated him three times. He is the Antichrist! declared his enemies, thinking of his heresy, his magic, his perjuries, and his Saracen court. But those who were loyal to him loved him so stubbornly that they battered their heads against a wall when they lost his confidence. And the poets affirmed that never had there been a lord more worthy of honor.

THE EAGLETS

The imperial German eagle was now Roman in name only, whereas the communes, in the process of breaking away from the feudal order, bore a heritage of Roman thought and lineage. Associations of citizens had gradually sprung up in those localities where the emperor had distributed his vassals as governors in the ninth century. The members of these associations pledged themselves to mutual assistance to safeguard their interests, to buy the lands belonging to the courts and barons, and to wrest as many liberties as they could for themselves, i.e., exemption from taxes and other public burdens. These civil associations became political bodies when they began to govern themselves with their own magistrates, called consuls. The communes had come into existence especially in northern and central Italy, differing in their origins and structure with each region. No two of them had originated and developed in the same manner. Some small communes held their parliaments on the church grounds with ploughmen as consuls, and pastors as teachers, chief judicial officers and peacemakers. The feudal lord of another commune might be a bishop—hence a man without family hereditary ambition and with a spirit more Roman than German—one who found it easy to side with the people, and free himself and his flock from subjection to imperial rule. Some communes were born of the struggle between big and little vassals. Others arose through the authority of a single family, or a group of powerful families, who organized the adjoining populations into a centralized administrative unit; and still others through the union of several villages for agricultural or commercial reasons. Some rose rapidly through the necessity of defending themselves against a foe, others grew as slowly as the incrustations on coral reefs, and some started with everything new, new laws and new magistrates. Still others assimilated and transformed the old institutions in such a way that the stewards or the barons, and other public officials were no longer agents of the emperor, but of the people. There were rich communes and poor communes, active and enterprising communes, like the maritime republics of Amalfi, Pisa, Genoa, Venice, as well as communes slumbering on a hilltop, or on the bank of a stream, between the belfry of the parish and the tower of the house of the consul, practically unchanged for centuries. A few communes were cultural centers, with traditions of scholarship to arouse the envy of capitals like Bologna, Pavia, Florence and Naples. And there were communes sunk in illiteracy where the pastor was the only person who could write, and where the consul signed his documents with a cross.

While elsewhere in Europe nations were being born from the disintegration of the empire, Italy seemed like a nest of eaglets which would suffer no one's foot on their necks. Nevertheless, they were not even at peace among themselves. Apart from their feeling of independence, they had nothing in common, each commune being determined to act on its own. And each commune was also self-destructive. Many communes, in fact, after driving out the nobles, who represented feudalism, and reducing them to the status of common people by forcing them to join the guilds if they wanted to enjoy civil liberties, started another struggle—between the bourgeoisie and the plebeians, the rich and the poor. Those who called upon the Pope for help were called Guelphs; those who appealed to the emperor were called Ghibellines. These internal struggles were further complicated by the struggles, sometimes very fierce, between commune and commune in which the eaglets gave evidence of barbarian blood in their veins. But when the barbarian eagle threatened their independence, as happened with Frederick Barbarossa and with Frederick II, they knew how to unite in the League of the Trevigian March, and in the first and second Lombard Leagues.

The communes, born of the Roman-German eagle, had the individual virtues of the German and the social virtues of the Latin. War and money, force and law, the boldness that made the knight, and the practical sense that made the merchant— these together contributed to their development. But the eaglets rejected any Germanic heritage, and recognized only the paternity of Rome as legitimate. The chronicler of the humblest commune sought gravely for its beginnings among the ancestors or contemporaries of Romulus. And the old woman weaving at her loom regaled her family with fabulous stories of Troy, Fiesole and Rome. Despite these social virtues, there was something savage about the wars, the vendettas and the factions. The barbaric blood, inoculated by eight centuries of invasions, mingled with the ancient blood of a lingering paganism, could not be transformed virtuously by the human justice of the legal codes. The power of the ancient civilization was no longer enough to tame the eaglets. The power of the new Rome was required: the Cross.

THE CROSS

Nine centuries had passed since the Cross had taken the place of the eagle in Rome to signify that a new empire had arisen. This empire would not be spread by praying, but by suffering. Nor would it be spread by eagle beaks and claws, but with love and sorrow. Rome, which had become the center of a new civilization, struggled through the centuries with a superhuman energy to demolish an old world and to create a new one—not only from the debris of classic paganism but from the virgin forces which not even the juridical wisdom of the ancients had been able to discipline. And its struggle was compounded with martyrdom.

Just as the first Christians had accepted torture and violent death to bear witness that Jesus Christ is God and that His doctrine is truth, Christians tortured themselves to eradicate the paganism rooted in the beliefs and customs of the time. They denied themselves even the legitimate satisfactions of nature. They forbade themselves beautiful things, despising the joys of life as transitory. They sought to purge life of all superstitions which peopled the sky with gods, the mountains with nymphs, the seas with ondines and sirens, the rivers with dryads, the woods with sprites and fauns. They abjured a philosophy which found the meaning of life in glory and pleasure.

The Christians also did penance to convert the barbarians, opposing the power of the spirit to that of force. The whole work of the Church of the Middle Ages tended to convert what was evil into good, what was human into the divine, and what was momentary into the eternal. The Church opposed the empire when the emperors forgot their duty as Christians and sovereigns; she disciplined the instinct of war and adventure with the spirit of chivalry, and restrained violence, using only the religious weapons of excommunication and the power exercised by the thought of eternity in a state of damnation or of grace. And to the Italian communes, fighting unitedly for the first time against the foreigner, she gave the *Carroccio* which had already become the emblem of charity. This wagon, drawn by oxen, travelled through the countryside, its bell or "Martinella" calling upon sub-vassals and tenant-farmers to bring a tenth of their harvest to the churches. Eventually it became a wagon of war with an altar, a crucifix, and the banner around which foot-soldiers gathered for the supreme defense of their town, like the ancient Jews around the holy ark. Every parish, in the day of general illiteracy, was its own school, with its own ceremonies, songs, sermons and paintings. At the same time every monastery was a library and a study-center where that intangible value, knowledge, was cultivated with respect. Outside, knowledge was often held of second or third importance.

The Church instituted works of mercy for the miseries of the body and soul. She established hospitals and lepresariums, and gave assistance to the poor, to pilgrims and orphans. But she did even more for civilization: She enlarged Europe's spiritual and territorial rule in the Orient by proclaiming the wars for the liberation of the Holy Land. The Crusades shook men, ideas, institutions, heritages and states, and, in shaking them, renewed them.

The Cross was raised above the suffering of the victors and the vanquished, of the oppressors and the oppressed, in those centuries most torn by war. The Cross was symbolized by the hilt of the sword, and was there to remind the knight of justice and pity, to cause him to mitigate the wounds, to console the agonizing. The Cross topped the belfries of the churches, as a symbol to reunite the discordant populations in an ideal of faith and in a nucleus of a fatherland. It was on the sails of ships setting out for the Holy Land to bless the Mediterranean and to make it doubly Italian in the new maritime commerce.

The Cross therefore held a dominant position between the end of the twelfth century and the beginning of the thirteenth century. Yet it was stamped more on things than in hearts. Like the eagle, it was more symbol than life. The Cross was there, but there was not yet a man crucified like our Lord. The standard was there, but there was no standard bearer. He was to come.

TEACHERS AND PUPILS

The eaglets could be most proud of their Roman blood in the cities where studies were cultivated, especially the study of law. In the thirteenth century, Salerno was distinguished for the study of medicine, Bologna and Pavia for jurisprudence, and, later, Padua for the sciences and Naples for philosophy. The "studies" originated as private, limited activities, involving only an able teacher and a group of eager students. They grew when other teachers joined the first one, and when other students joined the classes, making it necessary to engage more teachers. Thus they became *universities of studies*. Bologna had Irnerius, who taught civil law, and Gratian, who taught canon law, among its first lecturers. The Bologna doctors of jurisprudence had defended the emperor at Roncaglia out of love for the Roman eagle. But, in lavish self-praise, they also defended their institution and their city. "People come to us continually," they said. "Foreign students come, monies, and legal codes. We have so many beautiful things." And in a certain way they made the emperor pay for their ruling in his favor by requesting special privileges for Bologna to safeguard the studies.

The University of Bologna grew into a study center of international importance. Its student population eventually formed a city within the city. They were governed by their own rectors, elected from among the professors, and accountable to no civil authority in matters concerning the university and its jurisdiction.

In the twelfth century Bologna's student population rose to almost 10,000, with students from every part of Europe. They were divided into two corporations: cismontane and ultramontane, i.e., corporations of Italians and of foreigners, each having special rectors and counselors. The life of these youths was strictly regulated: they had to live in places reserved for them, a kind of boarding-school or boarding-house, and they had to wear a cape and a special kind of garment, the cut and color of which denoted the faculty to which they belonged. Further they were forbidden to make merry at night, or to leave the city without permission. They also had to pay the professors a fee, collected by two students assigned the task. Naturally the students evaded the regulations whenever they could. They dressed like other folk when it suited them. They spent their money on sprees instead of on books and fees. They filled the city with their songs, their pranks, their tumultous discussions and their even noisier squabbles.

The ultramontanes contributed a bizarre touch. They were

Germans, Hungarians, French, Poles, Bohemians. These foreign students came from distant abbeys and castles, bringing with them strange ways, formidable eating, drinking and working habits, along with a barbaric Latin and the strange accents of their native languages. And they also brought a different mentality to their studies, raising new problems and vistas in the minds of their teachers and companions, they absorbed the Roman spirit from the legal codes and the Italian glossarists. Bologna and the other university centers were frequently inundated by waves of wandering scholars and riotous students. Almost all of them were foreigners, who wandered from university to university because through misconduct they had lost the subsidy which had provided for them in their own places of study. And they lived by scrounging hospitality, books, lessons, and by amusing their companions with their practical jokes and witticisms.

The wildest of them were called goliards. They were the jongleurs of the student world. The goliards sang the praises of wine and pleasures, spoke ill of savants, the emperor, the Pope, and the world in general. They poured ridicule on holy things too, showing no respect even for the Mass. The goliards used to say that they were going to study law in Bologna, medicine in Salerno, the sciences in Paris, the devil in Toledo and good manners nowhere. The fame of a study-center was often at the mercy of their spiteful and scurrilous tongues.

In Bologna study was a serious matter. The lecturers were strict and demanding. It was said that Azzone, one of the most eminent lecturers, got sick only during school vacations so as not to lose any working time. In fact, he died during a school vacation!

These study-centers contributed to the formation of a new consciousness of the dignity of the communes and of Italy. It was in 1158, when four Bologna jurists decided in favor of the eagle against the eaglets. About a century later, however, Rolandino Dei Passeggeri, a lecturer on the notarial arts, made the following reply to Frederick II, who had furiously clamored for the return of his son, Enzo, king of Sardinia, who had been taken prisoner by the Bolognese: "If you come down, you will find us. We are not marsh reeds that bend to a breath of wind. We will fight."

Rolandino was a man of the pen, but he wrote like a man of the sword. The spirit of the communes breathed in his words. They no longer felt themselves tied to the eagle of the Caesars, much less to the germanic eagle. Instead they felt themselves eaglets of the empire of the Cross, new Romans—in short, Italians.

Long before Rolandino had written, however, someone had left a teaching to Bologna, the city of learning, not to be found in the legal codes: it was the teaching of the madness of the Cross.

THE TROUBADORS

Life was not all war, commerce, or concern with struggle, conquests, and study. Life, as always, was also song. For song is to work as dream is to duty, as hope to sorrow, as faith to death. Songs were sung in Latin or in the language of the people. The songs in Latin were sung in the churches, and those in the vulgar tongue were sung in the streets and squares, in homes as the women busied themselves with weaving and sewing, and in the shops as men worked. Brides whose husbands were away fighting in the Crusades sang of the sorrow of loved ones far away.

Young men sang serenades, ditties for May-day festivities, and gave half-serious advice in the matter of taking a wife.

The communes and the victorious parties also celebrated their feats in song to heap more ridicule on the vanquished. All these songs were composed in the vulgar tongue, no longer Latin, and not yet Italian, but in dialect. The dialects were many. Learned persons despised them for their unevenness and crudity. Cultured and worldly persons preferred Latin for scholarly studies, Provençal for poetry, and French for stories in prose, and for conversation.

Provençal was especially fashionable. It was spread by its

poets who called themselves *trovatori* (finders) because they "found" rimes, which they accompanied on the lute. They came out of that beautiful land which extends in an arc on the Mediterranean between the Pyrenees and the Alps, a land gentle in climate, dotted with vineyards, olive groves, meadows and kitchen gardens. Life was lived on a splendid scale there in the castles of the great feudal lords—a round of jousts, tournaments, poetry contests and court games, engaged in primarily for the amusement of the consort of the lord of the castle and her ladies-in-waiting. Amid the splendor and gaiety, morality and the law of God were forgotten, and the value of chivalrous love greatly weakened, and some ideas put forth by heretics, found ready acceptance. And they were spread to the ultimate ruin of Provence. The Provençals lost their freedom, which they had been unable to maintain in the framework of a sound morality, and were submitted to bloody repressions. The troubadors then took their songs, ballades, pastorales and their poetry of love and war to Italy.

Troubadors, of course, had come to Italy earlier, and they had distinguished themselves in the adventurous lives they led. Rambaldo of Vaqueiras was one of the most singular of these troubadors. He was the son of a knight of Vaqueiras, in the county of Orange, who had fallen to low estate. Rambaldo came to Italy—no one knows why—between 1185 and 1189 after winning his first spurs in "finding rimes" and in knightly combat at the court of his prince, William IV of Orange. He took to Italy his lute and fiddle, and his first years were hard. In Genoa he had an argument with a beautiful merchant woman to whom he had offered his love. He addressed her ceremoniously in his soft Provençal, but she replied rudely in Genoese, treating him like a dirty, poor and desperate jongleur. And in Lunigiana he quarreled with the Marquis Alberto Malaspina, who was also a "finder of rimes" in the language of Provençal. Rambaldo was given to sensual excesses. He knew what it meant to go hungry, and he roamed Lombardy on foot like a beggar. But his luck changed at the court of the Monferrato family. Marquis Boniface placed him under his protection. In exchange Rambaldo followed and served him faithfully in all his enterprises, including a Crusade to the Holy Land.

Rambaldo fought with the Marquis at Blacherne, at the gates of Constantinople, in Macedonia, in Epirus, and celebrated his patron's valor and his munificence in song. In return Boniface, one of the military leaders of the Fourth Crusade, bestowed great lands and revenues on the poet in the kingdom of Salonica. But the troubador, now a prince, was nostalgic for his past. Amid the beauties of ancient Greece, which had no appeal for his medieval Christian heart, among the Hellenes whom he called "griffins," he mourned the years cf his poor, adventurous and amorous youth, when he had secretly admired the sister of his lord, Beatrice of Monferrato. He wrote poetry about her as the "beautiful knight," for the young lady was as daring as a man. She went riding with a falcon perched on her wrist, and she liked to wear her brother's suit of armor. Beatrice, "the beautiful knight," died the same year that her brother and her poet admirer left for those lands beyond the seas where they were to meet glory and face death. Rambaldo never found consolation for the loss of Beatrice, nor for being so far from his native land. In Greece he sang:

"Neither winter, nor spring, nor fair weather, nor May-leaf come anymore to delight me. Adventures are as disasters, and every great pleasure but sorrow. Repose is torment, and waiting but desperation . . ."

"Of what value the conquest of wealth? I deemed myself wealthier when I was loved. At that time there I loved a greater pleasure than all my lands and possession here. The more my power grows, the more I grow angry with myself, for my so greatly loved beautiful knight—and with him joy—have fled."

Thus this troubador, who had begun as a wanderer and ended as a feudal lord, who had seen Provence, France, Italy, Constantinople, Greece, who had experienced the idyllic and the epical features of life, who had achieved all that he could desire, ended with a song of heartbroken melancholy. Thus worldly joys always end.

CHARLEMAGNE AND KING ARTHUR

By hurling the word *jongleur* at Rambaldo of Vaqueiras like an epithet, the beautiful woman of Genoa knew she was offending him. For the jongleur did not himself compose verses, he sang verses composed by others. He was a performer, not a composer, more a copyist than a writer. Nevertheless the jongleur was an important personage in his own right. He went from castle to castle with his lute or viol singing the songs of the troubadors, telling the news of war and court, recounting the curiosities of the world. The ladies in the castles, bored during the journeys and expeditions of their lords, awaited his coming with great impatience. He was also festively treated by the lords who found in the jongleur a man of wit, of surprising turns of mind, of songs, jests, and of vulgarity and poetry, an indispensable element of a social gathering and the joy of a banquet. The jongleur was never missing from the courts and the great feudal castles. If he happened to be an intelligent man, he played the rôle of a newspaper or book for those illiterate lords. And if he happened to be more shrewd than intelligent, more vulgar than cultured, he played the role of a buffoon.

Often he did not sing but read or told stories about King Arthur of Britain and his knights. They were all valiant knights of equal rank, who sat at a round table at which no one was first and no one last. And they performed wondrous deeds, defending helpless damsels, conquering lands, winning the most valuable prizes at jousts and tournaments, and breaking the magic power of sorcerers. The jongleurs told of the pure knight who set out to conquer the Holy Grail, the precious vase believed used by Christ at the Last Supper, or about Lancelot who accompanied Queen Guinevere to her kingdom, or about Tristan who suffered so much for the fair Iseulte; or about the enchantments of Merlin the Magician and of the fairy Morgana. Or about the mysterious disappearance of King Arthur who had not really died in battle, but was sleeping deep inside a grotto (perhaps in the center of smoking and snow-capped Mt. Aetna) with his enormous sword at his side, ready to hurl himself against the invading Saxons immediately the cry of revolt rang out once more.

The jongleur read or narrated these deeds of chivalry, and the barons listened near the fireplace on winter evenings, forgetting for a moment all thoughts of war. The handmaidens stopped the twirling of their spindles, and the fine ladies stopped embroidering their taffeta scarfs, lost in reverie.

The people also had their jongleurs and professional story-tellers who stopped at crossroads and public squares to celebrate the feats of Roland. In the monotonous rhythm of the long strophes they sang of how Roland, the nephew of Emperor Charlemagne, and Oliver, the flower of French knighthood, had been vanquished at Roncevaux by the Saracen army because of the betrayal of a perfidious knight, Gamelon of Margence. They sang of the desperate defense of the French, of the heroism of Roland who refused to blow his great ivory horn Oliphant, whose sound reached the ends of the world, to summon the emperor for help. And they sang of the death of his friend Oliver, and that of the Archbishop Turpin. Turpin, faithful to his sovereign as to his God, and true to the tradition that a good vassal never surrenders alive, encouraged the combatants to fight to the very end and died blessing the dead with an episcopal gesture, while his entrails and brains gushed out of his body. They sang of the death of Roland, of the belated arrival of Charlemagne who, in the light of the moon, found a field of knights, their arms folded cross-wise with their swords beside them, fixed in the earth like lilies. They sang of Alda, Roland's beautiful betrothed, who, upon hearing of the fate of her knight, fell to the ground, as though struck by lightning, without uttering a word.

When the professional story-teller sang of the feats of Roland the valiant, of Oliver the wise, of Charlemagne with the flourishing beard, and of Rinaldo da Montealbano and Ogier the Dane, boys ran to listen, their eyes wide at visions of palfreys and tournaments, war-horses and coats-of-armor, camps of armed soldiers and the glitter of halberds. The women of the people also formed a circle around him, holding babes in their arms. And at the siesta hour the woolworkers, the smiths, the tailors, the weavers, the goldsmiths from their little workshops, came to listen. They came with their frocks belted tightly at the waist, and listened, dreaming. And the wave of the epic passed over them all.

THE HERETICS

Studies, songs, stories of war and love were the most human aspects of a century which was quite ferocious in many other aspects. Nor did such enjoyments reach everybody, nor were they able to bring solace to all minds. There were some who were not content with momentary relief, and these could not forget or numb their sensibilities.

The contrast between religion and customs, between the love preached in the Gospel and the hatreds of the public square, was found to be even more intolerable when the crusades and the pilgrimages brought the men of the West to the country of Jesus. The sight of the holy places brought back to life the vividness of His example and doctrine.

From the East came a desire for religious renovation, but toward the end of the twelfth century there also came the heretical doctrines of the Cathars. The Cathars so called themselves because they claimed to be pure in thought and in their way of life. They revived the ancient heresy of the Manicheans, and certain philosophical theories of the Gnostics and Neo-Platonists. The Cathars believed that the universe derived from two opposing principles of good and evil. The principle of good created the world of the spirit and all the beautiful and pure creatures. The principle of evil created the world of matter and all sentient and terrestrial things. This antagonism of principles was reflected in every man: the soul was the good principle, the body the evil one. Between the two there was a struggle unto death. For the Cathars, however, the struggle had a limited value, for they believed that everyone followed an immutable destiny. Each, according to his star, was predestined to heaven or to hell. They also believed that a tremendous war would be unleashed between the two antithetical principles at the end of the world, between God and the Devil, Christ and the Antichrist, and that this final war was not far off.

The Cathars sought to oppose evil by living in a state of poverty like the Apostles and the first Christian communities. They did not believe in the family, property, authority, ecclesiastical hierarchy, or in the sacraments. They were opposed to the nobles, to the rich, to the clergy and to the bishops. In their secret societies, the brethren lived on a communistic basis, divided in two categories, the "humble" and the "perfect," that is, neophytes and elders. No one was admitted into the sect without a period of initiation, and the consecration took place by a laying-on of the hands. The members were linked together in secrecy as to their beliefs and practices.

These doctrines spread rapidly, especially among the poor. They were acceptable to the workers and small tradesmen because of the germ of social rebellion contained in the religious program, because of the new world which they promised, because of the mystery in which they were hidden, and because of the strength which they gathered little by little, when the great lords or the nobles, or the heads of one faction or another had recourse to the Cathars for political purposes.

The Cathars spread to all the trading centers of Europe, flourishing especially in the city slums. The names they chose for themselves were characteristic, with always an overtone of people living in a state of desperation. In Flanders they called themselves *tisserands* or weavers, in Spain *zabatai* or wearers of worn-out shoes, in Savoy *barbets,* the muddy spaniels, in the Dauphine *the poor of Lyons,* in France *bougres,* that is Bulgars, the common term for gypsies.

Northern Italy welcomed the Cathars. The first strong group settled at Monteforte near Asti. Milan became a nest of Cathars. Here they called themselves *patarini,* that is to say ragpickers, because the *pataria,* where they probably gathered, was the market for old clothes and second-hand goods. But the heretics claimed they called themselves *patarini* from the verb *pati,* to suffer, meaning they were ready to suffer for their faith.

The heretical sects sprang up and spread like weeds. In 1178 a merchant of Lyon, Pietro Valdo, presented himself to Pope

Alexander III to ask for permission to preach in the language of the people, although he was but a simple layman. The Pope granted his request. Valdo was excommunicated six years later, however, after permission had been withdrawn because his doctrines were contrary to the Church's teachings. His followers, Waldensians, as they were called, lived on alms, went around in rags and sandals, preaching to the people, finding fault with the clergy and criticizing the Church. On the other hand, the "humiliated," a brotherhood which, properly speaking, was not heretical and which had appeared in Lombardy, were under strict obligation to work, and they lived in imitation of the Apostles.

All these sects brought the ferment of disturbed and turbulent consciences into the Church and society, the subversive germ.

Viewed socially, the Cathars and all their numerous heretical offspring were the Bolsheviks of the thirteenth century. And as for their utopia of religious reform, they claimed they were making progress by walking backward in history.

THE FAITHFUL

The heretics were right when they preached against luxury and the wicked customs of the time, when with exaggerated and proud poverty they reproached the avarice of some men of the Church. For a forgetfulness of the Gospel was undeniably noticeable among many of the clergy.

There were priests who lived like secular people. They had families and business interests, they were intent on profit, and demanded payments above the tithes. Some were not ashamed to traffic in the sacraments, or to intrigue for benefices, or enter into litigation with fellow-priests over parochial rights, burials, legacies. There were clerics who, under the pretext of studying, went from one university to another without the permission of their superiors. On the way they took advantage of the hospitality that the monasteries offered to pilgrims, and in the cities they went on sprees like the most worldly of students. For more than seven-hundred years the Church boasted that the order of St. Benedict was among her firmest pillars. This order had helped her to convert the pagans, to tame the barbarians, to Christianize the ancient civilization, and to re-colonize the devastated and deserted countrysides. With its spirit of prayer and work the Benedictine Order had imprinted the Roman sense of balance on monasticism and the religiosity of the West. And with its spirit of discretion and hospitality it had known how to unite Latins and Germans in Christ. But now the great Benedictine abbeys, formerly complete cultural and agricultural centers, governed by a paternalistic legislation —the first to be compiled in the Middle Ages amid the oblivion of all written laws—in many places could not be distinguished from the feudal castles except for a more refined opulence. The sceptered and mitred abbots bore princely titles. Often they lived with the pomp and vices of the princes, imitating their arbitrary acts of power. The Popes were often forced to recall them to the simplicity of the Rule, of dress, of eating, conti-nence, and mildness toward dependents. Or the pontiffs had to intervene in the struggles between castles and monasteries, or between the monasteries themselves, none of which resigned themselves to being subject to another, or to being surpassed. And the monks' peasants suffered, whereas at one time they had been considered the privileged among the serfs.

But the Benedictine influence did not diminish only because of monastic corruption. There was another reason of a political-social nature. Created at the beginning of the sixth century to preserve the spirit of the Christian *domus* and the order of the municipality in the conflict between Roman classicism and barbarism, gaining strength under feudalism and opposing the ignorance, violence, and crudities of the castles with Greco-Latin humanism, the Benedictine abbeys expressed the work of Catholicism in a society based on great landed property. But gradually the Benedictines themselves had taken over the spirit and the forms of that society which they had converted. But the interlude of feudalism, which had been of foreign importa-tion, now came to an end in thirteenth-century Italy. Society was no longer divided into two distinct classes, lords and serfs. There was now the populace of the commune. Just as the castles were being dismantled and their towers lopped off, so were the monasteries being isolated and the monks becoming strangers to the new artisan, trading and banking society. What was bound to happen in the Church was like what happened later in the field of military tactics: a mobile, echeloned, light militia took the place of the Benedictine territorial troops.

Because of the sanctity of their founder, because of the flexible wisdom of their Rule, because of the infallible assistance of grace which infuses a perpetual historical actuality in the Church, the Benedictines might have become the vanguard of the new infantry. In many countries they did. But this did not happen in Italy, because many abbeys had lost the spirit of St. Benedict. Some abbots were not even monks but lay princes who had taken on the title in order to enjoy the revenues.

Above all, the urgent need in the clergy was for a return to the evangelical spirit. The term cleric was a synonym for a literary man. But there was nothing Christian about the writings of many clerics. For example, a Latin elegy dealing with the fickleness of fortune and the consolations of philosophy was composed at the end of the twelfth century by Arrigo da Settinello, a rector of Calenzano, near Prado. Seemingly he had suffered a dreadful humiliation, perhaps unjustly, at the hands of the Bishop of Florence. He sought the most subtle arguments of Stoic philosophy in order to free himself from this sorrow which made him rave night and day. Not once did he, a priest, give a thought to the philosophy of the Crucified. A humanist before the name had been coined, he had a greater feeling for literature than for faith, a greater love for the classics than for God. When the best elements of the clergy separated themselves from the thought of Jesus Christ, they also separated themselves from the people. A reform among the faithful was needed, and a return to the Gospel was needed in the life and the preaching of the men consecrated to God.

THE ANTICHRIST

Many, seeing so many wars, so much destruction, persecution, the sad end of the Crusades and the wickedness rampant among the people, thought that the end of the world was near. They believed the Antichrist would be born overnight, a kind of devil in human form who would deceive men with false miracles and false promises in order to drag them to perdition before the Last Judgment.

At the beginning of the thirteenth century there was an old warrior who, repenting his life as a youth which had been employed too often in the battles of men, wrote a little poem in monorhymes. The Antichrist, according to the poem, which is the most ancient one in Italian literature, will be born and grow up in Bethesda. He will live hidden for thirty years. Then he will begin to make himself known with sensational miracles which will induce the belief that the Lord Jesus Christ has returned to the world. But, in truth, they will all be diabolical enchantments: the waves of the seas will break out of their beds, rivers will flow backwards, fire will rain from the sky, the dead will rise from the graves and the terrified people will cry out, "O God Who created us, have pity on us! Help us for we are lost!"

Then the Pope is to gather all the princes of the earth, the King of France, the King of Italy, and bishop, abbots, dukes, marquis and counts of every region in a general assembly in Rome. To it the Antichrist will send his ambassador, named Nero, with 6300 false sorcerers, and tents and draperies in a great encampment. Trumpets will blare and the ambassador of the Antichrist, coming forward in the parliament, will say:

"Hear ye, good people, hear ye and listen! The time has come when the Antichrist must rule over the earth. He sends you greetings, happiness and peace, a thousand pounds of gold, and many other gifts, on the condition, however, that churches, altars, oratories all be destroyed, dispersed, desecrated and that no one any more make the sign of the Cross or adore the Cross. And on condition that Mass never be celebrated again."

All present will be terrified at these infernal proposals, realizing the trap that has been set for them. The Holy Pope will bless the war against the Antichrist, entrusting its command to the King of Italy.

"Rise, barons, raise high the standards, join the fray with the blessing of God. Cut off the heads of those wicked enchanters!"

And the King of Italy will say:

"Barons, listen for the sake of omnipotent God! The ages are disturbed, the times are ended! The end of the world is near! Barons, fight the last battle like brave men. May your sharp swords strike such blows as will be praised forever!"

The Christian army will fight overseas, in the Holy Land where the Antichrist is living. And the King of Italy will join battle with 11,000 knights and banners flying, and 300,000 armed men singing the *Pater Noster* and the litanies. But arms are powerless against magic. A star will fall from heaven piercing the earth, from the hole will issue terrifying man-eating dragons, until the poor King of Italy, in spite of the encouragement of the Pope, will believe himself to be born under an unlucky star and admit defeat, presenting himself to the court of the Antichrist, shouting:

"I renounce the throne; you are the Roman king!"

And the Antichrist will reply:

"Good sire, King of Italy, you are powerful, the center of the world is in your hands because you have Rome, the great. You accuse me wrongly, you do not know the truth about me. I raise up the dead, heal the infirm, feed the poor, clothe the naked, and will give gold, silver, and fine silks to those who adore me. He who does not want to adore me will lose his head. But I will say naught of evil to you, Roman sire. You have permission to do as you please."

The King of Italy will be driven to desperation by the false goodness of the Antichrist. After having prayed over the Holy Sepulchre he will renounce his kingdom and return the banner to the Pope. He will kiss the ground, he will make the sign of the Cross, and will shout so loud as to make blood stream from his eyes:

"God, help us, Thou! We are Thy servants. If Thou helpest us not, we are lost!"

Then the Lord will send the two prophets of the Old Testament, Enoch and Elias, to Jerusalem. They will fight the Antichrist with preaching, but they will end as martyrs under the blows of his persecution. The Antichrist, swollen with pride, will want to ascend to heaven with a new enchantment. But God, wrathful, will send Michael the Archangel to strike him down like lightning. And one hundred thousand devils will carry his body to hell together with his soul, damned, for all eternity.

Once the Antichrist is no more, Enoch and Elias will rise from the dead. And after forty days of calm in which the good people will have time to purify themselves, the end of the world and the Last Judgment will really come.

The author of this poem was called Uguccione da Lodi. He was a native of Cremona, a soldier and a man of a subtle religious conscience. In fact one can also say he was a man of a precocious national consciousness, if in his poem he gave the heroic role of fighting the last battle against evil to a King of Italy which nobody at that time believed possible. In the fantastic vision of the end of the world he fused the memories of his youth, the meditations of his old age, with the military realities and the religious terrors of his time. But understandably enough, the faith of an age oppressed by the nightmare of the Antichrist could not be a serene one.

DE PROFUNDIS

The higher one climbs the better one sees. Among the men who saw the evils of their time more deeply because of the height of their genius and office there was one called Lothair, of the family of the courts of Legri. Later he was to become a Pope, and a great Pope: Innocent III. Lothair was born in Anagni in 1160 of a patrician family, and had studied jurisprudence in Bologna and theology in Paris. He was nominated cardinal at thirty, and then voluntarily retired to the solitude of his castle of Anagni for seven years, until he was elected Pope after the death of Celestine III. Life had rapidly brought him to the greatest honor after having given him uncommon gifts of talent, nobility, wealth. Yet Innocent III suffered as did few men, because he perceived all human misery in the sadness of the times.

If not over himself, he certainly was right to be distressed over the state of Christendom. In all Italy, and particularly in the lands dependent on Rome, he saw a struggle rage between the mighty families and the people, between the feudal lords and the communes. He saw the German domination re-assert itself in many towns which, after the victory of the first Lombard League, should have governed themselves freely. He saw the rights of his ward, little Frederick II, threatened by Otto of Brunswick, and in southern Italy by a Marcovaldo, a very cruel German prince who preyed upon, set ablaze and laid waste the Molise and the Sannio, enrolling the Saracens in his arms, thereby uniting Teutonic barbarism with the Moslem. Beyond the borders of Italy he saw the acts of violence and the arbitrary abuses of authority of Philip Augustus in France and of John Lackland in England. He saw Provence shaken with the Albigensian heresy. He saw the Holy Land dominated by the Moslems, despite the Crusades which no longer achieved their true purpose. And in all Europe, and also in Italy, around Rome, under his very eyes, he saw the cities and countryside made desolate by war, famine, and misery; nobles reduced to beggary, those of humble birth reduced to hunger, sick people abandoned on the streets, and newly born babies drowned in the Tiber, where the boatmen fished out the naked corpses with their nets.

While helping in the distribution of food to the poor, and in erecting a hospital (the still beautiful one of Santo Spirito), and protecting foundlings, Innocent III in his heart suffered the weight of all the human sorrow, and almost felt disgust with life itself. He expressed both feelings in a little work, written at Anagni before his election as pontiff, entitled "On Contempt for the World."

Nobody has painted the human condition in blacker colors. Innocent III scrutinized the misery of human nature, the weakness of the flesh from birth to death. He described sickness, fragile and fleeting youth, with a pitiless realism. He observed the sorrow that strikes at every age and every class, the married and the celibate, the learned and the ignorant, the good and the bad. He smiled over the vain toil of men on works that last but a day, like children's toys, and he analyzed human passions:

pride and anger, the fever for gold and the fever for pleasure, gluttony for applause and power, gluttony for refinements and luxury. Finally he immersed himself in contemplation of death. Such a tumult of desires, of passions, of sorrows! So much adoration of the senses only for the body to end in a tomb with worms and ashes, and the soul to end in a frightening eternity, if it is not a blessed one. After original sin something happened to human nature. To Innocent III man seemed to be an inverted tree: His hair is the roots, his head and neck form the base, the chest and stomach the trunk, the ulna and the tibia the branches. What will be the end of these guilty plants? His meditation on death, the judgment, hell and heaven concludes a work which seems to summarize the most tragic aspect of medieval thought.

But the author of "On Contempt for the World" seems also to have been the author of the very beautiful hymn to the Holy Spirit which the Church sings on the nine days following Pentecost:

> Come, Holy Spirit . . . Come and shine
> On our souls with beam divine,
> Come O Father of the poor,
> Come consoler, kindest, best,
> Come our bosom's dearest guest,
> Sweet refreshment. But for you blest Deity
> Nothing pure in man can be,
> Nothing harmless, nothing good.
> Wash away each sinful stain,
> Gently shed your gracious rain.

It is all aspiration and hope, it is the hymn of the distressed who break out of their own *I*, in order to be absorbed by the Spirit. Thus while the man foundered in the contemplation of our misery, the Pontiff, inspired by God, invoked the Consoler and looked toward the East.

THE PROPHET OF SILA

Innocent III was not the only one to look toward the East. Four years after his election as Pope, a Cistercian monk died in Calabria. He had written about and predicted the coming of a new age that would transform the world. He was called Joachim of Fiore and he was born between 1130 and 1145 in Celico, near Cosenza. Some say he was of peasant stock, others that he descended from a lordly family who supposedly made it possible for him to study and travel. He visited Greece and Palestine. Taken sick in the Holy Land, he recovered and spent forty days of penance and contemplation in a cave on Mt. Tabor. On his return to Italy he sought solitude, living hidden in the woody hills of Calabria, wholly immersed in contemplative thoughts, until he became a monk in the Cistercian monastery of Sambucina, a territory of Bisignano, devoted entirely to the study of Scripture and to outdoor preaching. He was elected Abbot of Corazzo, near Catanzaro, because of his austere and studious way of life. But the active and administrative life of a superior of a monastery was not for him. He escaped, and found a hiding place on the highest and most woody crag of Calabria, where he gave himself entirely to the study of sacred books. But no matter how much he wished for solitude, his faithful managed to find him. So he founded his own congregation, which bore his name.

Joachim was a man of reverie more than a man of prayer and seemed to gather in himself all currents of thought irrigating the Calabrian-Sicilian land: something of the philosophical asceticism of Magna Grecea, something of the Nordic fantasies which had infiltrated with the Normans, and something of the oriental fatalism which had infiltrated with the Arabs. Abbot Joachim dreamed that the history of the world was divided into three epochs, corresponding to the three persons of the Blessed Trinity. The first epoch, already passed, corresponds to the Old Testament and was distinguished by the government of the Father. The second corresponds to the New Testament, to the redemption through the merits of the Son, to the institution of the Church and of the sacraments. This, he felt, would come to an end in 1260. The third, beginning from that year, would be the epoch of the Holy Ghost and of men wholly spiritual who would develop the ideas of the Gospel in a perfect and eternal way.

Abbot Joachim distinguished the three epochs with arresting images. The first epoch, he said, was that of the patriarchs, of the kings, of the married; the second that of the priests; the third would be that of the monks. The first was the epoch of servile obedience; the second, of filial servitude; the third would be that of freedom. The first was that of slaves; the second, of sons; the third, of the friends of God. The first was that of fear; the second, of faith; the third, of love. He also compared the first age to winter, to the stars, to nettles; the second to spring, to dawn, to roses; and the third to summer, to day and to lilies. And with these ideas he commented on the Gospel and the Apocalypse. His sermons and his books spread rapidly and found favor with worldly people and heretics because (without deliberate bad intention) they demolished the sacerdotal church and exalted monasticism. They were liked because of that promise of a new era which greatly attracted the superstitious masses who were starved for mystery. Prophecies were attributed to him that Abbot Joachim never uttered. Many revered him as a saint, the Church condemned him. Apart from the theological errors on the Trinity, however, and the fantastic construction of the three epochs, the voice of this solitary, which echoed continuously from the beginning of the thirteenth century up to the Renaissance, did sound like the song of a new dawn.

THE EXPECTATION

Thus a certain sense of expectation had spread through Italy between the end of the twelfth century and the beginning of the thirteenth. Uguccione da Lodi waited for the Antichrist and the end of the world. Innocent III invoked the Holy Ghost with a lofty faith. Joachim of Fiore looked forward to the time of the pure. Three men, three voices, three regions. The voice of the North, austere and fearful; the voice of the South, dreaming and ardent; the voice of the heart of Italy and of the world, the voice of Rome, divine. Innocent III who, in his double shout of desolation and invocation, summarized the Middle Ages and announced a new age within a few years, Innocent

III who seemed to close the period of demolition and expiation of Christianity to open that of construction and liberation, was to see before him a man, miserable in outer appearance, but of such inner greatness as to make him believe that once in a long while the inverted plant of humanity is born right, with its true roots in the earth and its leaves in the sky.

And this man was to be St. Francis of Assisi.

2

BETWEEN
THE WORLD AND GOD

IN THE INNERMOST heart of the Italian peninsula, so withdrawn in the interior that no sea touches any part of it, lies Umbria. A traveller, coming upon it from Perugia on a morning in May, enjoys a view of the Spoletan plain, and the wooded ridge of Mount Malbe the hills covered with fresh green, and thinks to himself: verdant Umbria. But a traveller looking down from the region of Gubbio, Nocera, Norcia, or Gualdo, sees chains of rocky mountains, barren peaks and bare stony ridges, cloudy at midday, purple or emerald green at sunset, and iron grey in storms. The traveller who sees the rugged, steppe-like hills with a small bell-tower and a cypress tree perched on a peak, the traveller who sees its meandering torrents, in whose beds the pebbles gleam with the whiteness of skulls, thinks: This is a land of passion and torment.

But the traveller who, from Montefalco or Todi, gazes upon the solemnity of its hills sloping in a circle, and understands the ineffable word of peace they whisper to the most tortured soul; the traveller who from Assisi, Città di Pieve, from Perugia itself discovers those horizons surrounded by mountains which nevertheless are as vast and as blue as the sea; the traveller who rediscovers the desire to pray on the deserted banks of the Trasimeno, whose silence encloses the tumult of bygone wars, or before the crystalline Clitumnus thinks to himself: holy Umbria.

In Umbria nature presents such contrasts of extreme gentleness and harshness, of the holy and the savage. History, like nature, presents the same story. From here came the greatest founders of the Western monastic orders, St. Benedict and St. Francis; from here came the most famous condottieri, professional adventurers, Braccio Fortebraccio, Niccolò Piccinino, Gattamelata; and from here also came illustrious jurists, like Baldo degli Ubaldi who was the glory of Perugian scholarship. The spirit of the former inhabitants of the region seemed to rise again in these diverse figures emerging from the centuries, impressing their civilization on them after millennia: the Umbrians with their dreadful duels, the hieratic Etruscans with their absorption in the mystery of eternity, the Romans with their mastery of law. As the centuries passed, warriors, priests, magistrates, men of arms, men of the Church, jurists, arose from this ethnic substratum and though they were in seeming contrast to one another, they still are well united in the discordant harmony of life. For holiness is militant, militancy is discipline, discipline is justice.

Umbria's saints, who by their very perfection summarized the genius of the race by sublimating it, were men of action rather than of study; men who loved, prayed, worked, praised the Lord and sacrificed themselves for their fellow men with military valor. But at the same time they were not warrior saints, they did not go into battle with armies, they did not live by action alone, nor did they live by contemplation alone. They did not aspire only to penance, just as they did not aspire only to ecstasy. With few exceptions they possessed the Roman virtue of measure, the Italian genius for harmony, and reconciled conflicts and victories in great serenity. It is that serenity that smiles on the most beautiful horizon of the Umbrian land, that serenity which all seek in a somewhat conventional way when they think about Umbria. But to avoid the commonplace, one must understand this so highly praised serenity.

It is the serenity of the olive tree.

The olive is the tree of Umbria. Grey-green olive trees engirdle the hills like necklaces, descending as far as the lake, from where they clamber up the mountains as high as they can go until they are repelled by the cold; content with little earth, they entwine their roots around the rocks. At these heights the olive trees are small, rent and splintered, hollowed out after a long resistance to the diseases of a too rigid climate. Here they are no longer trunks but perforated, knotty, twisted barks which at night look like tortured souls raising their arms to the stars. They spread a veil of melancholy over the landscape, yet yield the richness of an oil as flavorful as butter, and as yellow as the sun. If the dominant note of Umbria is peace, this peace is born of martyrdom. Like the olive tree.

ASSISI

Umbria has its pearl: Assisi. From a distance, Assisi is a handful of houses perched on the western slope of the Subasio that can be seen from the Spoletan valley, one half green, the other half bare and rugged. Viewed from nearby, the small town with its few long and level streets extends parallel to the mountains and then rises on the slope with many small steep streets, with steps and turns, winding between the houses which, in order to adjust as best they can to the grade, consist of three or four storeys on one side, and of only a door and a roof on the other. Anyone who passes through these streets will never forget them. Narrow, irregular, deserted, wherein lies their beauty? The houses are huddled close together and different in appearance: one is made of blackened limestone, another of that rose-and-ivory-colored stone found in the Subasio; another is unplastered, and one is low, another higher, and one has its tower lopped off. In some places they rise as iron-studded structures, heavily buttressed, connected with deeply shadowed large and small vaults, as if barricading themselves: fortresses. In other places they are smooth and secluded, with the occasional little windows doubly barred or with closed shutters like nuns with downcast eyes: convents. The passing centuries have touched and retouched them according to different tastes, and the doors and windows have preserved the marks: inside an ogival arch, with its beautiful rayed stones, are the traces of a Renaissance arch, and inside the arch is a modern squaring.

These houses are not like the big buildings of today. No automobile can pass through these streets. But on days when the weather is fair the turquoise-colored sky thickens darkly over them. This turquoise and a bit of the landscape, suddenly framed in an arch, and the old-fashioned geraniums at the windows, weave the spell exerted by these streets. Now and then a cypress rising above the garden wall, an olive or a fig-tree peering out from between two houses, a fountain murmuring in the silence, reminds one of the Orient. But there is a kind of watchfulness, absorption and pensiveness here that is not of the Orient. These streets are more than clean, they are pure, ingenuously more primitive than they are classically old. Their poverty is nobility, their silence is prayer. It is not the Orient but mystic Italy that keeps vigil here.

The whole surrounding countryside counsels prayer. Behind Assisi the Subasio rounds off in a great rocky ridge, which juts out in a wild, uncultivated valley carved out by the winding of the Tescio. It is a valley in which to meditate on the Last Judgment. Before it spreads the cultivated plain with its isolated plots of green and brown. Mountain upon mountain dot the horizon as far as the eye can see, four or five undulating chains that change from deep blue to purple according to the time of day. They make us feel no humiliation over our insignificance, as high mountains do, because they are far away. And because they are beautiful they arouse the desire to escape from this insignificance. These mountains say: One must climb! The sky overhead says: One must be pure! And mountain and sky promise a beauty infinitely greater than the one that is seen. And they engender such a passionate desire for it that one cannot help shouting the cry of the heart: "My God!"

THE HEARTH

Assisi was an eaglet hatched by the German eagle. In 1160 Frederick Barbarossa awarded it a diploma of defense against the oppressive feudal lords, but only to bind it more closely to himself than in 1117 when he gave it to a faithful follower,

Duke Conrad of Lutzem. But the eaglet, which guarded over the whole framework of ancient and new Rome from the pagan temple of Minerva to the Christian temple of San Rufino, soon broke out of the imperial shell. It dislodged the Ghibelline nobles from their castles and sought to live in freedom and independence.

Two purely Latin forces helped it to achieve liberation: the faith of its bishop and the money of its merchants. Its development was a typical case of the embryology of the commune. Toward the end of the twelfth century, in the very center of Assisi, near the Piazza del Popolo, where the old temple of Minerva still lifts its Corinthian porch, stood the house of a cloth merchant, Pietro Bernardone. It was a beautiful, comfortable, three-story house, with iron rings for tieing up horses, hinges for window bars, and four big doors with ogival arches leading to the warehouse and the shop. It also had a narrow entrance door, raised from the street, that was reached by means of a ladder, like a drawbridge. This was a necessary precaution in those days of civil warfare.

Messer Pietro Bernardone imported bales of uncut woolen cloth from France for carding, sheaving and cutting. At that time this was flourishing Italian industry. On one occasion he brought not only money and bales of cloth from France but also a wife, whose given name was Pica. She was of noble birth, and as delicate and gentle as the husband was hard, avid and violent. On one of Messer Pietro's business trips, Madonna Pica gave birth to a child whom she baptized Giovanni. But when the father returned he changed the child's name. Either out of gratitude to France where he had found riches, or out of eccentricity peculiar to upstarts, or just to contradict his wife, he named the boy Francis, Francesco, in Italian, a name rather rare in those days.

Francis grew up with a sincere and generous character, tenderly loved by his family, although sometimes they scolded him for a habit of giving away everything he had.

"We shall make a sharp merchant out of him!" said Messer Pietro, who could not wait to have an assistant in his business.

"We shall make a valiant knight of him, a soul of God," thought Donna Pica, secretly dreaming of the gardens and the chivalry of her native country.

From his father, Francis learned all the tricks and risks of trade; from his mother, the prayers of the faith, the songs of the troubadors, the tales of King Arthur and his knights; and from the priests, who were the school teachers at San Giorgio, he learned Latin and the abacus. But often he fled from the Latin, the warehouse, and the gentle words of his mother to run over to the square and listen to a jongleur sing the story of Roland the brave and Oliver the wise, or to watch the Swabian knights ride by. They were the guests of Conrad of Lutzem, who held the fortress in the name of the empire. Francis was excited by the sight of the knights riding in their shining armor with the silver eagle on the crest. "I too shall be a knight," he thought, his black eyes looking steadfastly into the distance like the eagles.

THE JOY OF LIFE

At twenty Francis found himself wealthy and almost free of tutelage. Educated by his father, he was as successful in business as his parent, not so much because of business shrewdness but because he knew how to handle his customers with a grace not at all related to merchandising. He had the gift of attractiveness. Whoever spoke to him had to do as he wished. And he was not stingy like his father. If Signor Pietro worked to accumulate money, Francis worked to spend it. From his mother he had inherited gentleness of heart and manners, the taste for beautiful things, the passion for music, for poetry, for a splendid and gay life. He was elegant to the point of being bizarre, generous to the point of dissipation. Using the most precious cloth from his father's stock he had garments made in the latest French fashion. And all the money that he earned or his parents generously furnished him he spent for dinners, riding parties, games and feasts with friends. For besides his gentlemanly refinement Francis had this special quality: a delicate and ardent feeling for friendship, the need to share his goods and happiness with others, to amuse himself and to amuse others, to enjoy himself and cause others to enjoy themselves with great lavishness. He was so fond of his friends that he often rose from the table before the meal was over and ran off with them, leaving his parents grumbling. But at heart they were not displeased with him, even when he indulged in eccentricities.

"Messer Pietro," said his father's neighbors, "did you know that your son's garment is of very bad cloth on one side and of very precious material on the other?"

"Oh foolish boy!" grumbled the father. But as an ambitious merchant who suffered when the noblemen of Assisi looked down their noses at him, he enjoyed seeing his son prominent at feasts, knowing that he had acquired the fame of being the *Flower of Youths.*

"Listen, Madonna Pica!" her friends informed her with great concern, "Francis is a spendthrift. He will ruin you!"

But the mother replied calmly, "You worry what will become of my son? You will see that he will be a son of God."

A mother's heart can foresee the future.

All Assisi loved the joyous, splendid youth. There was a poor man, half-crazed, who, whenever he saw Francis coming, rushed to place his mantle on the street before him, crying, "Peace and good things!" And the *Flower of Youths* passed by laughing, but in his heart he was also sure of the greatness to come.

VALOR AND COURTESY

Francis was always cheerful, never coarse. Rudeness, bad words, vulgarity repulsed him like a splash of mud on a garment or a spot of grease on the tablecloth. For Francis was more elegant in thought than in dress, and he loved the beauty of the soul more than the beauty of things. When a companion started to tell a dirty story Francis did not reprove him or become scandalized. He was silent. He was silent as one who was absent, for some things do not deserve attention or an answer. And the companion understood and was ashamed.

He was courteous to all by nature and chivalrous by intent.

Only once did he send away a beggar who had come into the shop at the busiest time. "Charity for the love of God," moaned the ragged beggar among the customers crowded around Francis' counter. *For the love of God.* That ordinary expression planted itself in the heart of the youth as if it had reached him for the first time and assailed him with remorse. "If that beggar had been sent by some prince to ask for alms," he said to himself, "you would have fallen over yourself to please him. And if he asks in the name of the King of Kings can you deny him anything? Or should you not be more courteous and generous to do him honor."

His elegance and courtesy were not vainglory but rather the expression of a passion to do well whatever he had to do and to be first in all things. In order to be praised? No, in order to be pleasing. In order to vanquish others? No, in order to be loved.

Although he was rich, fastidious, and spoiled, he did not place pleasant living and his interests before the public good. This was shown in 1198 when Duke Conrad was forced to render homage to Innocent III for the duchy of Spoleto and the county of Assisi. The Assisians took advantage of this to tear down the fortress dominating the city, the usual headquarters of the German garrison. But after this display of boldness it was necessary to defend Assisi against the inevitable German vengeance. Therefore the consuls, elected that year for the first time to govern a free commune, decided to ring the city with very thick walls, towers and bulwarks according to the art of fortification and the military science of the time. But speed was of the essence, before the enemy arrived! All the citizens, rich and poor, young and old were called to help in the frantic task. Francis too left the warehouse, and with the ardor of his seventeen years learned to carry stones, mix cement and handle the trowel. As good in the construction work as he was in business and in enjoying himself, because he put his soul into everything, Francis helped build the wall. And his companions followed him in work as in play, singing with him as he sang, fascinated by that flash of heroism that shone in every gesture.

A YEAR OF PRISON

After the destruction of the fortress the noblemen who were on the side of the emperor were besieged, warred upon and persecuted. The castles of Sassorosso, of Aguramonte, of San Savino, were destroyed by fire and sword by the violence of the people newly come to political power. Even the city palaces, defended by the lances of the lords in armor, yielded to the arrows of the communal archers and the cudgels and hatchets of the artisans. The exiled nobles asked Perugia for help in avenging themselves, promising in turn to recognize its authority over their city. The powerful Perugians did not have to be asked twice: They declared war on Assisi. The ranks of Assisi, composed of nobles still faithful to the commune of merchants and the populace, could not resist the blows of the more experienced and better led Perugian military. And at Collestrada, a height near the Tiber, Assisi was defeated with heavy losses.

Francis was among the many prisoners. He was taken to Perugia and imprisoned in the Campo di Battaglia with some nobles of his city. Perhaps the victors thought he resembled a gentleman in appearance and dress rather than a merchant, or perhaps they thought his father would pay a large ransom for him.

Thus Francis, who loved liberty more than life, found himself locked up within four walls in the company of haughty nobles who tried to exclude him from their intimacy and seemed to say, "Go away! You have your moneybags but we have a coat-of-arms. You may be rich, but we are what we are!" From behind the bars he saw the steep slope of the hills over the smiling valley, the Subasio radiant in the rising sun, Assisi where his mother wept for him and waited. But the youth of twenty did not weep. Without ever having read Seneca, for books were not to his taste, he knew that a magnanimous man never weeps. On the contrary, the more blows of misfortune he suffers, the more he sings. The paladins never admitted defeat. Yet his noble companions of high lineage were discouraged by prison life. Not he, a son of the people! Francis sang, he sang the most beautiful French songs, the sweetest Provençal ballades. And his song and joyful face were like a ray of sunshine in the prison. He conquered his companions. He even conquered a knight who was always grim-looking, ill-tempered and as prickly as a porcupine, who never spoke to anyone. Francis pitied such pride, and with courtesy and gentle words he was the only one to approach him, to make the prison bearable for him, and to bring about a reconciliation between him and the other prisoners.

"Messer Francesco, what did you do to tame that savage?" a fellow-prisoner asked him.

"What do you find to sing about in this prison?" asked another.

"Oh," replied the youth, "how little you know about my affairs! This is nothing! I shall be venerated by the whole world. I shall be a saint."

"He's crazy," said his companions.

He was not crazy: He was a prophet.

GLORY

After his experience in war and the year of prison in the company of noblemen, the usual daily life no longer sufficed for Francis. Was it worthwhile to work all day only for the purpose of enjoying himself in the evening? Such a reward for work was insipid, but the work was too dull and prosaic. Now he appreciated the pleasures of the table and of animated conversation only when they crowned a day of battle. There was no life without risk, no pleasure without joy. But when the battle was over, to cleanse oneself of dust and blood and to allow oneself as a reward for greatness a feast with friends inside the tent! There to drink a cup of Cypriote wine, to listen to a troubador sing one's feats together with those of the paladins and to carry news of them afar, to some gentle admiring lady! This was life! Yet he must not grow into a lout between business and good times, simply for the glory of being called the *Flower of Youths* in a small town like Assisi.

He wanted to create his own nobility. Men much more obscure than he had become knights and had risen to fame in the suite of a famous lord! Arms opened the road to honor. Events and conversations around him enkindled his dream. Foreign merchants came into the shop, reporting the latest news:

"The Venetian fleet has sailed for the Orient. Two hundred fifty vessels for the knights and soldiers, seventy ships for supply, fifty galleys. The finest lords of France knelt before the Doge in San Marco to ask for the fleet. Lucky fellows, those Venetian merchants!"

Would Francis never get the chance to begin to conquer glory? He did get his chance. And it came when a gentleman of Assisi began to muster foot-soldiers and horsemen for Gualtierri di Brienne, who was defending the rights of the Church in Apulia against Marcovaldo who wanted to deprive the Pope of tutelage over Emperor Frederick. At once Francis prepared a battle outfit for himself that a prince might have envied. His parents did not object. Army discipline might put some sense into his thoughtless head. Perhaps he too could fight for a crown like the nobles of France and the merchants of Venice.

Francesco had no doubts. But on the eve of his departure he heard that a nobleman of Assisi, impoverished by the war, was not able to participate in the expedition because he did not have the means to procure a suit of armor. Immediately Francis gave him his own most beautiful armor so that the nobleman would not cut a poor figure among his peers. Nevertheless he too had been so ambitious to shine! But his generosity won out over his ambition.

As if in recompense for this sacrifice, Francis had a strange dream on the following night. It seemed to him that someone called his name, and led him into a magnificent palace full of military implements, armor, shields, standards, trophies. Every room was an arsenal.

"Whose are these?" asked Francis. "Who owns these splendid arms and this beautiful palace?"

"They belong to you and to your knights," replied a mysterious voice. Francis awoke with a start of joy.

So, he would not be only a knight but a captain of knights! He left for the expedition in Apulia with this happy presentiment. But he was forced to stop at Spoleto. He was ill. During the drowsiness of the fever the same mysterious voice called him:

"Francis, who can do more for you, the Lord or the servant?"

"The Lord."

"Therefore why do you leave the Lord for the servant and the Prince for the vassal?"

"O Lord," replied Francis excitedly, "what do you wish me to do?"

"Return to Assisi. And you will be told what you have to do. You must interpret the dream you had in another way."

Francis slept no more that night. At dawn he slowly returned to Assisi, meditating on the words he had heard: So there were other arms, other battles, another kind of glory! The Assisians, who had seen him leave the day before, with the boldness and dash of a knight, shook their heads: "One more of his jokes!"

But Francis had begun to glimpse the true life, and confidently and pensively he awaited the orders of his Lord.

LOVE

Besides, the change in him had not begun that night. For some time now he had felt consumed by something he could not define. The merry life he had continued after the war was interrupted by a serious illness which had reduced him to a shadow. He recovered. Death, however, is a wise counselor. When he began to get up and walk about the house leaning on a little cane, he felt a kind of inner torment that engendered a discontent with life. One sunny morning he went outdoors for the first time and walked beyond the gates. The verdant plain, the Subasio looming gigantically in the blue horizon, the distant mountains seemed like new things to him. Everything quivered and palpitated in the sun: the streams, the buttercups, the lizards. In the languor of convalescence Francis felt a sense of sweetness and of pain. The pain arose because all such beautiful things were outside him, and therefore he could not make them his in a single embrace. Their beauty escaped him, as did their soul. And they changed continually. The sky darkens, flowers fade, leaves fall, mountains envelop themselves in mist. Now everything was smiling, later all would be dark and forbidding. It was the same with friends. They loved one or not, according to their moods. One could never know how they really felt, never be sure their affection would last until to-morrow. How then to attach one's heart to something which is here today, and gone tomorrow? To whom or to what could he give himself with a vow of perfect love? And if he took the vow would he be sure of keeping it? Did he not also change like the others? From that day on his heart was fixed on the desire to take up the life of a soldier in order to conquer the disgust he felt with himself and with the mediocrity around him.

But after the mysterious admonition of Spoleto that way seemed also to be cut off. What should he do? He took up with his empty-headed and scrounging friends again. He no longer enjoyed himself, but it pleased him to make others enjoy them-selves. One night, after a splendid dinner in which Francis had been crowned king of the feast, the brigade of revellers took to the narrow streets of the silent city serenading girls with their lutes and viols. Francis was last, carrying a scepter of flowering verbena. The others were singing their love songs, he was remembering his dream of battles and the superhuman voice that had called him to unknown feats. What feats?

Suddenly he was struck by a thought. What if glory were to be found where it was least suspected? What if in order to be great before the Lord one had to be just the opposite before men? What if the enemies were not outside him, but within? What if true wealth were poverty, true glory contempt, true love death? This idea permeated his being entirely. He was now alone, as if lost, when his gay companions noticed that he was missing. "Where's Francis?"

They retraced their steps, and one of them tapped him on the shoulder, laughed openly and frankly and asked,

"I say, Francis, are you in love?"

In love? Yes, that was the word. But he was in love with an idea that no one before him had ever loved like this, save Jesus Christ. For this reason it was an idea more worthy to be loved than any other. Immediately Francis grasped in this friend's word the image that he had lacked to give form to his feelings. And he embraced the word like a bride that no one would ever take away from him.

"Yes," he said. "I am in love, and my lady is the most beautiful among the beauties of Assisi."

His companions guffawed:

"Would it be Monna Laudonia? Or Monna Ortolano?"

Francis stood still and silent, and as he looked up at the stars, he saw Poverty nailed to the Cross with Christ. It was Christ who was giving him his bride.

FIRST MEETING WITH POVERTY

That night Francis had understood. His lord was not to be Gualtierri di Brienne, or Frederick II, nor any other prince of this world, but Jesus Christ. And if the insignia of his Lord was the Cross he would follow the Cross, and if the love of his Lord was Lady Poverty, he would marry her. His new thought was so absorbing that he could no longer stand to be among people. He went off alone to meditate, where the countryside was most deserted, as men do who have discovered a treasure and hide to count and contemplate it. But from meditation he immediately passed to action. For Francis was not one of those who, after perceiving the ideal, discouragingly stop to ask, "Will I ever reach it?" Francis immediately tried to do what would lead him to become what he wanted to be: a most faithful follower of Christ.

He began with the poor. At that time many wandered the roads, driven by poverty, wars and famine. To those he saw Francis gave without measure, as he had formerly given to his friends. And when, after giving all, he no longer had any money he gave his brooch, his belt, his cloak, his cap. And when he no longer had anything he could decently remove he hid himself, undressed, and gave his shirt. One day during the absence of Messer Pietro, Donna Pica found the table covered with bread that would have sufficed for a family twice as large as theirs.

"Why all this bread, Francis?"

"For the poor, mother. I have promised to give alms to all who ask."

The gentle woman looked at her favorite son in silence. Francis, who loved his friends, felt his heart heavy as he forbade himself to do what had previously been his joy. He gave up his attention to his cronies, his courtesies, his splendid gifts that anticipated and divined the taste of the recipient. His Lord had spoken clearly: "If you do good to one who loves you, what merit do you have? But even a glass of water given to the least of the poor is given to me." Therefore, in order to serve the Lord, one must serve the poor. They were His representatives.

But being poor is not the same as loving poverty. To give is wealth itself, superiority and joy. One does not know poverty until one descends to the point of not being able to give any more, to the sting of necessity and the humiliation of begging. Francis himself did not know this degree. He decided to try it, but this was not possible in Assisi.

He decided to make a pilgrimage to Rome. Perhaps this desire came to him as a result of the pilgrimage his fellow-citizens had made the year before, in 1205, when Innocent III had granted plenary indulgence to all who visited the tomb of St. Peter. The Assisians were under the interdict for having rebelled against the Church and for electing a mayor who was both a Ghibelline and a heretic. These citizens had gone to Rome in the hope of obtaining pardon and peace of mind through the pilgrimage.

Francis left with a well-filled purse, thanks to his mother. Accustomed to that assured mastery of self and of the world that comes with wealth, he did not dare to travel without money. He took the Via Flaminia from Assisi all the way to Rome. In St. Peter's he was struck by this majestic evidence of Catholicism and the power of the tomb of the Apostle. But when he saw the small change left behind by the pilgrims, he was overwhelmed by magnanimous generosity. He said to himself: "The prince of the Apostles should be honored magnificently. Why do they make such small offerings?"

Impetuously he put his hand into his purse, drew out a

fistful of gold pieces and threw them through the bars into the tomb below. The coins clanged on the marble, making a great noise. The pilgrims stared wide-eyed at the unknown benefactor. Francis repeated his clamorous gesture and, as if to punish himself, since he no longer had even a copper, he hid among the beggars in the atrium of the basilica. To the most miserable one among them he suddenly said:

"Let's exchange clothes . . ."

No sooner said than done! He took off his fine clothes and put on the beggar's cloak and cowl, torn, patched and dirty.

Neat and delicate by nature, Francis shuddered at first but soon mastered his repugnance. In fact he went even further. In his evil-smelling clothes, he, the most brilliant gentleman of Assisi, always the giver and never the petitioner, who would have starved sooner than ask others for food, extended his hand like a beggar to the passers-by. At first he trembled, as he waited for the frigid alms of others. But then the victory that he had won over himself, his act of begging "for the love of God" infused him with such joy that he began to ask for alms in a loud voice in his mother's native language. He felt supremely happy in his rags. Now, for the first time, he was embracing poverty. And he felt that he really loved poverty in which he now wished to live and die.

But Rome did not give him only the experience of poverty. Rome, the city that has the unique capacity of humbling and exalting the spirit in a transcendent act of conversion and revelation, closed the old path of his life and opened a new one.

In Rome the young provincial arrived at an understanding of the supernatural element inherent in the Church and in her ministers. Suddenly he understood her universal mission and the pressing problems of the hour: the evangelical reform of life, the struggle against heresy, the liberation of the Holy Sepulchre. All the undertakings launched by Innocent II for this purpose, and the sights of the Eternal City made a deep impression on Francis, transforming him overnight into a Roman. And they began to suggest to him what the mission of his life should be henceforth.

THE LEPER

He returned to Assisi and to solitude. Who could understand him? Francis had discovered the secret of that glory that is called holiness. He listened to the voice of God speaking softly in his heart (whereas passions scream) and obeyed instantly. The more he obeyed the clearer became the voice. Now it said:

"Do not sing victory songs because you have found poverty. This is only a skirmish. You will not have defeated the enemy within you until you find those things to be sweet that were formerly bitter and bitter those things you once thought sweet."

One day he was riding through the countryside in bloom, when a gust of wind brought the stench of rotting corpses. He looked around and realized he was not far from the leprosarium of San Salvatore between Santa Maria degli Angeli and Assisi. He spurred on his horse but held his nose, imagining the repugnant sight of these poor wretches, segregated from society like corpses, whom he had often helped by sending alms. But he had never been able to go near them because the lepers terrified him. But the inner voice spoke to him. "You see? There is a poverty greater than the one you came to know in Rome. One must rise to it." But the landscape was bathed in a smiling sunlight, and the joy of life slowly crept back into the heart of the youth with the rhythm of a Provençal song when, at a turn, his horse suddenly reared. A man was standing on the side of the road. The man was a leper. Francis saw only the hollow-eyed purulent face and his first impulse was to rein in and turn into the side road. But the inner voice said to him, "Knight of Christ, are you afraid?"

He jumped to the ground, grasped the hand of the leper, kissed the thin fingers, breathed the stench of his skin and left him a coin that was nothing compared to the charity of that kiss. Then he re-mounted his horse and galloped away, mad with mingled sensations of nausea and sweetness. On the next day he went to the lepresarium with a courage he had deliberately instilled in himself beforehand and washed and bandaged the sores of the sick, and gave each leper a coin and a kiss. Repugnance writhed inside him like a truncated snake, but he enjoyed exercising his will and planting a heel on this monster within, as on a conquered foe. War and love were the glory of the knights. Francis, however, looked for glory and love in a way directly opposite to the way of the world.

3

LADY POVERTY

OUTSIDE THE GATE on the road to Spello stood a little church dedicated to St. Damian, a rustic structure with cracks and fissures in the walls traced like bolts of lightning. One day the priest who had custody of the church, an old man as poor as his church, saw a young knight come riding down the steep hill.

When the knight reached St. Damian he jumped down from his saddle, hitched his horse to an olive tree and entered the church. There he remained all night. That visit became a daily habit.

"What fantastic notions has Messer Pietro's son now?" the kindly old man wondered.

The love of God had grown in Francis after the kiss he had bestowed on the leper, and out of preference he went to St. Damian where he found his Lord alone amid the squalor of its unplastered walls, uneven floor, and bare altars. All around was lofty silence and peace, the shade of olive trees as pale as melancholy. Behind stood Mount Subasio, rugged as a penance, and in front a sky as vast as a dream, and a series of blue-tinged mountains disappearing in the distance, as rugged as sanctity. Francis looked about him and pined for his God. Then he fell to his knees in the little church in front of a Byzantine crucifix, praying to it to teach him what to do, for love without works is gold without alloy. The figure on this crucifix had round eyes, an emaciated body, and wounds the color of wine. It was not beautiful, and at first Francis found it painful to look at, but faith opened his eyes and he saw. He saw his Lord Jesus Christ nailed on the Cross for him, and he convinced himself of an idea which when it fixes itself in the mind of a man is capable of making a hero of him.

"God loves you. He loves you, precisely you, it is you He wants."

And in what a manner He loved him! To die, crucified for him. Not even his father would have done as much; therefore it was necessary to recompense it with the same passion, all the more so because all had forgotten it and were living as though they did not believe in the crucifix. The deserted little church aroused the throb of ardent invocation in the heart of the youth.

"What do you wish from me, Lord?"

At last a voice replied.

"Francis, don't you see that my house is falling down? Go, then, and repair it."

The youth recognized *that voice.* Not for a moment did he doubt that the crucifix had spoken, that the house to be repaired was the little church in danger of collapse, and that it was up to him to restore it with money and with work. He said, "Willingly, Lord!"

Immediately he sought out and emptied his purse into the hands of the amazed old priest, instructing him to have a votive lamp burn continuously in front of the crucifix. Then he hastened to the city to obtain money for the new enterprise.

From that day on Francis no longer suffered for himself; only one sorrow seemed worthy of being wept over—His Passion. And he had but one desire: to die crucified with Him. Often, he wandered through the countryside lamenting loudly.

"What's the matter? Are you feeling bad?" people asked him.

"No, I weep over the Passion of our Lord Jesus Christ, for which I must not be ashamed to go weeping all over the world."

And the passers-by, amazed over the unexpected cause of his weeping, were deeply moved and wept with him.

FATHER AND SON

Money was needed to reconstruct the church. Remembering his experience as a merchant, Francis decided to do for God that which before he had done for gain; he took three arm lengths of scarlet cloth out of the draper's shop, mounted his horse and went to the market of Foligno where he sold everything, including the horse. Then, tired and happy, he returned to St. Damian, and handed his swollen purse to the old priest.

"Take this to restore the church, and keep me here with you. We'll begin to work immediately."

But the priest shook his head. Was the boy really serious?

"Messer Pietro, your father is an irascible man," he observed. "I don't want to get into any trouble with him on your account. These monies belong to him. I won't touch them!"

"And neither will I!" exclaimed Francis, sending the purse flying along the sill of a little window of the church. And he remained, to live with the old priest, never returning again to his home.

Messer Pierto Bernardone lost his self-control at this new extravagance. He could overlook the fact that his son squandered money to enjoy himself. The escapades of youth were pardonable, but that money should be wasted on a little church going to ruin so that Francis could live like a hermit was a stupidity the honest merchant could not forgive. What a fine use to make of his good horse and his choice cloth! Since Francis persisted in staying away from home, the father one day armed himself with a club and accompanied by kinsmen and friends, went down to St. Damian. He looked everywhere, but there was no sign of Francis. There was only the old priest who handed him the purse which was still lying on the window sill, and he advised Messer Pietro to go with God. Pietro, mouthing imprecations, took the road back to Assisi—after all, the money had been recovered. As for his son, he would fall into his hands one of these days—if he did not want to die of hunger.

Father and son no longer understood each other: One travelled the way of the world, the other the way of God. But the mother understood. Poor mother! She secretly sent relatives to St. Damian to take the youth food and messages. She implored the priest to hide her favorite for charity's sake! Francis spent a month in a cave, weeping and praying, until such a rabbit's life made him angry with himself. *Knight of Christ*, he asked, *are you afraid?* The enemy was not outside him, not in the men who threatened him; the enemy was in his heart. He feared scorn, blows, and persecutions. Forward, forward in the name of Jesus! Have you not the weapons of the Lord? One day he hurried out of his cave, and took the steep ascent to Assisi in an assault, thinking, "In this first battle I will know whether I am worth anything . . . and if I must be valiant, it is better to die an upright knight than live in cowardice."

He was confronting Assisi for the first time since his great change had set all tongues wagging. He had left the city boldly on horseback with his mantle of rich cloth and pack of provisions; now he was returning barefoot, dusty, emaciated, red-eyed, his face skeleton thin, his hair in wild disarray, his beard, long and ragged.

"The simpleton! The madman! The one who wanted to go to Puglia and conquer a barony!" Street urchins shouted. "Come and see Messer Francesco who has gone out of his mind!" And from the gate of the square came hoots and whistles accompanied by a hail of stones, mud-pies and rotten apples. But the knight of Christ passed amid that uproar as though he were deaf and dumb, rendering thanks to God, because his weapons were humility and patience. When Messer Pietro, who was in his shop learned that his son was the cause of the tumult, his Francis, the *Flower of Youths* and the *King of Banquets*, of whom until yesterday he had been so proud, he was blinded with rage and hurled himself into the crowd. He grabbed the youth, and dragged him home, with blows, to lock him in a tiny closet.

Pietro was not exactly a wicked man. His heart was in his purse and his heart was moved only by his ambition to achieve the status and refinements of nobility. What offended him in

Francis was that he had exposed the family to ridicule, and for a peasant who has climbed the social scale ridicule is more tormenting than dishonor. But what drove the father to fury proved the heroism of the son; Francis had the same mania of showing off, the same fear of cutting a ridiculous figure. By facing up to the ridicule, he conquered the most sensitive part of his ego, and by overcoming the repulsion of being taken for a madman, he tested his courage. Henceforth, there was nothing more to fear, not even death.

THE MOTHER

For several days Francis lived on bread and water in the closet under the stairs, a place so small he could not lie down in it. Then his father gave up scolding and beating him and left for a business trip. Then began the most terrible of all the attacks against Francis: the attack of the heart. The new adversary did not inflict blows upon him, but caressed him, indulged in no rages, but wept with sweet and gentle words: It was his mother. Francis, who since childhood had known how that gentle woman had suffered with her big peasant of a husband, Francis who loved with her same delicate and ardent heart, found it more painful to resist her tenderness than the violence of his father. But the struggle was brief, because that which could not happen with his father occurred with her. Mother and son understood each other.

What had she dreamed for her boy? A dominion beyond the seas, a crusader's lot? The glory of verse, as with Rambaldo Di Vaquerias? The most beautiful bride in the world? None of these, for Francis made her understand that those dreams were the shadow of truth. He would indeed become a prince, but in the Kingdom of Christ, and a great troubador, but of the Most High, and the happy bridegroom on earth of Lady Poverty. Pica understood. If she loved him, she had to become his mother in his soul as she had been the mother of his body. Stirred to her depths, she released him from his chains, and permitted him to take money for the reconstruction of St. Damian, and left him free for his mission.

But after Francis left, Pica returned to the house, shattered in spirit. He would never come back, of this she was sure. Instead, her husband returned and upon discovering the flight of the prisoner, Signor Pietro unleashed a torrest of abuse. Donna Pica, who was expecting this, said nothing, ready to suffer the designs of God on her Francis. Her Francis? Then she felt that pang in her heart that mothers feel when a son leaves the house to take a wife or to follow an idea.

"He is no longer mine!" He was no longer hers, but neither did he belong to the world: He belonged to God. All that remained for Donna Pica to do was to pine away willingly, in silence, which is the mission of women called by Providence to participate in the life of a great man.

THE BISHOP OF ASSISI

After having vented his wrath against Pica, Signor Pietro decided to disinherit his son legally. He denounced Francis to the consuls of the city, and sued for the restitution of the money which the youth had taken from the family coffer. Pietro Bernardone was one of the leaders and one of the benefactors of the commune. The consuls, seeing him in such a state of fury, sent for Francis who was praying and working at St. Damian. But Francis replied to the messenger:

"I have been made free through the grace of God, and I am no longer beholden to the consuls, because I have become a servant of the Most High God."

"See?" said the consuls who, though they feared thwarting Messer Pietro, could not, on the other hand, force Francis, toward whom public sympathy was already veering, to comply with their request. "If he has taken on the service of God, he is outside our authority."

Messer Pietro then took his case to the Bishop of Assisi. Fortunately, Bishop Guido knew Francis very well, indeed, he had been his confidant ever since the youth had begun to change his life. Francis obeyed the voice of God, which spoke to him inwardly, but for the very reason that he was embarking upon a path never before taken, he wanted his intimate aspiration confirmed by the authority of the Church. Bishop Guido had the merit of discovering the seed of sainthood where others saw the mark of a madman; and because he himself was of a fighting temperament, he liked Francis for having set himself in opposition to all in defense of his ideal. But he received the father in order to define an affair which was scandalizing the city. And being a holy and discreet man, he invited Francis to appear before his court to answer his father's denunciation.

"I want to come to Monsignor Bishop," said Francis to the messenger, "because he is father and lord of souls."

Guido received him with open-hearted joy, determined to defend him. In spite of his irascible temperament, Guido combined the characteristics of the Church of Rome: human common sense and supernatural faith.

NUPTIALS WITH POVERTY

It was the morning of April 10, 1207. The audience chamber of the bishopric was crowded with curious Assisians. In front of Bishop Guido, looking solemn in his garnet-colored mantle, stood Messer Pietro with a retinue of friends. Near him stood Francis, alone in the boldness of his twenty-five years. The father repeated the charges, and since the son gave no sign of defending himself, the bishop spoke:

"Francis, your father is very angry with you. If you wish to serve God, return the money that you have taken, and your father's fury will be mitigated."

A wave of whispering swept through the Assisians. So the bishop was declaring Messer Pietro right! Pietro's face cleared. But the bishop continued:

"Perhaps the money was obtained unjustly, and through the sins of your father; God does not wish it to be used for the needs of the church."

Messer Pietro's face fell. The bishop continued: "My son, have faith in the Lord, act manfully and fear not because He will be your help in all that is necessary for the restoration of the church."

"Monsignor!" exclaimed Francis, completely happy, "not

only is the money his, but I also gladly wish to return the clothes which he has given to me."

And Francis disappeared into an adjoining room, returning a minute later to the audience chamber naked, with his thighs girded by a hair shirt. He laid the clothes between the bishop and his father, and he placed a little heap of money on the pile. Then addressing the amazed public like a town-crier, he solemnly proclaimed:

"Hear ye all! Hear and understand! Hitherto I have called Pietro Bernardone my father, but since I have proposed to serve God, I return to my father the money over which he has become wrought, and all the clothes I received from him. Thus, henceforth I can with full right say: 'Our Father, Who art in Heaven,' and not father Pietro Bernardone."

The merchant, who had expected anything except a twist of this kind, gathered up the money and clothes, and left the chamber in a rage amid the jeers of the spectators who were angry that he did not leave his son even a shirt, while the bishop opened his arms and wrapped the youth in his mantle, respecting in him the mystery of that inimitable act which forever cut the bridges between Francis and the ordinary path of the world. The clothes and the money belonged to his father, and he returned them to the father. His body and soul belonged to God. The Lord had placed him on the earth naked, and it was naked that he committed himself to Him, as though he were being born for the second time.

As for Francis, he finally felt himself as poor as Christ on the Cross. Legally, before God and men, the authority of the Church and of the people, he had now broken with his family to wed the poverty of the Master, so disrobing himself that only the veil of the flesh was left between his spirit and God. It seemed to him that he too was as naked as a crucifix. The five wounds were missing, but even these were to come.

THE HERALD OF THE KING

Meanwhile, he must cover himself. The bishop's gardener, with the common sense of the people, brought Francis one of his old frocks. Francis threw is around his shoulders, letting it be marked with a huge cross in chalk to show that he belonged to God. And he took the road to the mountain. He was living through one of those great hours of life in which any company is disturbing, when it is necessary to remain alone with our love. Alone with his poverty, Francis sang to the trees, to the wind, to the clouds in the language of his mother, which for him was still the language of love. Suddenly, some brigands stuck their ugly faces from the thickets.

"Who are you?" The rogues had hoped for some booty but they found themselves before a man in rags.

"Me? I am the herald of the great King!" replied Francis in a loud voice. "What does it matter to you?"

The assailants roared with laughter.

"You make a fine herald in those clothes. Get down, you peasant proclaimer of God!"

They jumped on him, pummelled him and threw him into a ditch still half filled with snow. But Francis, precisely because he was an authentic herald, shook off the snow and resumed his way, singing as happily as before. Even those words had a quality of mystery about them. What did Francis announce in the name of the King? Herald of what?

But one cannot live on air and songs. He walked and walked through the mountains. The youth felt the bite of poverty, namely brutal hunger. Finally, he arrived at a Benedictine monastery, where he asked for a little bread and a discarded tunic in exchange for his services. The monks, who had taken him for a vagabond, put a shirt on him and kept him as a scullery-boy in the kitchen. Yet even here he suffered from hunger to the point of desiring a little soup. Saints and brigands treated him in much the same way. Francis, who was most content in his implacable love, understood that these were the real straits of poverty, the true signs of the predilection of God. But he could not stay long in the monastery, and one day he set out toward Gubbio, where he had a friend who made him a gift of a hermit's tunic.

He remained for some time at Gubbio, devotedly nursing the lepers. But the voice of the crucifix of St. Damian called to him again: "Francis, go and repair my house which you see is falling down."

It was sweet here not to hear even the echo of the petty gossip of Assisi, but it was best to obey the Lord, depriving himself even of the intoxication of solitary poverty. So he returned to St. Damian.

THE STONES

In his first journey with Lady Poverty, Francis had understood the difference between hunger for penance and hunger imposed by necessity, and the difference between being able to do good with one's own means and the necessity of doing it with the means of others. In order to reconstruct St. Damian, stones, lime, a mason's tools, masons were needed, in short, money. And he had shown contempt for his. Who would give him any now? Now poverty brought its first virtuous consequences: the exigency of labor not for oneself, but to do good, the deployment of one's own forces for an entirely non-egoistic end, the abandonment of oneself to Providence.

One morning the inhabitants of Assisi found Francis on the square singing like a jongleur, but not of the feats of the great of France or Brittany; he was singing the praises of the Lord. Was this not just? And was it not fitting that this reform of popular song should begin precisely with him who had so much sung the praise of earthly joys? After finishing his laud, he went around like a jongleur, begging alms for his little church.

"He who will give me a stone will receive one reward, he who will give me two will receive two, he who will give me three, will receive as many."

One day two young girls, accompanied by an older woman, passed through the square. And the younger one said, "Let us too give a stone to that poor youth."

The older one, with the blonde hair under the pearl-colored bonnet, did not answer. But she placed some money next to the stones piled up by the singular beggar.

"Will we also have a great reward, sister?" asked the little one. Then Francis, in a gladness of spirit, began to shout:

"Come to help me in the work of the church of St. Damian. Here one day will rise a convent of nuns by whose life and fame our celestial Father will be glorified over the whole Church."

"What is that fellow saying?"

"Don't pay attention to him, Donna Clare, he's crazy."

But the young girls gazed at the madman, fascinated, little knowing that they themselves would be the most precious stones of St. Damian.

THE SOUP BOWL

In the evening, Francis plodded down to St. Damian bent under the weight of a load too heavy for him. And while the sky lit up with stars, and the hedges with fireflies, the valley with little lights, and while the mountain top vanished in the shadows, the song of the most perfect labor poured forth from the new poet in rhythms that had never been heard before. When he had collected sufficient material, Francis built walls all day long and prayed at night. This was no new trade for him, since he had already worked on the walls of Assisi. But now he brought a new aim: to obey God, to imitate Jesus, the worker. And he also found something new in it: the knowledge and the comfort that are born from humbly doing primitive and indispensable things with one's own hands. Francis put his consciousness into every stone that he cemented and every stone in turn enlarged his consciousness. Having abandoned what is called the world, he re-entered society through that which constitutes its great constructive force: work illumined by faith.

But he loaded and unloaded, cudgelled and hammered, prayed and fasted and became as thin as a rail. The priest of St. Damian, fearing for his health, bartered his own bread to obtain eggs and milk for Francis. The kindly old man became something of a mother to him, but when Francis realized this he said to himself: "This is not right! Where would I find another priest who would treat me with such humanity? This is not the life of the poor that I wished to elect! What a poor man does out of necessity, I must do for the love of the most poor Jesus Christ!"

With these thoughts, one day he took a soup bowl and did what he had seen done at Assisi: he begged for alms from door to door. The housewives looked out in amazement, because they knew how magnificently he had lived until yesterday. Some gave him a handful of "pasta," others a spoonful of soup, some a little ragout, others the drained liquid of their pots. Some who offered a piece of meat hesitated to throw it into such a gruesome mixture. But Francis would say courageously: "Throw it in. God will reward you for it."

When, however, he sat down on the steps of a church to eat, he rested the soup bowl on his knees for a moment, with tears in his eyes and his stomach rumbling in revulsion. It was a meal for dogs. In other days, the mere sight would have made him nauseous. But a voice within him said: "Knight of Christ, do you wish to fail your word?" He thought of the gall which poverty gave to the Crucified One, closed his eyes and opened his mouth. Hunger, the will to penance, the victory over himself, gave the taste of joy to the inhuman concoction.

Messer Pietro Bernardone, informed of Francis' new prowess, found no peace in such self-abasement. "If only he would take his shame and ours away from here! Instead he remains in Assisi to degrade us all!" And between rage, remorse, and the sorrow of seeing him reduced to an "ecce-homo" state, every time he met his son he swore imprecations at him: "Cursed be the day that you were born!" Francis' heart felt a wrench at these maledictions (blood is not water) and he found it necessary to seek refuge with the Father of the Heavens, remembering that it had been for Him, that he had repudiated his terrestrial father. To make this idea more concrete to himself, Francis took on a beggar as a father, entering with him upon the following pact: "I will give you a part of the alms that I receive, and you, whenever you hear my father curse me, will make the sign of the Cross over me and bless me in his stead." They did just this, and Francis could now answer Messer Pietro with tranquillity of conscience: "Don't you believe that God can give me a father, who blesses me against your maledictions?"

It was a good lesson to administer to Messer Pietro, who had forgotten that children are not there for their parents but for the mission to which Providence destines them.

THE OIL

Francis wanted the lamp always lit in his church, but oil was lacking. One day he went to the city to beg for some, and passing a house he could hear from the voices that his old friends were gathered for one of their usual reunions. Should he appear among that brigade, abject as he looked, to extend a begging hand to those who knew him by name and considered him crazy? Francis had a presentiment of the pranks they would play. He feared the scorn of his world and turned back. But immediately the inner voice shouted: "Are you afraid?" Then, as if he were fleeing from himself, running, he went back to the house where they were gambling. He went in and confessed to those present that he had been ashamed to ask for alms. And then in a fervor of spirit, and in French, the language of gentlemen, he asked for a little oil for the lamp of St. Damian.

It was like the apparition of a prophet in a company of sybarites, although a prophet accuses and threatens, whereas Francis accused and humiliated only himself, and his humiliation struck at the heart more than an anathema.

Interrupting their games and their conversation, the cronies listened to the beggar madman, who until so recently had dominated them with his generosity and who now dominated them with his courage. After he left they made many comments, but few laughed. No one said anything in derision. Some laid down their dice and one said, "That fellow is wiser than all of us."

LA PORZIUNCOLA

After repairing St. Damian as best he could with the help of a peasant and a day-laborer, Francis decided to restore another church in the countryside, dedicated to St. Peter; and then another one, a little church, squatting among the woods of the valley, of which he was particularly fond because his mother had taught him to love it and because it was dedicated to the divine Mother of all creatures, St. Mary of the Angels. At that time it belonged to the Benedictines of Mount Subasio who, however, had practically abandoned it. It was called "Porziuncola" (small portion) because of its small size and because of the small parcel of land surrounding it.

One February morning when Spring began to glisten in the cold air, the priest of St. Damian, who had been invited by Francis, came down to celebrate Mass at the Porziuncola. Deeply engrossed in contemplation, young Francis assisted at the Mass, praying that the Lord illuminate him. To what restoration should he set his hand, now that St. Mary of the Angels was also finished? And was this actually the great enterprise to which the Lord had called him in the dream of Spoleto: to be a mason for churches all his life?

The answer came with the Gospel of the Mass of that day, February 24, 1209, the Feast of St. Matthias. The priest was reading in a low voice, and the eternal words fell like diamonds in the heart of him who waited. "The Kingdom of heaven is at hand . . . Freely you have received, freely give. Do not keep gold, or silver, or money in your girdles. No wallet for your journey, nor two tunics, nor sandals, nor staff; for the laborer deserves his living. And whatever town or village you enter, inquire in it who is worthy; and stay there until you leave."

Francis thrilled with joy. Jesus Christ spoke very clearly to him who wanted to follow Him. Here, then, was his mission: to preach the Kingdom of God from land to land, from town to town. But with what rule of life? With one even much stricter than that which Francis, though presuming to have wed poverty, had observed until now, even though he dressed like a hermit, with a leather girdle, sandals, purse and staff. That was too much luxury! At the end of the Mass, not trusting himself, he asked the priest to comment on the Gospel of the day and the priest confirmed it for him. Indeed, this is what Christ wanted from His followers, an apostolate in poverty.

Immediately with the impetus of a spring that has found its course, he happily threw away his sandals, staff, pocket-purse and girdle and all duplicate things. He fitted a rough tunic with a cowl around himself, in the manner of Umbrian peasants, girded a rope around his thighs, and by the divine instinct of evangelical perfection, he began to preach penitence in public.

The Porziuncola marked the third call of God in the life of St. Francis, after that of Spoleto and of St. Damian. The first brought him to his separation from the world, the second to work, the third to the apostolate. But the third would not be possible without the other two because the Gospel cannot be brought to others if it is not first lived in oneself. And it cannot be lived in a saintly way in the world if we have first not removed ourselves from it. Now Francis would not be building with stones but with souls, he would no longer found chapels, but religious orders. He would not restore this or that church, but the Church. And in order to arrive at such a height, it was necessary to begin as he began, from the penitence of the hermit and from the labor of the manual worker.

WELCOME, LADY POVERTY

The call of Porziuncola implied something that had to be further deepened and something that had to be started in the life of Francis. That which had to be deepened was poverty, that which had to be begun was the apostolate. These were two facts difficult to reconcile because one can live like the poor in solitude, but to live like the poor in the world, where everything is a play of money, seems like madness. On the other hand, in order to convert men it is necessary to live among them, demonstrating by example that there is a power much greater than all the monies of the earth: love. But who would have believed it, if Francis had lived like others, counting upon human means?

Therefore, the idea was to possess nothing, not even a pillow on which to rest one's head (in fact, when they gave him one, he had to throw it away and go back to lying on a stone, because it seemed to him that there were devils inside). Provide for the nourishment of the day with work if possible, with alms if this were not possible; and if while begging he picked up only refusals and acts of rudeness—so much the better! To him, a sinner, contempt! To God alone glory! He erased the possessive pronoun from his vocabulary. Once somebody said to him; "I am coming from your cell." Francis rebelled, "Mine? I have nothing of my own." He never went back to that cell.

He said that he had wed Lady Poverty, and like a bridegroom he was loyal to and jealous of her. He loved all the poor because they wore, he said, the uniform of Jesus Christ. But he also envied them as if they beat him in the competition of poverty, and he could not tolerate that another might be poorer than he. The tunics that they gave him lasted a very short time on his back, for he gave them to the first beggar that he met, at the cost of freezing to death. And when he did not have a mantle, he tore his cowl or a piece of cloth from the tunic or he took off his breeches. And when he no longer had anything, he asked the rich to give to the poor, saying with his courteous joyousness, "Don't expect to get your gifts back anymore!"

He gave with a most delicate manner not only without a shadow of that satisfaction which discounts the benefit, but with the deference of one who pays a debt or who makes restitution. One time at Rieti through a friend he sent his mantle and twelve loaves of bread to a beggar woman he had met on the road with this singular message: "That poor man to whom you lent the mantle thanks you for the favor and returns what belongs to you."

The beggar woman thought she was being made fun of and was about to send the ambassador packing, but when she saw that he was serious, she took the unexpected gift and ran off, fearing another prank.

One day going from Rieti to Siena for treatment for his eyes, he met three young girls on the highway who looked and dressed completely alike and who, bowing their heads humbly, said to him:

"Welcome, Lady Poverty!"

Francis was as gladdened by these words as a knight who hears himself greeted in the name of his lady, and he asked the doctor who was accompanying him to give alms to the girl pilgrims. They continued along the road for a while, but when they turned to look back at the three mysterious girls, they saw only the white road among the hedges. Who were they? Perhaps the three virtues whom Francis always had in his heart: Poverty, Chastity, Obedience. But since he loved and saw the favored one in all, they all had the same smile and the same aspect of his bride, just as he himself was so much identified with that ideal bride as to be taken for her by name.

THE BRIDE IS PLEASING

During the long journey on foot to preach the Gospel in the manner of the Apostles, Francis and one of his companions, Friar Masseo, arrived very tired and hungry at a city exactly at noon. Each taking a different street, they went from door to door asking for alms. Francis was emaciated looking and timid in asking. One had to look into his eyes to feel any sympathy for him. Friar Masseo instead, was tall, well-built and a seductive talker. If they managed to eat outside the city, near a spring of clear water, next to which was a beautiful large stone, each one would put the alms collected on this stone. But whereas Francis brought back only a handful of dry and mouldy pieces of bread, Friar Masseo, with a flourish contributed beautiful loaves of fresh bread and even white rolls. For men do not give to him who merits more, but to him who cuts a better figure and who knows how to please.

"Look," it seemed that Friar Masseo was thinking before his abundant haul, "look, how good I am!"

Francis, instead, happy to have been surpassed by his companion, never ended showing his happiness with that courteous joyousness that was uniquely and completely his.

"O Friar Masseo, we are not worthy of such a great treasure!" Francis exclaimed.

That word "treasure" did not persuade the good Friar Masseo, who finally observed:

"Dearest father, how can you call it treasure, where there is so much poverty that even the needful things are lacking? Here there is neither cloth, nor knife, nor chopping block, nor bowl, nor house, nor table, nor man-servant, nor maid-servant?"

"But that's just what I consider to be a great treasure," exclaimed Francis, "where nothing is made by human industry, but all is prepared for us by Divine Providence, as can be manifestly seen in the bread given as alms and spread on this table of stone so fair and this spring so clear. Therefore, we should pray to God that He may make us love with all our hearts the noble treasure of holy poverty that has God for its servant."

Friar Masseo, who had an earthly mind, called treasure the luxury that money brings; at heart he mourned for well-set and well-serviced tables. Francis, a poet, saw the beauty of the stone, of the spring, of the bread, of that dinner composed of humiliation and served up by charity in the open countryside under the sun of God. Francis understood that while the rich have other men for servants, the poor have God as servant, in that it is He who provides for them, sending simple, unexpected, and ever new and gladsome things to him who is never surfeited because he possesses nothing.

On this journey Francis proposed to Friar Masseo that they go to Rome.

"Let us go to St. Peter and St. Paul and let us pray to them that they teach and help us to possess the measureless treasure of most holy poverty. Poverty is that virtue that tramples upon earthly and transitory things and therefore poverty is the queen of all. Poverty is that virtue that removes every obstacle from the soul so that it can join with eternal God; it was poverty that accompanied Christ from the manger to Calvary, and prepared for Him a rude Cross, rusty nails, a beverage of gall, a tomb not His, with a winding sheet and unguents given out of charity."

In Rome, when they entered the Church of St. Peter, Francis went off to pray in a little corner of the church, and Friar Masseo went off to another. The sainted Apostles Peter and Paul, who in their blessed heaven hear mortals invoke them for a hundred thousand favors save for that of being poor, did not delay appearing to this most singular supplicant and they said to him:

"Our Lord Jesus Christ sends us to you to announce that your prayer is heard, the treasure of most holy poverty is granted to you and to your followers. And still from Him we say to you that whosoever will follow your example is certain of eternal blessedness."

EACH DAY HE LOVED HER MORE

Later, Francis had an illustrious protector, Cardinal Ugolino, Bishop of Ostia. This venerable old man loved him, advised him, and defended him with that practical sense that the saint, precisely because he was a saint, could not have. Whenever he could Cardinal Ugolino wanted Francis to be his guest and he always had him sit near his table. But that cardinal's table was too luxurious for Poverty's bridegroom.

One day, at the dinner hour, Francis went out to beg. Then he went to the cardinal's place when the Cardinal was already at table with his ecclesiastic and aristocratic guests. In the dining room Francis lined up on the table before him the gray crusts of bread that he had collected as alms. The cardinal felt bad, both because Francis had gone begging when he was expected at the cardinal's residence, and because he had displayed his alms at the table. But he said nothing out of regard for his guests.

After having eaten a little, Francis rose and in the name of the Lord he distributed a part of the bread he had begged to the knights, chaplains and prelates, who received it with delight and devotion, removing their cowls or berets as though they had received a singular favor, and sensing, in that gesture of the man of God who gave the rich the bread of the poor, something that according to the world could also have been called wrong, but which according to the spirit was a warning and a benediction.

The cardinal beamed when he saw that his distinguished guests either were eating the bread or were preserving it like a relic. But later, when he retired with Francis to his chambers, he could not resist asking him:

"Why, my dear most simple brother, did you make me blush by going begging alms when coming to my house, which is the house of your brothers?"

Then St. Francis explained to him that he was honoring

God, who is pleased with poverty by distributing the bread given by brotherly love to the rich, and by his example showing them the nobility of asking and giving for love of Jesus Christ. And he added frankly, "I prefer a poor table, served up with alms, rather than one where you can hardly count the number of knives and forks and spoons."

Cardinal Ugolino understood that if the saints push against convention, it is because they judge things in a more lofty way than is common, and that certain eccentricities veil a profound wisdom which cannot be misunderstood by righteous men. Therefore, opening his arms to Francis, he said:

"My son, do what seems good in your eyes, because God is with you and you are with Him."

4

The knights
of Lady poverty

AFTER THE EVENT of Porziuncola, St. Francis began to preach in the Piazza San Giorgio without asking himself whether he was prepared or unprepared, worthy or unworthy. His humility entertained no such scruples, certain as he was that the word of God is true and that the way of hearing it would come from on high. He penetrated the heart of his listeners because when he spoke he was always illuminated by the Lord and in a fervor of spirit, and he amazed them to the point of stupor. He began his sermons with the greeting: "The Lord grant you peace." And he desired that the citizens should repeat that greeting when they met, because he perceived that a war of covetousness and hate lurked in the depths of souls.

Among his frequent listeners was a certain Bernard of Quintavalle, one of the richest and wisest men of Assisi. For two years he had been observing Francis' conduct, marvelling at how a youth of his age and nearly of his own social class could arrive at such prodigies of sanctity or madness. Then, after hearing him preach, he felt a desire grow within him to imitate him. But, being a prudent man, he first wanted to make certain that Francis was really a man of God, so one evening he invited him to his house. At dinner he took note of what Francis said and what he ate. After dinner he led him to sleep in his room in which a lamp was always left burning, thinking, "We shall see if he acts like everybody else." Although Francis was somewhat annoyed by the company of his host and the light, because it was his custom to get up at night in order to pray, he dissembled his feelings courteously. He threw himself on the bed and immediately made believe that he was asleep. But as soon as he heard Bernardo snore like a contra-bass, he left the bed and fell on his knees with his hands and eyes fervidly lifted to heaven. Lost in prayer he forgot where he was, and he remained rapt there, pining away in tears, repeating only two words that expressed everything, "My God! My God!", until the bells rang for the matins of the April dawn.

Messer Bernard, who had been only half asleep, stopped his pretended snoring, and beheld Francis admiringly and he himself also wept. He made up his mind then and there.

"Francis," he said to him later in the morning, "What should one do who has had many goods from one of his lords, and who has enjoyed them for many years and who now no longer desires them?"

"Render them to the lord from whom he has received them," replied francis.

"I will give all my temporal goods to the poor, for the love of the Lord God who has lent them to me," said Bernard. "And I will distribute them as you see fit, because in my heart I have decided to abandon the world and to follow you in whatever you will command me."

At other times, when he had cut a brilliant figure among knights, Francis had run into youths ready to follow him in order to win honor for themselves, but so far not in his new life. Indeed, he had known no one so disposed. This man was the first. He rejoiced over the situation as though his fervent prayer of the night before, in which he had asked God for help in his mission, had been answered with a companion. Something new was happening to him. He was no longer solitary, he was about to become a teacher; and in his humility he invoked the guidance of the eternal Teacher.

"Messer Bernard," he answered, "what you say is so great and difficult a thing that it behooves us to seek counsel from our Lord Jesus Christ. Let us go to the bishop's house together, where there is a good priest. We will hear Mass and remain in prayer until tierce (that is until 9 o'clock) beseeching God that in the three openings of the missal He point out to us the road that it would please Him for us to choose."

The priest who celebrated the Mass was a learned canonist named Pietro Cattani, who had studied law at Bologna, and who was attached to the Church of San Nicolo of Assisi. He was an admirer of Francis and had already showed an inclination to follow him. Thus, Bernard's example of that morning also decided things for him. Bernard took the proferred missal and opened it three times in homage to the Blessed Trinity. The first time it fell open on the passage, "If thou wilt be perfect, go and sell what thou hast and give it to the poor . . . and come follow me." The second time it opened on the passage: "No wallet for your journey, nor two tunics, nor sandals, nor staff; for the laborer deserves his living." And on the third time the passage read: "If anyone wishes to come after me, let him deny himself, and take up his cross, and follow me."

The Gospel had responded exactly to the ideal of St. Francis, who, taking the word of God literally said: "Brothers, this is the way of our Rule and of all those who will desire to join our company. Go, therefore and do faithfully what you have heard."

Messer Bernard at once distributed his patrimony to hospitals, monasteries, orphans, pilgrims, widows and the poor. The learned canonist, Pietro Cattani, a man of few belongings, liquidated his earthly goods in a short time, renouncing his canonate, an honorific post, a comfortable life, gentlemanly and literary tastes, for evangelical poverty. It was a spectacle never before seen in Assisi when, with Francis present, they began to distribute money to the poor in the Piazza San Giorgio. The poor sprang up from all sides, even more ragged than was necessary, and Francis who by now knew them all, pointed out the more timid and deserving to his friends. There were comments from many that the three men were throwing away indifferently sums for which others in the square might have given their lives. A priest of Assisi, Messer Silvester, approached Francis and said: "You did not pay me completely for those stones you bought from me. Now that you have money, pay me!" It was an act of public insolence and reprehensible for a priest. St. Francis' blood boiled, more for the latter than for the former reason, and he took a handful of money from Bernard's tunic and gave it to Messer Silvester. "O father priest," he asked, "are you yet fully paid?" And then he gave him a second great handful, "Are you paid?"

The priest took the money, and he went away. But something inside him grumbled, "This is not right!"

GILES AND SILVESTER JOIN FRANCIS

The three friends lived in a hovel between Porziuncola and the leper hospital, a place which Francis never forgot, not even in his preaching, because works of such mercy are a priest's concern and the foundation of the apostolate. For he who does not know how to help his neighbor in his body can never know how to safeguard his soul. In addition some nostalgia for maternal caresses kept Francis near the little church, which bore the name of Mary, Queen of the Angels.

Meanwhile, there was much talk in the city of these conversions. A boy of eighteen, an orphan called Giles, was so deeply moved by them that he too began to wonder how in all his actions he too could please God alone. Certainly Francis must possess this secret. So one April morning, after praying in the Church of St. George, he set out looking for him, and as he was standing at a cross-roads, uncertain of which way to turn, he met Francis just coming out of the forest. Giles threw himself at his feet and Francis, who had the perceptive eye of a teacher, welcomed the youth as though he had been expecting him.

"Welcome to this new knight!" he said. Knight, he said, because the day was April 23, the feast of St. George, patron of knights. "If the emperor should come to Assisi and desired to nominate a citizen as his private chamberlain, should not the man be glad? All the more so should you rejoice whom God has chosen as his knight to follow the perfect way of the Holy Gospel." The first knightly act imposed on the newly chosen was to give his tunic to an old woman beggar. Then the youth distributed all his other belongings to the poor and joined the followers of Francis.

Some time later even Silvester, the priest who had demanded full payment for the stones, also appeared at the friary. And he explained that since that day of the restitution in the town piazza the example of Francis had been gnawing at him continuously.

"Here I am an old man, I told myself," he said, "and I still desire temporal things, while this youth despises them." That night, he said, he had had a dream: He saw an immense cross of gold come out of Francis' mouth and rise up to the sky and shed its beams from one end of the world to the other. When he woke up he understood that the dream meant that Francis was truly a friend of Christ, and that his Order was to spread throughout the world. Silvester then began to do penance at home, and after he chose to follow the bridegroom of Lady Poverty he became a friar of such lofty contemplation that often his teacher Francis turned to him for advice.

GILES FIRST JOURNEY

With the arrival of Giles they now numbered four at the Porziuncola and they lived happily. But since they all sought the glory of God more than their own happiness, they separated. Francis sent Friar Bernard and Friar Pietro Cattani to Tuscany, and he and Friar Giles set out toward the March of Ancona. Francis was as happy as if he had found a treasure, and he walked singing the praises of God as the larks sing flying. Behind him humbly trudged Giles reciting the *Pater Noster*. Suddenly, Francis interrupted his song in the French language and called out:

"O Brother Giles!"

"My father!"

"Listen to what I say to you. Our religion will be like the fisherman who catches so many fish in his net that he throws the little ones away and puts the big ones in jars."

As they strode along, Francis stopped passers-by, whether they were knights, peasants or artisans, and asked them bluntly, "Brother, do you love God?" Those queried stood openmouthed. They had never given the question thought.

Francis did not preach openly to the people, but as he passed through cities and castles he admonished and corrected men and women, saying, "Love and fear God and make a worthy penance of your sins." When he had finished, the good Giles added, "Do what my spiritual father tells you to do, because he speaks excellently well."

But the people were dumbfounded. "Where do they come from and what do these bizarre people want?" they said because the world had almost forgotten God, however often it had Him on its lips.

THE FRIARS MINOR

When Francis returned to St. Mary of the Angels, three men of Assisi, Sabbatino, Morico and Giovanni della Capella, came to beseech him to receive them among his followers. Francis welcomed them in a fatherly fashion. Then these six, by their example and words, attracted to the group Filippo Longo, Giovanni of San Costanzo, Bernard of Viridante. In 1210 they numbered twelve. Francis loved them intimately knowing them one by one, and he called them and wanted them to call each other *frati*, that is, brothers. Later he added an adjective which was to remain forever in the definition of the Order: *minor*. *Friars minor*, in remembrance of the Gospel which promises heaven to the little children and those who care over them; *friars minor*, out of christian humility, which prescribes that one put oneself last; *friars minor*, out of a social intention, since in the life of the communes and especially of Assisi, the rich and the powerful were called the "majors" and the artisans and the poor were called the "minors." Through the vicissitudes of concessions and insurrections, of peace and of reprisals, and the alternating tyranny and misrule of the factions, it was the minors who always ended by getting the worst of it because there is no true and enduring elevation of the poor little folk without charity. St. Francis called his followers *friars minor* because they had to take pride in being among the oppressed and always to side with them without, however, hating the oppressors, indeed, loving even the nobles and the rich, even the worldly and the sinners, because all are children of God, all can be converted, all can be, or do become, superior through we know not what virtues.

If to earn the title of knight it was necessary to submit to a symbolical ceremony, and to assume a habit of the knightly order every part of which represented a duty and a commitment, to become a friar minor involved also the wearing of a special habit: shedding shoes and wearing the tunic and tightening the girdle could mean more than putting on golden spurs, a blouse of white silk, a crimson robe, and buckling on a sword. And if the faith of the knight was to maintain his loyalty to God, and to His Church and to his own lord, to keep himself pure, to renounce all commercial trafficking, never working for profit—to defend the weak, and women, and the oppressed, to oppose all injustice, to be brave and courteous in every encounter, loyal and daring, all this also was expected of a friar minor. But with a loftiness of intention infinitely superior—nothing for oneself, everything for God.

THE NOBILITY OF WORK

By nature and training, St. Francis worked willingly and, even when he had worked in the world, he stood at the drapery counter without blushing. This was because he came from that mercantile bourgeoisie which formed the economic soul of the Italian commune, and which vis-à-vis the nobility of the castles asserted a new nobility, derived from themselves and not from the lineage of blood. His conversion quickly turned him to manual labor. When they were not praying, the twelve were working, first, at works of mercy, serving the sick and nursing the lepers, then sweeping out the churches, and then working at their regular trade. The teacher set the example and prescribed: "I desire that all my friars work and humbly excercise themselves in good works in order to flee idleness, the enemy of the soul, to be less of a burden to people, to earn their livelihood honestly. Those who know how to work will work and excercise the trade that they already know, those that know nothing, will learn to work, but let them take care to work with faithfulness and devotion in such a way as not to extinguish the spirit of prayer, which all temporal things must serve, and let them take care to receive in compensation only the things needful to the body, excluding money however; and all this humbly as is fitting to the servants of God and to the followers of most holy poverty. '

With these precepts Francis avoided the twin dangers of action, that of loving one's work overmuch and one's own self in one's own work; and of neglecting the inner life for work or glory. Brother Giles became one of the most perfect personifications of this aristocratic ideal of work.

Giles prayed, walked, worked and sang. As a young man he had already travelled along the roads of the most celebrated pilgrimages to Rome, the Puglie, Galicia, the Holy Land, earning his daily bread by any job that came to hand. In Brindisi he had been a water-carrier, in Cairo a grave-digger, in Ancona a basket-maker, in Rome a wood-cutter, and in Rieti a scullery-boy. And in the countryside through which he roamed he was a wine-maker, a gleaner, an olive-gatherer, a walnut-beater, refusing any compensation in money, and giving the remains of what he consumed to the poor. He changed jobs as he changed towns, despising money. He worked to live, he did not live to work. He did not wish to be anybody's servant, not even of his work, not even of his heart.

The guest of a cardinal who loved and respected him like a saint, he did not sit at the table if he did not first earn his day's keep; and he ate dry bread. One day of heavy rain, the cardinal was pleased, thinking, "Friar Giles must rest today. He can't go out working today!" But Giles went to the kitchen and cleaned it up. It was still raining on the next day, so he earned his keep by sharpening all the knives in the cardinal's house. And when a priest met him on the street and saw him looking so poor and yet so happy, he shouted at him, "Ne'er-do-well!" Friar Giles, convinced of his own worthlessness, wept with remorse.

St. Francis looked on the lazy as sterile drones. He once told a friar who neither prayed nor worked nor begged for alms,

"Go your own way, Friar Fly, since you want to eat of the labor of your brethren and be idle in the work of God."

No nobility has been known more complete than this transcendent industriousness, which gave all and retained nothing. But there is a nobility even more difficult to understand, the nobility of begging.

THE NOBILITY OF BEGGING

The virtue that St. Francis recommended above all to his friars was poverty, but he also understood that they were ashamed to beg. Since he loved and venerated them, as if each were better than he, and since, preserving the intuitive delicacy with which he was born, he greatly sympathized with that shame, he did not tell them to go begging for alms but went himself, every day, in place of the others. Perhaps he hoped that they would learn from his example, or that if only out of a little discretion they would say, "We will go!" But they were hesitant. Meanwhile, Francis overtired himself, delicate as he was by nature, and by the life he once led in the world and now weakened by fasts and mortifications. Therefore, being unable to cope with so much work all by himself, and knowing it was not just to deprive the friars of the perfection of poverty, he sought for more persuasive arguments to conquer their shame. So he said: "My dearest brethren and children, the Son of God was more noble than us and still He made Himself poor in this world. For love of Him we have chosen the absolute poverty which is His inheritance, therefore we must not be ashamed to go begging, as the heirs of a kingdom are not ashamed of the commitment of their inheritance." He selected another point to prick their self-love.

"The time will come when the most noble and learned will enter our congregation and they will esteem it a great honor and grace to go begging for alms. You who are the first should be glad and enjoy serving as models for the saints of the future." But even this was a rather remote argument. What was required was one that would destroy the humiliation of begging. And St. Francis found it:

"You must ask for alms for love of the Lord more willingly and more gloriously than one who out of liberality should offer a thousand marks in gold in exchange for a single coin, because you are offering the love of God in exchange for a little bread and in comparison with this love all the treasures of heaven and earth are as nothing."

He was right: the world's ambition is to give and not to ask. St. Francis, on the contrary, humbled himself to ask in order to give with the greatest generosity of one who hides himself in the gift so completely that he passes for the benefacted whereas he is the benefactor, and gives the highest gift, that which is neither bought nor sold: love. Between him who asks and him who gives, he who asks is the more generous and the more powerful; the other is aware of this because he often gives alms as he would conduct a business deal in order to obtain some good outside human possibility, and he looks with a kind of superstitious respect at the poor man who mysteriously promises: "God will reward you." Thus, by turning the principles of the world upside down, St. Francis revealed to his friars that there is more merit in asking than in giving, because it offers others the opportunity to do good without having the air of so doing, and because there is no greater humility than his who extends his hand and confesses: "Brother, I need you."

The friars understood the admonition. From then on each asked permission to go beg for alms. Upon returning, each would show his alms to Francis, and one would say to the other, "I collected more than you."

Francis rejoiced to see them so happy, but he wanted them only to keep the indispensable; the rest must go to the poor.

POVERTY AND FREEDOM

Bishop Guido, who continued to be a friend and adviser to Francis, one day brusquely observed: "Your life seems too harsh and bitter to me. How do so many of you manage to live together without having even the essentials?"

"*O domini mi,*" answered Francis in Latin, "if we had possessions nobody would believe us when we speak of charity and penitence. And then we would need arms to defend them, because quarrels and troubles are born of property and it generally impedes the love of God and of neighbor in many ways. Therefore we do not want to possess any temporal thing."

This reply, which pleased the bishop, contained the core of the idea that animated St. Francis in desiring the collective poverty of his Order in contrast to the pre-existing ones which permitted, not the monks personally, but the community, to own houses and lands in order to provide for its members. St. Francis thought that property occupies, preoccupies and binds one's thoughts and feelings, whereas the man dedicated to God must be free as the wind, to go with all, fear nobody, with nothing to lose and nothing to gain. Francis and his friars wanted to be obedient but dependent on no others but the Church.

St. Francis did not despise the rich. On the contrary, he prescribed that his followers should respect those who live affluently and dress with luxury, but he maintained that the first condition for truly serving one's neighbor, as they wished to do, and for giving themselves entirely to all, is not to have anything for oneself, not even a hovel. In fact, St. Francis wanted no household furnishings nor provisions; he forbade the friar in charge of the kitchen to keep vegetables in water for the next day, since, according to the Gospel, one should take no thought of the morrow. Was not every day sufficient to the day thereof?

THE KNIGHTS ERRANT

To his first companions gathered at Porziuncola, St. Francis said, "Let us consider, dearest brethren, that God has so mercifully called us not only to save our own souls, but also by example and word to exhort all peoples to do penance and to remember God's commandments. Do not be afraid because you are poor and ignorant, the Spirit of the Lord will speak in you. You will find good people who will welcome you with joy, and you will find wicked people who will resist and mistreat you. Prepare yourselves to endure everything patiently and humbly."

After having encouraged them, he blessed them, and they

went away two by two like the Apostles, preserving his benediction and admonitions in their hearts. They did not own anything, not even the cloak they wore because they had to be ready to give it away to anybody who asked for it; they ate the fruits of the forest or crusts of bread begged for charity, they slept under a portico, or the step of a church, at the foot of a tree. When they found a church or a Cross they knelt in devotion, remembering the Passion of the Lord. When they entered a city, a town, or a house, they presented themselves with the greeting of St. Francis, "Peace and good things," comforting all as they taught them to fear and love the Creator of heaven and of earth, and they patiently put up with hunger, cold, tribulations, distresses: they were men destined by their will to suffer and to be despised like the Lord Jesus.

Their fellow-townsmen and kinsmen gave them little or nothing in the way of alms: "Why did you leave what you had in order to live at the expense of others? Now fend for yourselves as best you can, simpletons!" Even in those times nobody left his own belongings in order to beg alms from door to door.

Even though it was not rare in the thirteenth century to see wanderers, pilgrims, penitents, in wild, strange dress, leading lives that appeared to be of desperation, the followers of Francis created a great impression. Some feared them as madmen and fled from their presence. Those who listened to them, said, "Either they are crazy, or drunk, or they are so perfect that we cannot understand them." Many overwhelmed them with questions, "Who are you? Where do you come from? To what Order do you belong?" They confessed that they were penitent men from the city of Assisi and that their Order had not yet been constituted. But idlers and street urchins amused themselves by hurling insults at them, by putting dice into their hands and inviting them to gamble, and by ripping off their shabby tunics to leave them in a state of semi-nudity, because these men did not ask for the return of things taken from them. If their clothing was returned they humbly thanked their benefactors. Malicious ones grabbed them by their cowls from behind and carried them suspended like sacks. What purpose did this self-abasement serve? And did they render glory unto

God by letting themselves be stepped on in this way by men? Indeed, they did render glory, as their adventures demonstrated.

FRIAR BERNARD'S ADVENTURES

Friar Bernard and Friar Giles went to Florence, preaching along the way, as St. Francis desired. But when they got to the city they could not find a hospice. They stopped at a house with a portico and an oven in front, and humbly beseeched the mistress of the dwelling that if she would not lodge them indoors, she should at least let them spend the night next to the oven. The woman consented, but when her husband came home and saw the two friars he reproached his wife: "Why did you allow those vagabonds to lodge in the portico?"

"What danger is there outside?" she asked. "At most, they may steal some wood." She also wanted to give the poor devils a blanket because it was so cold, but the husband objected. "Nothing! They're rascals and thieves who roam the highways."

Friar Bernard and his friend rested near the oven that night, warmed by the love of God and covered only with the blankets of Lady Poverty. And when matins sounded they went to church. At daybreak the mistress of the house also went to church and upon seeing her guests kneeling in a corner absorbed in meditation, she thought, "I was right! If these men were rascals and thieves as my husband believes, they would not be so devoutly in prayer." But her amazement increased as the result of what followed. After Mass a certain Messer Guido, a very charitable person, distributed alms to all the poor who were in the church. But when he came up to the two friars he heard himself told that they did not desire any money.

Messer Guido persisted. "But since you are poor, why don't you take money like all the rest?" Friar Bernard answered, "Because we are voluntarily poor through the grace of God and in order to follow the Gospel."

"And did you ever possess anything in this world?"

"Many things, but we sold them to give to the poor."

The parishioners stood around in amazement. The mistress

of the house with the oven stepped up to say that she would lodge them for the love of God: "God will reward you for your good will," replied the friars. But Messer Guido, with greater right, wanted them to come to his house, saying, "This is the hospice that the Lord has prepared for you. Stay as long as you like."

Thus, the friars, by refusing temporal goods and promising the eternal ones, also obtained the goods of the world as a reward.

Around 1211, St. Francis sent Friar Bernard of Quintavalle to Bologna to convert souls to God. The preparations for the departure were brief: a sign of the Cross, the benediction of the teacher and off he went. Anyone else, confronting so hypercritical a city as Bologna, would have prepared a repertoire of flowery sermons and taken on a grave, dignified air. Bernard, on the contrary, entered the city wearing his shepherd's tunic and silently endured the mockery of the idle bands of street urchins; indeed, not to seem to avoid ridicule he stopped in the largest square. He sat down patiently and children, artisans, shopkeepers, and students gathered around him in a circle. One plucked at his cowl from behind, another hurled a clod at him, one pushed him on this side, and another on that. But Bernard smiled, not however, the smile of an idiot, but of a man who knows what he is about. He exposed himself voluntarily to such public ridicule for several days, until a doctor of laws, and a lecturer at the University of Bologna, Messer Niccolò dei Peppoli, who had been observing him, came up and asked: "Who are you? And where do you come from?" For answer, Bernard drew out the Rule of St. Francis from his tunic and gave it to the professor. Messer Niccolò read it with interest. Was wisdom, so searched after in books, perhaps to be found there? Then turning to some of his students, he said: "Verily this is the most exalted state of religious life that I have ever heard of, and this man and his companions are the most saintly men in the world. To revile him is the greatest sin, indeed, he should be honored as the friend of God." He invited Bernard to his house and later gave him a cottage to lodge his companions. The professor furnished it at his own expense, and became a protector of the friars. Thus honored by so esteemed a doctor, Bernard was sought after by the Bolognese who, once they knew him, became enthusiastic over his holy conversation and vied to see him. Anyone who could touch his cloak held himself to be blessed as though Bernard were a saint.

"This is bad," thought Friar Bernard. So one day he fled from the learned city and returned to St. Francis. "My father," he said, again amid the holy rusticity of Porziuncola, "the place has been taken in Bologna. Send other friars to live there and maintain it, for I have no profit there. Indeed, because of the great honors paid me, I fear I should have more to lose there than to gain." He left the harvest of souls to be reaped by his companions while he went looking for other insults and conversions. Meanwhile the germ which had been planted grew like a mustard seed. Niccolò dei Peppoli became a friar minor and the great jurist Accursio left a new place to the friars and soon after the foundations were laid for the Church of St. Francis, one of the most beautiful in Bologna. Common folk and nobles, learned glossarists and artisans asked to be buried in the shade of the cypresses of its church-yard, holding death sweet under the protection of St. Francis.

THE ROUND TABLE

As the knights of the Round Table returning from their feats gathered around King Arthur and were all served with perfect equality, at the same time and in the same way, so did the knights of poverty gather around St. Francis after their missions. And they loved each other and honored each other in a brotherly manner, even though the twelve of the first hour who formed the Franciscan Round Table were different in age and social class. They were nobles and rich men, like Bernard of Quintavalle; doctors of law and theology, like Pietro Cattani; priests like Silvester; peasants from the countryside around Assisi, and genuine knights like Angelo Tancredi of Rieti, whom Francis had conquered at the first stroke, when one day on the street he brusquely said to him, "Brother, you have been wearing the belt, sword, and spurs for a long time. Now it is time that you change the belt for the rope, the sword for the Cross, and the spurs for the dust of the street. Follow me and I will make you a knight of the army of Christ."

When the friars reassembled they were so happy to be together that they forgot all the world's insults and injuries. They spent their time either praying or working with their hands. They lived in purity and poverty; they conquered evil inclinations with virtues; they had nothing of their own at all, they used the books in common, and rose every night to pray together. The peace and harmony among them was wonderful. They loved each other with an intimate love; one served the other, one took care of the needs of the other, as a mother might take care of her son. One was ready to give his life for the other; those who had to command tried to be the most humble of all, those who had to obey never criticized the superior, because in him they saw only the authority of God, and they found every precept good and easy to follow. They were careful never to use offensive words, and if one said or thought something that might displease another, he asked his forgiveness on bended knee and beseeched the person offended to set foot on his mouth. Although very poor they always found something to give those who visited them.

Both rich and poor came down to the forest of Porziuncola where the treasure of poverty had been found. The friars were courteous with the rich, receiving them joyously and devising ingenious means to invite them to penitence. They rejoiced always because there was nothing in them or among them that disturbed them. But at a sign from the teacher they were ready to separate from each other and wander along the hard roads of the world.

Francis sent them out at random, and they like the errant knights had their king, Christ; their lady, Poverty; their land to be conquered, the world. But in the world St. Francis carefully distinguished one point, his little Assisi, and whereas many converts feel the need to flee from the people they know in order to be alone in an idyllic communion with their secret, Francis remained in his native region and began his apostolate there. It was there that he established his headquarters, it was there that he desired to die. And he desired that his friars, though moving with the freedom of the wind, should work habitually in their native place. For Francis, who was a genius in addition to being a saint, and a Latin genius at that, understood that the charity begins at the place of one's birth, and that there is no humanity where there is no fatherland.

ROME

The number of friars was twelve when St. Francis chose to transfer his Round Table from Porziuncola to a hut on the plain between Santa Maria of the Angels and St. Damian, which was called Rivo Torto because of a nearby gravelly torrent. The responsibility of directing the twelve was becoming a serious one. In May or June of 1210, Francis, who the year before had already sketched out an extremely simple Rule transcribed from the Gospel, thought that it was time to submit his work to the Church, especially in order to obtain permission to preach. One day he simply proposed to his fellow friars: "Let us go to our holy Father, Messer the Pope." All twelve set out on the journey, with the speed of one who leaves nothing behind and carries nothing to where he is going. St. Francis named Friar Bernard head of the expedition.

On the way they joyously sang the praises of the Lord, they talked about God and souls, they prayed without worrying about the necessities of the journey, lodging wherever night might catch them. When the *poverelli* presented themselves and asked for alms in His name, they did not fear being refused.

In Rome they found their own Bishop Guido, who at first was dismayed to see them, because he thought that they wanted to abandon Assisi. But when he learned of their intentions he rejoiced and promised to present them to the Pope, availing himself of his friendship with Cardinal Colonna of St. Paul.

Innocent III, who was princely of lineage and spirit, had an extremely acute sense of compassion but a great scorn for human misery. He scrutinized this mendicant, Francis, who had asked him for the privilege of living and preaching in the poverty of the Apostles. He questioned him carefully, fearing that he too might be one of those Waldensians or Albigensians, who under the pretext of following the Gospel, really wanted to dictate the law to the Church, and who were plaguing her with heresies. He looked directly into his eyes. Francis did not lower his, but expounded his simple Rule with a firmness that was equal to the regalness of the Pontiff who, sensing that he was confronting a man of his own stature, limited himself to observing:

"Children, your life seems too hard to us. We do not doubt that you, who are so full of fervor, can endure it. But we fear those who will come after you."

"Messer Pope, I commit myself entirely to my Lord Jesus Christ. How can He not keep the promises that He made to him who abandons everything for Him? Can He refuse what is needful to our humble life?"

Before a faith which would not have retreated without obtaining its intention, Innocent III told Francis and his fellow friars to pray to God to receive his will in regard to them and to come back when he called them.

The waiting period would have been a tormenting one for anyone with less faith, but St. Francis did not doubt the outcome. He spent his days in Rome nursing the sick in St. Anthony's hospital.

THE PARABLE OF THE KING'S LOVE

Meanwhile, the cardinals, meeting in a Consistorium, expressed their opposition to the approval of the new Order, because of the irreconcilability of communal life and of preaching with a collective absolute poverty, as no other Order had. But Cardinal Giovanni Colonna defended Francis with an irrefutable argument:

"I fear that we may displease God by refusing the petition of this poor man. And if you say that his Rule founded on the Gospel is against human possibilities, then you are saying that it is incompatible for men to follow the Gospel."

Innocent III then recalled Francis and his eleven companions. Tense, the night before, the Pope had dreamed that the Lateran Basilica was about to fall and that a man in motley dress had run to prop it up with his own shoulders, which had suddenly assumed an enormous size. Who believes in dreams? But the Pontiff did not believe his eyes when in the emaciated and radiant face of the poor man from Umbria he recognized the man of the dream. Meanwhile, Francis, in the presence of the Pope and all the cardinals, defended his ideal with a parable. Although the parable was a mode of didactic eloquence peculiar to Jesus, it had never occurred to anyone to speak in parables to a Pope. But Francis, of a poetic and dramatic mentality, inclined to incarnate his ideas in imagery, and thus he conceived the relation between his Order and Providence:

"A great king fell in love with a very beautiful woman who was poor and lived alone in a desert. He married her, he had many children by her and then left. When the children grew up, the mother said: 'Fear not and be not ashamed because you are the sons of the king. Go then to his court and he will minister to all your needs.' They went and the king was amazed at their beauty, and perceiving that they resembled each other he asked, 'Whose sons are you?' and when they answered that they were the sons of a poor woman who lived in a desert he embraced them with joy, saying, 'Fear not, you are my sons. If servants are nourished at my table, all the more so should you be nourished there who are my legitimate sons.'

"I," explained St. Francis, "am like the poor woman loved by the Lord and through His goodness I have had so many sons from Him. The King of Kings has promised me that He will nourish them, for if He nourishes strangers, how much more shall He provide for His legitimate sons? If the Lord bestows temporal goods on sinners for love of their children, He will bestow much more on evangelical men through His own merits."

Resting his chin on his hand, Innocent listened attentively and thought, "But is this really the man in my dream?" The cardinals, seated around the Pontiff, looked at Francis in amazement. They had never heard anyone talk about God and the soul in that modest and daring way, yet his parable would not have been out of place in the Bible.

That indefinable regalness about him which had already flashed in the pupils of the saint's eyes during the first interview, shone through even more brilliantly in the parable. No matter how poor his soul, it was beautiful and favored by God, precisely because it was poor. And as the sons of love, the men of his Order would be beautiful and privileged persons at the court of the King. One who was certain of being so loved by God could only be a saint. Innocent III understood and embraced Francis. He approved his Rule, and, in order to confer a greater authority on his work, he expressed the wish that Francis and his eleven followers wear the monastic tonsure.

This was the knightly investiture of the standard-bearer of Christ.

RIVO TORTO

Happy at having received the approval of the Church, the group returned to Rivo Torto. It was a miserable, almost uninhabitable hut, so narrow and low that it was a great effort for one to stand up straight in it. St. Francis had written the name of the friars above the rafters so that each could find his place when he wanted to pray or to rest. At Rivo Torto the penances were even more harsh, there was a lack of bread because of their great distance from human habitations and many languished for sheer hunger. One night one of the friars cried out, "I am dying! I am dying!" Francis was the first to get up and light the lamp.

"Who said he is dying?" he asked.

"I," a friar answered.

"What ails you? Why are you dying?"

"I am dying of hunger!"

Immediately St. Francis had the little reserves brought out; he prepared a table with all the elegance of poverty and invited all the other friars, himself included, to eat so that the hungry one would not be ashamed to eat by himself. For St. Francis taught his followers not to notice such straitened circumstances, to live in their own hearts enlarged greatly enough to lodge God there, to work externally only in order to perfect themselves internally, and to prize above all the honor of the apostolate in which the Church had confirmed them.

Some friars who could not read, one day said to Francis, "Teach us to pray."

"Say the Our Father," replied Francis, and then having the Passion of Jesus in mind, he added, "Say further: We adore Thee, Christ in all Thy churches that are in the whole world, and we bless Thee because Thou hast redeemed the world with thy Holy Cross."

They could not be poorer and therefore happier than this: For shelter, no convent, not even a cell; for a "refectory," the grass, where they ate raw turnip, crusts of bread and drank pure water; for a cloister they had the horizon; for a garden, the valley; for recreation, the leper hospital; for joy, prayer; for a feast, a day of meditation on the Carceri on the slopes of Mount Subasio, where caves and chasms opened amid a thick forest, inviting and welcoming one to contemplation.

It was an idyll with Lady Poverty. It was too much joy. One day while the friars were praying at their place, the pious silence was broken by a loud, rude voice.

"Whoa, my beast! We shall do very well in this place!" It was a peasant who was carrying on like a proprietor, pushing his donkey forward with the intention of using Rivo Torto as a stable. St. Francis trembled as the tyrannous invasion disturbed the prayer of the friars. Francis immediately abandoned the place saying, "My sons, the Lord has not called us to prepare a hospice for asses and to have frequent visits from men, but to preach and pray."

Thus the friars took leave of Rivo Torto, learning that no matter how small one makes oneself, reducing oneself to a hole like a beetle, he can never be sure that some donkey may not come along to drive him away. And this is just, since even a hole can become a palace, even a penny can become a million for the heart that loves it.

Driven out of Rivo Torto, the Round Table returned to Porziuncola where it had been born. Francis asked the Benedictines of Mount Subasio for permission to use the little church that had been restored with his own hands, and for permission to construct some huts of wattle, wood and clay nearby as dwellings for the friars. The Benedictines consented but Francis, to prevent the consent being perverted into a donation and therefore into a property for him, proposed to pay rent. This consisted of an annual tribute of one basket of fish caught in the river Tescio. And in order not to be outdone in generosity, the abbot of Subasio reciprocated with a small jar of oil.

THE CODE OF THE NEW KNIGHTS

The number of friars continued to increase. One proof of the sanctity of St. Francis was that where he passed by he aroused a desire to serve God as he served Him. A nuclei of the faithful were formed in the cities and towns, ruled like the community of Porziuncola, electing a superior who was called warden, who directly obeyed a superior who directed all the places of the province. The superior was called minister (or servant) and all the ministers were dependent on the minister-general who at first was St. Francis and then Pietro Cattani. Every now and then the general gathered all his sons together for a great chapter at St. Mary of the Angels.

The very short Rule of St. Francis, composed of versicles from the Gospel and approved by Innocent III, could not suffice an Order now become so vast. After the compilation in the spring of 1223 of another Rule which encountered great difficulties and which was lost, Francis, having retired to the hermitage of Fonte Colombo near Rieti, with Friar Leo of Assisi and Friar Bonizio of Bologna, wrote the definitive Rule in solitude and prayer. It was then approved on November 29 of the same year by Pope Honorius III.

There is no briefer or broader legislation in the world, or one that is more simple in its lines, more formative of character and yet more respectful of all individuality than this Franciscan code—its author called it the *Key to Paradise*—which summarized and prescribed evangelical perfection in twelve articles. The principal ones were:

Obedience. Obedience was required to the Pope and the Church before any other authority. (Francis held the priests of

Christ in such honor that he kissed the ground they walked on.) Obedience to direct superiors in whatever "place" the friars should happen to be, and not only to the superiors of a specific convent as the Rules of the preceding religious Orders prescribed. The friars, possessing no fixed properties, could not have any fixed superiors, yet even this privileged consequence of poverty was immediately corrected by this strict bond of obedience, which introduced a new element in medieval monastic legislation. Thus, their winged freedom of movement was curbed: they were as birds, but restrained through the heart by a thread of renunciation.

Poverty. Entrance into the Order was impossible without first renouncing one's own goods, and selling them, and giving the money to the poor. This done, the friars could possess nothing else, except a tunic, the cowl, the girdle. And if the tunic was patched so much the better, for it would do honor to the wearer. Nor was the friar to receive money for any reason at all, nor appropriate anything for himself; and he was to work without gain and beg without shame.

Purity. The friar was to live a life without voluntary defects; one marked by a continuous mortification, a maternal love for all creatures, but especially for the brethren, for the poor and the sick; a life of continuous intention of perfection.

Prayer and Work. These two activities were to be assiduously alternated. Through work each friar had to exercise decorously the trade that he knew, persevering in his vocation.

Apostolate. The friar had to preach, with the permission of the ecclesiastical authority, for the good and the edification of the people, but briefly, because the Lord pronounced brief words on earth. Those friars who wished could go to distant missions to bring the Gospel to the Saracens and other infidels, but only with the permission of the provincial ministers.

There was then a fourth precept implied in the whole of Franciscan life: *Gladness.* Gladness had a capital importance for St. Francis. A melancholy friar was a bad friar. Sadness is a sickness of the devil; sadness is to think of oneself, to mourn the past and sin, to desire impossible goods and impossible goods are false. Gladness is gratitude to God, trust in God, appreciation of the value of life, purity of heart, a denial of oneself and others. "Try always to make a show of gladness of countenance," Francis said. "If an act, however good, does not seem to be done willingly and fervently it generates disgust rather than promotes good."

POVERTY AND STUDY

There is a wealth that is not seen: knowledge. There are very heavy coins which do not have much of a ring but which can make others feel more inferior and ourselves more proud than do genuine coins: books, for instance. How then could Lady Poverty be in accord with study? Moreover, in the thirteenth century books were parchment manuscripts, bound in wood or in leather, with metal studs which cost much. Special rooms were required to keep them and they were not as handy and manageable as today. Could therefore they be possessed by the knights of poverty?

This was the very question that Richard of March, who was a nobleman and cultured, and who could give of everything except study, asked one day of St. Francis when he visited him in the bishop's house in Assisi. And St. Francis replied: "The friars must have nothing except the tunic which our Rule allows them, plus the girdle and breeches."

"But," objected the other, "what shall I do who own so many books, worth more than fifty pounds!" He was saddened at the thought of having to give them up.

"You see!" exclaimed Francis, "you wish to be considered by men as a friar minor and observant of the Gospel, but in reality you wish to have money!"

But in the young men of the time the desire for books was not born out of a covetousness for rich and rare things, but out of a thirst for knowledge and glory.

When a novice friar asked him for permission to keep a psalter, the saint, who knew the secret of reading consciences— the most interesting and complicated books of the world— answered, "Charles the Emperor, Roland and Oliver and all the paladins, mighty in arms, who chased the infidels with much sweat and travail to their deaths, won a memorable victory over them and finally conquered the glory of martyrdom, dying themselves in battle for the defense of Christ. But now there are many who would win honor and praise among men by the mere recital of their feats. Even among us there are many who would receive honors and praise by reading and preaching about the works accomplished by the saints."

Thereby, wisely, Francis sought to bend the youth's ambition toward virtue by counterposing the glory of action to the glory of words, the heroism of war to the heroism of the study table. But the young novice returned to the attack because he wanted to ransack all possible ways leading to an escape from the rule of strict obedience, and yet he did not want to disobey. Francis, seated near the fire, listened. Then pointed out the consequences of his attitude.

"After you will have had a psalter, you will want a breviary. And when you will have had the breviary, you will sit in your chair like a great prelate, and say to your brother, 'Bring me the breviary.'" Then, as if he could not reproach others without also accusing himself, Francis picked up a handful of ashes from the fireplace and sprinkled them over his head saying, "I want a breviary too! I want a breviary too!" And while the novice blushed, the saint confessed:

"Brother, once I too was tempted to have books, but not knowing the will of the Lord concerning this, I took up the Gospel and I prayed the Lord that He show me His will at the first opening. And at the end of my prayer, at the first opening of the book, my eyes lighted upon these words, 'Unto you it is given to know the mysteries of the Kingdom of God, but unto others in parables.'" And he added, "There are so many who willingly rise unto knowledge, that whosoever makes himself barren for the love of the Lord shall be blessed."

He meant that true knowledge does not come from books, but from faith, from humility and from works.

But when a youth appeared later at the friary in whom the love of study was a sincere, authentic vocation, unmixed with curiosity, vanity and pride, and when he tried to suppress it like a temptation, then St. Francis said to him, "Study and

teach, as long as the spirit of prayer be not extinguished in you."
That youth became St. Anthony of Padua.

For what St. Francis fought against as contrary to the poverty
of heart was that inflated knowledge which is not converted into
life, study without thought, thought without works, admiration
without imitation, egotistic study which is smugly pleased with
itself and never sacrifices itself for others.

Lady Poverty is in accord with study only when the study is
caritas.

THE CHAPTER OF THE MATS

One of the most memorable gatherings of the friars was that
held at St. Mary of the Angels on Pentecost in 1221. It was called
the Chapter of the Mats because the friars, divided in squads
according to their diverse provinces, were sheltered under
wicker cots of willow and rush matting. There were five thousand of them and yet not a sound of the usual raucous hustle
and bustle of crowds was audible in this army of penitents. They
slept on the bare earth with blocks of stone for pillows, praying, reciting the divine office, weeping for their sins and those
of others, especially of those of their benefactors. Or they were
seated in companies of forty, one hundred, two hundred, listening to one of their order discoursing about God, happy to be
together, united in a single heart and soul on that blessed plain
girded by dreaming hills. Barons and knights, noblemen and
common people, high prelates and clerics came to behold the
wondrous assembly of saints. And Messer Raniero Capocci,
cardinal deacon, expressed the opinion of all when he said,
"Verily this is the camp and the army of the knights of God."

But, above all, the people came to see their leader. And the
blessed Francis, raised high above the devout throng of his
sons, preached to them with that fervor that transhumanized
his thin and exhausted body.

"My children, we have promised great things to God: but
God has promised even greater things to us if we observe those
we have promised Him. Brief is the joy of this world, but the

pain that follows it is everlasting. Small is the pain of this life, but the glory of the life to come is infinite."

A great wave of hope enveloped the attentive friars as he spoke. He continued, recommending the observance of the fundamental rules of the Order, and ended his sermon as follows:

"I command by the merit of holy obedience that none of you that are assembled here have care or solicitude for what he shall eat or drink, nor for aught necessary to be body, but attend only to prayer and to the praise of God. Leave the solicitude for your body to Him, for He has special care of you."

This command seemed like stupidity to the prudent ones of the world. But soon people from Perugia, from Spoleto, from Foligno, from Spello, from Assisi came with mules, horses, loaded with bread and wine, with beans and cheese, and other things to eat, along with tablecloths, pitchers, bowls and glasses, and all required for five thousand poor of God. And they competed with one another as to who brought the heaviest load, while noblemen and knights held themselves honored to serve with humility and devotion. St. Francis' immense faith was immediately rewarded as if Christ, his King, were, in another form, renewing the Gospel miracle of the loaves and fishes for his five thousand. Thus he, who desired nothing, received even more than was needful from Providence.

During this chapter, Francis, having learned that many friars were sick and could not pray and were dying because of excessive self-imposed penances, ordered them to surrender to him their breastplates of iron, iron rings, chairs, and hair shirts with which they mortified the flesh. They obeyed and they made a great heap of these objects before him. Then, after receiving his blessing, they all left for their own provinces, free and swift as birds.

THE TEACHER

St. Francis loved the friars and with his natural gentleness he would not have been capable even of reproaching them. Indeed, he inclined to be silent, to endure, to assume the most painful duties, to work and to atone for them. But he understood that this was not the way to lead them to perfection. Therefore, knowing the weakness of each one, he brought them together or corrected them with great wisdom without being afraid of seeming to be very harsh and fantastic.

In order to mortify Friar Masseo for his pride in being a man of fair countenance and of eloquent speech, St. Francis, finding themselves together at a cross-roads where three roads met, one leading to Florence, the other to Arezzo, and the third to Siena, commanded him in the name of holy obedience to turn around and around like a top, and not to stop until ordered. Friar Masseo obeyed, albeit he was slightly ashamed since passers-by stopped and laughed to see him spin around like a child. But he obeyed so well that even after he fell to the ground from dizziness, he straightened himself up and started all over again. He did this several times until Francis cried, "Stay still!" And Friar Masseo stayed still.

"In what direction is your face turned?" asked Francis.

"Toward Siena."

"That is the way which God wills that we go."

They arrived in Siena during a fight between men of opposed factions, in which two had already been killed. St. Francis spoke to them with such devotion that the enemies made peace among themselves. Peace was also restored to the city and the bishop invited Francis with great honors to his house in appreciation of the good done to his Siena.

But on the following morning Francis wanted to leave without the knowledge of the bishop, because public demonstrations were displeasing to his humility. Friar Masseo followed behind him in silence, thinking his teacher certainly very eccentric. Only the day before he had him spin round like a top, and now here he was slipping out of the bishop's house, a guest to whom his host could bid no farewell, indeed, without even a word of thanks to the good bishop who had done him so much honor. But his conscience admonished him that such thoughts were not humble, that he was mistaken in wishing to judge a man like Friar Francis because, after all, that journey which had begun with his childish spinning and had ended up with that morning flight had, after all, had the result of preventing a slaughter in Siena. And he walked with lowered head when St. Francis, who read the secrets of his soul, said: "Hold fast to these thoughts for they are good and useful and leave your first murmurings, which were suggested by the devil."

On another occasion in order to tame the instinctive presumption of Friar Masseo, he said:

"For this very reason you will take upon yourself the offices of doorkeeper, almoner, and cook, and when the other friars are eating, you will eat outside the door and attend to all who come there. Before they knock you will say a kind word, and you will send them off in peace, so that your companions need not be disturbed."

Friar Masseo drew back his cowl, lowered his head and for several days discharged the three offices, to the admiration and compassion of his companions who were pained to see a man of such great talent wasted in the performance of that triple task. Together they went to discuss the matter with St. Francis, who consented to their brotherly request and said to Friar Masseo:

"Your companions want a share of the offices that I have given you, and I too wish them to be shared."

"Father," replied Friar Masseo, "whatever task you lay upon me is for me like one laid upon me by God."

Thus, the lesson in humility for one had been a lesson in humility and charity for all.

The teacher stressed humility more than all the other virtues, indeed he did not believe in the other virtues and especially in the spirit of prayer and contemplation of his friars, if he did not see them founded in humility. Friar Rufino was a solitary so rapt in God that he had almost forgotten the faculty of speech since he so often hid himself in the forest for prayer. Therefore, one day Francis commanded him to go to Assisi and preach there. Friar Rufino thought to defend himself against this command by answering, "Reverend Father, I pray that you forgive me and send me not because, as you know, I have not the grace to preach, and I am simple and unlearned."

Francis' reply was prompt:

"Since you have not obeyed quickly, I command you to go to Assisi in your breeches, to enter into a church and to preach thus to the people."

It was a very harsh command for a noble gentleman like Rufino who was born in Assisi and who had his family and many acquaintances there. Nonetheless he obeyed and seeing him in such a get-up, the people jeered at him and said he was crazy from excess of penance. Meanwhile, St. Francis, reconsidering the command he had given and Friar Rufino's prompt obedience, felt remorse. "Whence," he said to himself, "O son of Peter Bernardone, you wretched little man, whence comes this presumption to command Friar Rufino, one of the noblest gentlemen of Assisi, to go there and preach like a madman? By God, you will prove in yourself what you command others to do."

He stripped and, followed by Friar Leo who carried his and Friar Rufino's habits, he went to Assisi, and entered into the same church where his companion was preaching. In breeches like his friar he mounted the pulpit and began to preach on the poverty of Christ and on voluntary penance with such fervor that the people, instead of laughing, began to weep.

Thus did the teacher correct his possible excesses of severity and through the divine spirit that animated him he plucked miracles of conversion from seeming eccentricities. His counsels were collected in twenty-eight small chapters which place especial stress on poverty, on charity, on obedience, on the imitation of Christ, and on the wisdom of the humble. There is an intense content in their very brevity that deserves to be meditated upon and to be revered. But in order to understand their full power it would be necessary to liberate them from the prison of their pages and to hear them as they were pronounced by the teacher at Rivo Torto, at Porziuncola, at Carceri, at Fonte Collana, on Mount La Verna, in the verdant depths of the forests, in touch with the beauties of nature created by God and newly interpreted by St. Francis.

But example is worth more than precepts. St. Francis knew this well.

As soon as the Lord entrusted the friars to him, he confessed in his Testament, he felt the responsibility of a teacher and founder. And this sense of responsibility became even more acute, a concern marking all his acts, committing him to perfection. His fundamental thought was this: "It is needful that I myself be as I desire them to be, and even more so." Even more so; a gigantic model in order to render visible the virtues others must copy, and in order to convince the weak that they can be copied. He became pitiless toward himself, imposing on himself a superhuman discipline. And the more the friars deviated from his ideal, the more he mortified himself to atone for their shortcomings, and in order that they might mend their ways.

This responsibility of example, in which the awareness of his mission was asserted, increased the power of his personality as teacher, which had on its credit side all the gifts of a profound and keen genius, of a magnificently generous soul, musical, solar, free from every formalism, which made joy spout out of sorrow, beauty out of ugliness, and goodness out of apathy or of fault.

5

The Poor Ladies

As SOON AS Francis returned from Rome with the permission to preach, Bishop Guido thought to make use of him for the good of his diocese. So he entrusted him with the task of delivering Lenten sermons for the year 1211 in the largest church of Assisi. The beautiful San Rufino church was filled by the local citizens burning with curiosity to hear the son of Pietro Bernardone preach with apostolic authority, a man now recognized as a man of God by Rome itself. Unfailingly present were the women-folk of the Offreducci family, Donna Ortolano, with her three young daughters: Clare, Catherine, and Beatrice. The Offreducci, one of the most powerful noble families of Assisi, occupied a palace-fortress on the Piazza San Rufino, and were boastfully proud of the seven knights of their lineage who were valiant and cruel, tenacious in their hates and loves, ferocious in vengeance and thirsty for military glory, booty and for adventure in distant lands.

The three girls had grown up amid the clamors of war. They had gone into exile to Perugia when the nobles had been driven out of Assisi. The girls were reserved in bearing and pious; they never looked down from the balcony when knights and soldiers paraded on San Rufino square, or when the people gathered to listen to the town-crier, or when the little army filed into the cathedral to receive the benediction of the patron saint before leaving with its *Carroccio* and its banner to fight against the neighboring communes.

108

From her mother—who had gone on a pilgrimage to the Holy Land as soon as she became a bride—Clare had inherited a fervid piety, and from her father and warrior ancestors a firmness that would not make her bend to any violence. She understood the Latin of the Mass, she read the lives of saints, she worked for the poor more than for herself, she often set the tastiest dishes aside to give to the poor, and she prayed much, counting her Our Fathers with little beads. The recitals of the jongleurs had no attraction for her, the antics of the buffoons did not make her laugh, the talk of her friends did not interest her, and the songs and the love-poetry of the troubadors gave her an anxiety not of ordinary love but of the Absolute. And when her kinsmen talked about marriage to her, she would answer, "Let's wait!" This was to avoid having to say "I don't want to." But why didn't she want to?

While she was asking herself what she wanted and what she was to do with her life, St. Francis began his preaching mission. He was then on the threshold of thirty and there was nothing beautiful about him save his voice and eyes. And as he talked with that voice and with those eyes he transported his listeners. The overwhelming power of his preaching consisted especially in the fact that he lived as other men spoke; he really did the penances and practiced the virtues that many preachers recommend but often do not always follow themselves. And he put into words the joy and beauty which men were seeking in life, in order to make the virtues more attractive. His action was word and his word poetry, doubly beautiful for what he did and how he did it. Clare sensed the response that her conscience awaited from her in the ideal of this wondrous preacher and she said to herself, "I must talk with him."

ST. CLARE'S VOCATION

Clare told one of her friends, Bona of Guellfuccio, about the impression the jongleur of God had left with her since the time when he sang on the square to beg stones for St. Damian, surrounded by jeering street urchins. No feat of war or tournament could rival his courage, no richness of court pleased her as much as his marvelous poverty. The two friends managed to approach St. Francis through Friar Rufino and Friar Silvester, who were kinsmen of the Offreducci.

At the first meeting in the little chapel of Porziuncola, Francis, who knew her by sight and reputation, knew that among the thousand souls, who shared a crowd's easy susceptibility to enthusiasm and sudden changes of mood, there was none who understood him more thoroughly and who was more capable of following him courageously than Clare. And while she, vibrating with admiration revealed herself to him, asking him to teach her how to live only for God in perfect poverty, the saint remembered and reflected. The maiden on her knees before him came from the clan of the Offreducci who had looked upon him with contempt when he was but the son of a merchant. He had looked upon them with a certain envy when he had dreamed of wearing golden spurs. His Uncle Monaldo had fought against Offreducci and his faction at the battle of Collestrada, as an exile in the ranks of the Perugians. And now the flower of that proud house rendered the most coveted homage that a knight could ever dream of. Who among the knights of Arthur's Round Table had ever experienced a similar adventure? The herald-troubador of Christ immediately felt the mission of bringing the virgin to his King. And he agreed to talk to her clandestinely in her own house, in the houses of friends, in Porziuncola, teaching her the vanity of the world, the loftiness of the religious life, his ideal of poverty, without hiding from her the serious sacrifices that they would impose on a young girl like herself. But he would also enflame her with love for Our Lord which conquers every obstacle.

The immediate preparation was brief. Clare became more fervent about her intention and immediately showed her spiritual affinity with the teacher, since she did not want time to lapse between decision and deed. The practice of the Gospel, to the letter, even for her, a delicate woman? So be it! Poverty for the daughter of knights, to whom even the superfluous was necessary? So be it! And it was not a question of entering an already well-known convent, of taking the highway of an ancient and accredited Order, but of making her way by herself and of starting the Order by herself, on the word of a new man who in the eyes of his elders still had something of the madman about him.

A few days before Palm Sunday of 1211, Clare went to St. Francis with the ardent desire to know when she would be able to give herself completely to God, by leaving her home. The teacher explained to her what she should do. On the morning of Palm Sunday the Assisians saw Donna Clare of the Offreducci in the cathedral at a High Mass in her richest velvet gown. She was elegant, beautiful and happy among her sisters and friends, as she had never been before.

"Certainly Madonna Clare is going to become a bride!" whispered the curious. But during the Mass she was so rapt in meditation that she did not notice that everybody was rising from their places and going to the altar to take the blessed palm. When she emerged from her rapture, she did not dare to cross the church by herself. Then something of a prophetic nature occurred. Bishop Guido in person, who was privy to everything, took a palm frond, descended the steps of the altar and placed it in the hands of the praying girl. Even with St. Clare, as with St. Francis, it was the Church herself, who, in the person of a bishop, blessingly welcomed the new ideal of religious life.

FLIGHT AND RENUNCIATION

Assisi was asleep under the moonlit sky. Even the palace of the Offreducci seemed to be shrouded in sleep. The seven fierce knights were asleep, Donna Ortolana and her smallest daughters were asleep, the hand-maidens were asleep and even the crossbow-man at the main gate was taking a nap stretched out on his plank. Clare was preparing to run away from home. She tiptoed out of her dark room, anxiously holding her breath, and went down the stairs. Since she could not go out the gate that was under guard, she went to the gate of the "dead man," the small gate that was part of every medieval house and which was used as an emergency exit by knights only. It was barricaded by rocks and logs. Laboriously, tearing her dainty hands and startled at every sound, Clare removed the logs, and finally opened the gate. A friend, Pacifica di Guelfuccio was waiting for her outside. The two girls ran swiftly down the hill in the dark.

Friar Rufino and Friar Silvester, leaving the other friars singing Lauds in the little church of St. Mary of the Angels, were dispatched to meet them, and then all the knights of poverty moved out with blazing torches to receive the fugitives, and to escort them through the forest in a cortege in the reddening dawn to the church where St. Francis was waiting for them. Prostrate in front of the altar of Mary, Clare consecrated herself to the Lord promising to follow Him according to poverty and the Rule of her teacher Francis. To seal the nuptial pact, she changed the gown she had been wearing that morning, the dress of velvet, the necklaces, the gem-studded girdle, and the satin slippers, for a coarse gray tunic, a rope girdle, and a pair of wooden clogs. But this was not enough. Clare bared her head, and St. Francis sheared off her hair. The scissors cut the thick tresses with difficulty, again and again they snipped noisily over rebellious locks which now were strewn all over the floor like spun gold.

Clare acquired an incorporeal beauty, and the knights of poverty with an admiring tenderness gazed upon the noble girl who had made herself like one of them, subjecting herself to the same harsh life for the same ideal. And Clare had the virile heart to live this life to the full, to the point of begging from door to door, of going on missions to countries beyond the seas—even to the point of martyrdom. But a black veil now covered the shorn head and the white forehead: under that veil the friar minor was still a woman. Dawn was awakening the fields when St. Francis entrusted his daughter to the Benedictine sisters of the convent of St. Paul, near Assisi.

THE PERSECUTION

Dawn was awakening the hills when the inhabitants of the palace of the Offreducci noticed that Clare's chamber was empty, the bed intact, the little gate "of the dead man" forced open by some miracle of strength. Immediately the palace was thrown into an uproar as if from an enemy assault. And an assault had been made—a new ideal, breaking the family traditions, had stolen their "silver dove" from the nest, sweeping her along the dangerous path of that poverty which had unhinged the mind of the son of a merchant. Donna Ortolana counseled peace, the sisters wept, the handmaidens ran hither and thither at a loss as to what to do, but the seven knights rallied kinsmen and consorts, leaped on their horses and galloped wildly to the convent of St. Paul.

Clare took refuge in the church where, under the right of asylum, they could not touch her without committing sacrilege. She clasped the altar, as the knights alternately showered her with promises and threats, now reminding her of the nobility of her birth, in comparison to the meanness of the life that she was choosing; now trying to move her to remorse by picturing the sorrow of her mother and her family, now swearing to take vengeance and violent action. This was all that was needed to re-confirm Clare in her intention, because, like them, she had the heart of a lion.

Suddenly, still holding to the altar with one hand, she swiftly removed the veil with the other and revealed her shorn head.

The knights drew back without a word because a shorn head was the sign of consecration to God. The men of iron, who had cursed and sinned, were afraid of God's thunderbolts, and Clare was lost forever to them and their egotistic love. For after a few days of useless struggle, the defeated kinsmen lifted the siege and returned to their palace.

Then Francis came with Philip and Bernard to take the valorous Lady of Poverty to a safer place. And all three cavalierly escorted her through the blossoming forest to another Benedictine monastery on the slopes of Mount Subasio, St. Angelo of Panso.

CATHERINE'S FLIGHT

Two weeks later Clare's sister Catherine knocked on the door of that convent. She was a sixteen-year-old adolescent, with blue eyes.

"I also want to live like you, for the Lord."

The new flight caused another tumult in the house of the Offreducci and on the following day twelve armed men attacked the convent. The Benedictine sisters imprudently allowed some knights, her close kin, to enter the courtyard in order to talk with Catherine. Unable to persuade her to return of her own free will, they dragged her out of the monastery. And since the young girl resisted like a lion cub, shouting, "Help, Clare, my sister! Christ Lord, have mercy!" her kinsmen brutally dragged her, by the hair, at times, down the mountain path. Streaks of blood and locks of hair marked her passage on rocks and briars until the heroic child fainted. For a moment the warriors stood perplexed before the pale immobility of the girl, but when they tried to pick her up it was impossible; her weight was like lead. And her fierce Uncle Monaldo, who had raised his hand to strike her, remained with his arm suspended in the air as though paralyzed.

A miracle? Doubtless. Clare was praying on her knees in the church of the convent and the Lord had answered her prayer, teaching those men of violence that might can do naught against a will, and that even the will of a child is invincible if it is linked to His.

St. Francis came later and received Catherine as a nun, changing her name to Agnes (from *Agnello,* meaning lamb), because she had sacrificed herself like a lamb to the divine Lamb. Was she too young? Unprepared? But she had already made the novitiate of martyrdom, and she had first been shorn of her hair by the brutality of her kinsmen. But the two sisters were not even safe at St. Angelo of Panso, and besides the way of the Benedictines was not theirs. St. Francis accordingly asked the Bishop of Assisi for permission to use St. Damian as a habitation for the poor girls and it was granted.

THE CASTLE OF LADY POVERTY

Clare knew what St. Damian represented for her teacher. She knew that since she could not go through the world like the

friars, without a house and without a roof, the most worthy
habitation that Francis could offer her was that which he himself had reconstructed with his own hands in the first fervor of
his conversion, and which still contained his precious memento:
the crucifix that had spoken to him. Clare therefore advanced
to become a custodian and an initiator: she was to keep custody
over the ideal of the teacher in order to transform it into the
Second Order which would be born from his brain and her
sacrifice.

Clare and Agnes did not remain alone at St. Damian. Their
extraordinary adventures set all Assisi and the neighboring
towns agog. And many other young girls felt a desire to imitate
them. The religious life appeared to be the only ideal good
without deceptions, and this new religious life started by Clare
held greater attraction than that of the established convents
where the sceptered abbesses dealt as equals with bishops and
with feudal lords. Clare's life seemed to be closer to the poverty
of Christ, the crib and the Cross.

The first to come to the peace of St. Damian were the friends
of the Offreducci girls, those who had played with them as
children, spun and embroidered with them next to the fireplace or on the terrace blooming with flowers. They were
Pacifica of Guelfuccio, Benvenuta and Filippa. Then came
other cousins or kinfolk, the others from distant castles, among
them the beautiful Amata of Corano, who suddenly had run
away from home on the eve of her marriage, leaving on the roof
her white bridal gown and the garland of roses that had been
prepared for the ceremony. She had fled to St. Damian as if
summoned by an irresistible call, and she remained until her
death. Later even Clare's mother and her little sister, Beatrice,
came. Thus the good Lord paternally reconstituted the family
around the virgin who had abandoned it for His sake.

St. Francis found a name for the daughters of his ideal that
expressed this ideal. He did not call them sisters minor, as he
had called his sons friars minor, but chivalrously he called them
the *Poor Ladies* to remind them and others that in the harshest
poverty they must consider themselves noblewomen, brides of

Christ, rich with all for having renounced all, and ladies, *Dominae* in the Roman sense, in order to respect themselves and to be respected.

With his troubador fantasy Francis called St. Damian the Fortress of Poverty, for even though it had the superiority of stone and walls over the hovels of the friars, poorer than this it would be impossible to be. The church was low, dark and bare: a bare room, with a prison-like window, served as a choir, five steps below the church, with tables chained to the walls and hinged seats for stalls and a bench for a kneeling-stool, with two rustic lecterns which looked like havens for doves. They had a dormitory without beds—the healthy ones slept on straw, the sick on straw-mattresses—a refectory with a rough-hewn table and earthenware pottery, and for St. Clare, a terrace as small as a flower-bed. Yet amid this squalor everything was warmed with the smiles of people consecrated to mildness and peace. The sliver of light which came into the small choir illumined it as brightly as though the sun came from within, the hanging flower-bed was as blooming and fragrant as a big garden; it seemed impossible that it could contain so many geraniums and passion flowers, sweet basil, mint and pink-root. The horizon appeared infinite from that little garden, and the more the soul beholding it was in a state of grace the more the horizon broadened.

The Poor Ladies, like the friars minor, took vows of obedience, poverty, chastity and gladness. They were never idle; they worked for the churches and the poor; they prayed and nursed the lepers whom St. Francis sent to them, and they often suffered hunger because they could not go begging for alms but they had to wait until they were brought to St. Damian. And they suffered the biting cold of the winters under Mount Subasio, and the freezing north winds even in spring.

But they loved their poverty because it signified total dedication to the Father of the Heavens and the vigorous imitation of Christ Crucified. Their teacher Francis comforted them in this.

TEACHER AND DISCIPLE

Francis, however, did not go to St. Damian as often as the Poor Ladies would have liked. He reduced his visits when he saw them well on the way to perfection: a perceptive teacher, he wanted them to learn to get along without him, to follow the ideal, not the man, to love the great King and not his herald. Besides, Francis did not go willingly to where he noticed that he was admired, and the humble nuns admired him without limit.

One day he was expected for a sermon. "He's coming! He's coming!" repeated the sisters, happy to hear the will of God in the words of their teacher. When Francis entered into the church, he sensed this eager expectation in the air and said, "Bring me some ashes." He plunged his hands into the gray dust and spread it on the floor in a circle around him. Then he sprinkled the rest on his head and while a shiver of death went through the virgins, he loudly intoned the *Miserere,* the psalm of repentance and of mercy, of annihilation of man and of exaltation of God. Then he left. The sermon was over.

He was severe, but paternal. He watched over them and helped them, even when he feigned that he had forgotten them. And he promised them in writing, in a letter sent to Clare in the first years of their foundation:

"Since, through divine inspiration, you have become daughters and handmaidens of the most high King, the Heavenly Father, and you have met the Holy Ghost, electing to live according to the perfection of the Holy Gospel, I myself wish and promise, also in the name of my friars, to take a vigilant care of you and a special interest in you, as I do of them."

Sometimes the thought of that Rule, without any mitigating provisions, which he had dictated to those noblewomen, weighed on his conscience. Was it not too much for Clare and her companions?

One evening, after having been driven out of Siena, Francis and Friar Leo were laboriously crossing the treeless countryside. It was a stark, naked landscape which conjured up the idea of souls devastated by a great passion. And he was so tired that it was hard for him to drag himself through that caved-in terrain. Among the thoughts that weighed him down, one pounded insistently on his brain: "Clare is suffering tribulations too great in behalf of your poverty. Penances that break a man are not suitable for women. And that soul has entrusted herself to your guidance and you do not know how to keep account of her strength. You will have to answer to God for this. Clare is suffering. She is dying."

Oppressed by this thought, Francis, foundering in the clayey path, came to a well lost in that solitude, and he threw himself on the parapet, instinctively seeking the coolness of the water at the bottom. Friar Leo sat down on the side of a ditch. The moon was rising over the clay. Suddenly, the saint found his voice again.

"Friar Leo, little lamb of God, do you know what I see in the mirror of this water?"

"The moon, father," replied Friar Leo.

"No, I see Clare's face, pure and resplendent, like that of one who lives in the perfect grace of the Lord."

And feeling once more lighthearted, he resumed the journey, praising God for Sister Clare and for the comfort that He had given him.

The great consideration in which he held his spiritual daughter was manifested by the fact that he turned to her for advice and comfort. When he was seized by doubt that the solitary life was better for him than a militant apostolate, he asked for an opinion inspired by prayer from only two persons. One was Sister Clare. Having heard the commission from Friar Masseo, she immediately threw herself into prayer. Then she went back to Friar Masseo and said:

"God says that you say this to St. Francis: that God has not called him to this state only for himself, but that he might produce fruit in souls and so that many may be saved through him."

Thus, the humble disciple became herself a teacher at a decisive moment. St. Francis could find himself in her, just as the artist finds himself in his work, but with something different which was lacking in him and which in her came from the involuntary pride of her innocence and from her feudal blood: self-assuredness and the taste for resistance.

THE BANQUET OF LOVE

Nonetheless, Clare felt like a little girl before St. Francis. And, like a little girl, she desired to dine for once alone with him. Perhaps a memory of the banquets in her home or of the courteous friendship of the past came to flower in that childish desire. The teacher always responded "no" to her entreaties, perhaps because he too at bottom desired the same thing. So he refused that consolation to his daughter in order to deny it to himself. It was his friars who convinced him.

"Father," they said, "it seems to us that this rigidity is not in accordance with Christian charity. Why do you not desire to grant so trifling a favor to Sister Clare, a virgin so holy, so beloved of God, that through your preaching she left behind the riches and the pomp of the world?"

St. Francis who desired nothing better than this justification, and willingly committed himself to the opinions of others, said:

"Since it seems thus to you, so it seems to me." But with that princely delicacy that was his by nature, he sought perfection in courtesy. "In order that Clare may be more comforted," he told them, "I desire that this banquet be held at St. Mary of the Angels. She has been cloistered for a long time in St. Damian, thus it would do her good to see the place where she got her tonsure and became the bride of Jesus Christ. There we shall dine together in the name of God."

Finally on the appointed day, Clare left St. Damian with a companion, and accompanied by the knights of St. Francis acting as a guard of honor, she went down the flower-strewn hills to Porziuncola and knelt, in commemoration and deep emotion, before the altar of her nuptials and then, while awaiting the dinner hour, the friars showed her around this convent without buildings, consisting only of huts and chapels in the depths of the forest. Meanwhile, Francis was having the dinner prepared on the ground, as usual. When everything was ready, St. Francis and one of his companions, and St. Clare and one of her companions made ready to sit down, after which all the others humbly sat around them in a circle, on the carpet of moss, in the shade of the oak trees. Never had the Round Table had more beautiful company and a childlike happiness spread among the knights before the Princess of Poverty.

At the first course, St. Francis began to talk about God so sweetly, so loftily, so wondrously, that the abundance of divine grace descending upon them made them so rapt in God they forgot the food, the place and even themselves. In one stroke the saint had transported them from the gladness of this life to another, infinitely greater.

Meanwhile from Assisi, from the Bettona, from the surrounding countrysides, the bright light of a fire was seen in the plain around St. Mary of the Angels. "Fire! Fire! The place of the friars is burning!" And the inhabitants came running to extinguish the fire, but they found no flames in the forest, only the holy company, around the humble table, rapt in ecstasy, with their eyes and hands lifted to heaven. Then they understood that the fire was only a sign of the divine ardor burning in those exceptional souls, and they left edified and comforted in their hearts.

THE LITTLE PLANT

In 1215 St. Francis asked that Clare officially assume the administration of St. Damian with the title of Abbess. The virgin had to accept out of obedience and, feeling the responsibility of her charge, only one thing preoccupied her: namely, to be the first in every virtue and the last in every concession.

She slept on the bare ground or on twigs, she wore a hair shirt, and ate only what was necessary. Yet, to see her smiling, with that bearing of a duchess in her worn tunic, patched but clean, none ever would have said that she was wracking her body in penance. When the sisters were still sleeping in their little cots at dawn she rose, went into the church, lit the lamp and then, not without a twitch of pain for having to break their youthful slumber, she would call the others with a bell which prolonged its peals through the little convent. But even more silvery than the bell was the voice of Clare which rose above the others in the choir singing praises to the Lord. Late at night, she walked through the poor dormitory, observing the sleeping sisters one by one, covering them with love, stopping at the bedside of the sick, while for the younger, the weaker, the more tempted ones, she always had a maternal caress.

She never gave an order that she herself had not first carried out; she preferred doing to commanding, serving to being served. She always chose the most uncomfortable place, the stalest bread, the most tattered tunic, and she nursed the most repulsive illnesses. For humility she washed the feet of lay sisters who came in from the outside. She not only nursed them materially as the Rule provided, but she educated them. She taught them how to pray and read, she directed their labors, those beautiful embroideries which were sent to the poor churches and which are still one of the glories of Assisi. She kept them happy. And when she divined remorse or temptation in the heart of a sister, she would call her aside, knowing so well how to talk understandingly, going so far as to kneel before her so that the sister might confess her torment to her, that she succeeded in comforting her. She also concerned herself with their spiritual culture, seeking good preachers. Once when Pope Gregory IX forbade the friars to visit convents without special permission, Clare reacted like a feudal lady. "Henceforth take away also the mendicant friars, since you have taken away those who give us nourishment of life!" At the risk of dying of hunger, she sent away the mendicants since she could not have the friars who brought them spiritual bread.

Gregory IX then referred the prohibition to the minister-general.

Her unconquerable faith was never discouraged by adversity. Was there not enough bread at the hour of repast, let the housekeeper begin the distribution and the bread would increase gradually, sufficing for everyone. Was there no oil even for the sick? No fear: with her delicate hands, the abbess washed the water pitcher in boiling water, she put it on the little enclosure wall outside and before the almoner Friar Bencivenga arrived the pitcher was full, so that the rustic friar grumbled, "Those women called me just to fool me."

St. Francis had felt the Lord through direct inspiration and found Him among the lepers and the poor. Clare had felt Him through Francis and she had absorbed the spirit of the teacher as a plant absorbs solar energy from light. Therefore, she declared herself to be the little plant of the blessed Francis and sought to re-live his inclinations, piety and ideal as a daughter.

St. Francis rose up to God in the contemplation of beautiful and holy nature. Clare wanted flowers in her little garden and when she sent the serving sisters outside the convent she admonished them that upon seeing beautiful, blooming and leafy trees they were to praise God. St. Francis went to lands beyond the seas to convert infidels and St. Clare too wanted to leave her homeland and die as a martyr for Christ. St. Francis made an ardent cult of infancy and of the Passion of Jesus, so much so that he instituted the crib at Greccio and received the stigmata on Mount La Verna, and St. Clare so loved the Infant Jesus that she merited seeing Him and holding Him in her arms, and she suffered so from the sorrows of the Lord that one year, from Maundy Thursday to Holy Saturday, she remained in her cell like a dead person, while her soul relived the torment of the Passion. St. Francis, permeated by the mystery of the Eucharist, swept out churches in reverence of the body of Christ, and St. Clare made the Blessed Sacrament the fulcrum of her hidden life and worked to adorn the church, fixing the ideal of her teacher in embroideries either with designs of flowers, trees, birds, as simply as he saw and loved them, or with that cross-stitch which both recalled and engraved the sign of redemption at every drawing of the needle on the fabric.

Because of this identity of ideals, there is nothing strange about the legend of the roses.

St. Francis and St. Clare were walking together through the countryside white with snow. Upon coming to a cross-road near St. Damian, the teacher spoke first and said, "We must now go our separate ways."

The word of renunciation came always from him, the word

that signifies strength. Clare fell to her knees on the snow with that humility which came to her spontaneously only before the teacher, and waited for him to bless her. But upon rising, her heart trembled like a sparrow in the desolation of the winter landscape, and human desire forced her to formulate a little girl's question:

"Father, when shall we see each other again?"

"When the roses will have bloomed," replied Francis briefly, because he too was deeply moved. He had gone forward only a few steps when Clare called him back.

"My father!"

He turned around. The shrub in front of Clare had become a rosebush of flaming blossoms and wherever the two saints rested their eyes, roses bloomed in the snow as in May.

When two people separate for love of Him, the Lord unites them forever. The thread of gold which unites is not nearness nor affection, but duty lived and suffered together for the same ideal.

THE FEMALE KNIGHT OF POVERTY

But where St. Clare most showed the identification of her thought with that of St. Francis was in the defense of his bride, Lady Poverty. The virgins of St. Damian lived under a brief Rule similar to that St. Francis had given his friars. Around 1216 Clare requested Innocent III for the privilege of poverty for herself and her sisters. The Pope granted it, indeed, he wrote the first words of the brief with his own hand, observing with a smile that such a request had never before been presented at the court of Rome. In 1219, while Francis was in the Orient, Cardinal Ugolino, who protected the Poor Ladies in the name of the Holy See approved the very strict Rule, which had been suggested to him by Clare. When, after the death of St. Francis, the same cardinal became Pope Gregory IX, he told her that such poverty and such fasts were excessive for young women. In the belief that her resistance derived from her respect of the vow, he said, "If it is because of the vow of poverty, we absolve you of it." Clare rose up as if the ideal of the departed teacher were burning in her warrior blood, "Holy Father, absolve me of my sins, but not of the vow to follow our Lord."

The more some followers of Francis attacked the dream of the founder, the more the abbess armed herself to defend it in her fortress, gathering around her the most faithful who considered St. Damian as their bulwark and Clare as the surviving spirit of the inimitable teacher. Other converts came into the Second Order asking and receiving permission to own lands and houses. Over this, Clare suffered acutely. How could they call themselves "Poor Clares" when they despised the admonition that the teacher had written for her, for them? "I, humble Friar Francis, desire to follow the life and the poverty of our most high Lord Jesus Christ and of His most Blessed Mother and to persevere in this to the end, and I beseech you, my ladies, and I counsel you to live always in that very holy life and poverty, and keep watch attentively so that, either by the teaching or counsel of someone, you do not ever stray from it for as long as you live."

These words were Clare's dominating thought. She had no peace, and knew how to put off death itself until Innocent IV approved the Rule in twelve articles like that of the friars minor, written by her and fully in conformity with the principle of absolute poverty.

THE GREAT ITALIAN WOMAN

St. Damian did not only have to fight battles of ideas behind its peaceful walls. In the summer of 1241, Frederick II, at war with the Pope, hurled his Saracen troops against the inhabited places of the valley of Spoleto.

The Saracens fell upon the country like a cloud of locusts, devastating fields and sacking towns. Even the fortress of poverty was besieged. The infallible cross-bow men had already scaled the enclosure wall, and they leaned a ladder against the old gate of the convent to invade it with the fury of the satanized, sneering and jeering in the certainty of finding prey. Terror reigned within. The sisters huddled around the bed of the ailing Clare like a flock of doves. Clare did not tremble. The shouts of the assailants kindled her blood and stiffened her nerves, just as the risk of battle affected her kinsmen. She was the kind of a woman who would have climbed the main towers to help the armorers to prepare the incendiary materials against the besiegers. Now she did not even have a halberd with which to defend herself, but she had her heart and her God. She rose from bed, sent for the ciborium of ivory and silver, which contained the Blessed Sacrament, and she knelt before it, praying:

"Lord, dost thou desire to hand Thy unarmed handmaidens, whom I have nourished for love of Thee, to the pagans? Lord, Thou defend them, I cannot!"

Immediately the voice of a child answered from the small tabernacle.

"I will always watch over you."

Clare's soul, lifted up in hope, could not forget its own native land, and, with the gratitude of a daughter, she prayed: "My Lord, if it please Thee, defend further this city, which sustains us for love of Thee."

And the voice was heard again. "The city will endure some tribulation, but it will be liberated through My grace."

Then Clare confronted the virgins, "You will not suffer anything, if you will have faith in Jesus Christ." Then she had the gate opened and appeared before the furious Saracens, armed only with the Sacrament. If they wanted to enter and seize the sisters they would first have to trample over her dead body. But suddenly they withdrew: whether from superstition, or fear of sorcery—since they could not understand such daring in a defenseless woman—or whether it was from a sudden miraculous respect inspired by God, the fact is they scurried down the ladder again, leaped wildly over the walls and disappeared in the fields in frantic haste.

These were frightful times. The following summer another wave of Saracens and Normans rolled over the Umbrian countryside, especially against Assisi. Vitale d'Aversa, one of Frederick II's captains, swore that he would not leave until he had conquered the city. The terrorizing news reached even St. Damian.

"The siege is growing tighter. Assisi cannot hold out. There is no food. It will have to open its gates to those demons—it is merely a question of days."

Assisi! There were the families of the sisters, their kinsmen, their beautiful houses. But St. Clare was not concerned about this. Her thought took higher flight. Standing among the virgins in the little choir, she said:

"Dearest daughters, every day we receive many benefits from this city. We would be cruel and ungrateful, if at the opportune and necessary time we should not help them as much as we can."

She sent for ashes and repeating the gesture of penance dear to her teacher, she unveiled and scattered them over her head. Then she sprinkled ashes over the heads of each of the sisters.

"Go to our Lord and with all your affections beseech Him to liberate the city."

That night, the Poor Ladies prayed, flagellated themselves, wept and offered themselves as victims to God for their city. That night the Assisians carried out a bold sortie and victoriously repulsed Vitale d'Aversa. Dawn, rising over the shoulders of Mount Subasio, saw the victory banners waving on the towers of Assisi and the imperial troops in flight along the plain. Through the small window of the tiny choir of St. Damian dawn saw the virgins, exhausted in their stalls, like lilies after a storm. But the city was safe. Seasons and years went by and Clare's fame crossed the Appenines, and crossed the Alps. The feminine aristocracy of all the European courts, Agnes of Bohemia, Isabel of France, Elizabeth of Hungary, Ermetrude of Bruges, and later Elizabeth of Portugal and Bianca of Castille, turned to the ideal of poverty so amiably personified in Clare of the Offreducci. Thus, her Franciscan and Italian apostolate was extended beyond the confines of her own country. The four letters that she wrote to Agnes of Bohemia, the first great daughter of the world who lived and propagated the ideal of St. Francis, attest to the mystic wisdom, the educational finesse, the maternal ardor of her administration. Exquisitely a woman and a noblewoman as well, Clare was also an Italian in her supernatural spirituality. Without moving and almost without talking, St. Clare accomplished the most glorious of womanly missions—to help a great man, to educate souls maternally to God, and to defend one's native land.

6

The Militia
of the Penitents

FRANCIS HAD received the authorization to preach the Gospel from Innocent III on February 24, 1209, yet, returning from Assisi he had been seized with the gnawing doubt of his worthiness to give sermons and of being duty bound to prefer the hermit's life. At heart there was still in him that conflict between the jocund and brotherly soul of the King of Festivals and that need of solitude which the vocation had given to him like a second nature.

He expounded his doubts to the friars. "I am too ignorant to preach. Preaching purifies, preaching unites men and dusts off the soul of terrestrial things. But the Lord Jesus has given us the example of the apostolate in which the body wracks itself and the will mortifies itself more than in prayer. Therefore, perhaps the apostolate is better. What is better for me, action or contemplation?"

The friars could not answer, so it was then that Francis humbly asked the opinion of St. Clare and of Friar Silvester. And St. Clare, of the olive trees of St. Damian, and Friar Silvester of the forests of Mount Subasio, replied that it was the will of God that he preach. When the ambassador, Friar Masseo, returned, St. Francis did not immediately ask him for the answer. Instead, he embraced him affectionately, washed his feet, and prepared his dinner as was wont to be done at the friary for important guests. Then he led him into the forest, knelt down before him and respectfully drew back his cowl, made a cross of his arms, and asked:

"What does my Lord Jesus Christ command me to do?"

After hearing the answer, he rose, girded his rope around his waist and said:

"Let us go forth then in the name of God!"

In the company of Friar Masseo and Friar Angelo, he took the first road that presented itself and together they arrived at the castle of Cannara where Francis, now certain that he was doing the will of God, began to preach. But the swallows were chirping so loudly as they flew back and forth over the square that they drowned out his voice. So the saint commanded them to keep silence until he had finished his sermon and the swallows obeyed. The people of the town, partly on account of this miracle, partly on account of Francis' compelling manner of speech, were so deeply stirred that all, men and women, wanted to follow him, then and there, forsaking their homes and families. At other times similar events had taken place as the result of the preaching of some heretic who had thus formed sects opposed to the Church. The idea then came to Francis that he could turn toward the good what those fanatics had turned toward evil: he would organize a vast congregation of lay people who would live according to the dictates of evangelical purity and poverty, but who would be fully subject to the directives of the Church. For many men among the enthusiastic crowds were saying to St. Francis, "Friar Francis, we would like to follow you, but we have a family and children whom we cannot leave. How then can we imitate you?"

The saint replied, "Be not over-hasty and do not depart from hence. And I will ready that which you must do for the salvation of your souls."

Then it was that he conceived the idea of the Third Order opened to secular people, disciplined in spirit like that of the Order of Friars Minors and the Poor Ladies, yet free in its organizational structure so as to be adaptable to the lives of all.

WHEN ST. FRANCIS SPOKE

Besides his intimate inspiration and the counsels of the fellow friars, there was another reason which convinced Francis that he should preach. Often he had heard some Cathar Albigensian, bound for Rome, speak at the crossroads of Assisi, drawing audiences greater than the churches. After all there was a big difference between hearing a priest who explained a point of Scripture from the pulpit with a great flourish of Latin and hearing a man, a poor man at that, who talked about Jesus and His eternal promises in the open and in a way that was closer to their own lives. It was necessary to steal the heretics' thunder and to employ the powerful weapon of lay preaching in the vulgar language, always as a reinforcement of ecclesiastical preaching, of course, in the service of the Church. St. Francis had also noted that the sacred orators explained theology rather than the Gospel and that a jongleur or a minstrel was listened to by all, whereas a preacher was heard only by a few, since one look at him sufficed to know where and how his sermon would end. Francis concluded that to make men love God it was necessary to return to the great art of Jesus, to speak in similes, to recount parables, exemplary and interesting deeds—in a word to steal the intuitive, imaginative, poetic art of the jongleurs. To sing rather than to philosophize.

By temperament and intention Francis had already brought this renewal to preaching. And he and his fellow friars encountered more favor with the public insofar as from the very first words they pronounced, however simple, it was quickly understood that they were far from being simpletons as they were so fond of declaring themselves to be. In their simplicity, there often sprouted forth the chivalry of the born knight, the lyricism of the poet, the erudition of the savant and above all the love and insight of the man of God. Just as a peasant, however rich he may become, always has some earth under his fingernails, so does a nobleman, however he may abase himself, always have the gesture of a nobleman. The power of St. Francis' preaching lay in his poetic and dramatic genius, not only the power of the word, but the eloquence of the eyes, the voice and the gesture. Any place, any public, any moment found him prepared, because his mind, above all his ego, continuously revolved around a single argument. Now the crowd, rather than intimidating him, excited him. He spoke to thousands of persons as to a single friend and to a single person with the same fervor with which he would have talked to a thousand.

The sermons, which he prepared beforehand, were not those which met with the greatest success; indeed, it sometimes happened that on the point of speaking he would forget the whole. This did not in the least dismay him, but with that simple humility which was his grace and his strength, he confessed, "I had prepared a beautiful speech for you, but I have forgotten it." He improvised, and was happiest in the act of improvisation because it put him in immediate contact with his audience. Since by nature and grace he had the gift of empathy and of grasping the soul or the infinite in things, his word either pierced like a scalpel or cut like a blade, or it rose up like a lark. It was at once analysis, reproach and song, but more often song, and it transported listeners from the beauty of things to the eternal beauties. He commented on the virtues as follows:

"I salute you, O Queen Knowledge, may the Lord save you with your sister, holy pure Simplicity. O holy Lady Poverty, may the Lord save you with your sister, holy Obedience. O all you holy virtues, may the Lord, from whom you proceed and come, save you!"

Therefore it was difficult to repeat a summary of his sermons. How right was the doctor who said, "I can retain the sermons of others, word by word, but not those of St. Francis. And even if I manage to remember something, it no longer seems to me to be what he said." St. Francis exerted an irresistible attraction by being learned with the learned, simple with the simple, chivalrous with the chivalrous, most poor among the poor, accusing always himself and never others, castigating the sins and never the persons or the classes of persons who could impersonate them, surpassing all and yet holding himself to be the least among all. His entire person was a sermon just as his entire life was an example. No schematic summary could be made of his sermons. Who summarizes a musical composition? Yet they were music and as such they reverberated in the soul arousing that which educates one better than any treatise: a true desire for God.

THE WOLF OF GUBBIO

Francis not only set a good example and pronounced holy words in the towns through which he passed, but he also performed works of mercy for persons and cities. Once he arrived at Gubbio when the city was being terrorized by a wolf, which devoured animals and men. Toward evening the famished beast left its lair in the forest above the city and pounced on any unfortunate passers-by, tearing them to pieces. The country roads were no longer safe, women and children did not dare to venture beyond their doorways, men went out armed as though going to war. In short, things were so bad that nobody was bold enough to leave the town. St. Francis felt compassion for the people of Gubbio. That panic which debased an entire population menaced by a beast, enkindled courage in the knight of Christ who, although counselled to prudence by the citizens of Gubbio, made the sign of the Cross and went out against the wolf, unarmed, placing all his trust in God. And the people followed behind him, because the courage of one can inflame a thousand. But when they saw the wolf come running down the mountain with his gaping jaws, they all took to their heels, leaving only the saint who approached the beast without trembling. He made the sign of the Cross to the wolf and called out, "Come hither, Brother Wolf, I command you in the name of Christ that you inflict no hurt, neither on me or any other man."

At that sign, the wolf closed his jaws and stood still, and at that command he meekly laid himself down at the feet of Francis like a little lamb. Then one of the fleeing persons turned around and moved up to a respectable distance. And the saint, fixing his eyes on those of the savage creature, talked to it as to a man.

"Brother Wolf, you have committed many evil acts in these

parts, destroying and slaying God's creatures without His leave. And not only have you killed and devoured beasts, but you have dared to destroy and slay men made in the image of God, for which reasons you are worthy of the gallows as a most wicked thief and murderer, and all this city is in enmity with you. But, Brother Wolf, I desire to make peace between you and them, so that you will no longer harm them and they will forgive all your past offences and neither man nor dog will anymore pursue you."

The wolf beat his tail against his flanks, lowering his eyes, making signs that he accepted what had been said. The saint continued, "Since it pleases you to make and observe this peace, Brother Wolf, I promise to obtain for you a continual sustenance from the men of this city for as long as you live, because I know well that you worked all this evil from hunger. But in exchange, Brother Wolf, I desire you promise never again to harm either man or beast. Do you promise this to me?"

The wolf bowed his head. Francis spoke further, "Brother Wolf, I desire that you pledge to keep this promise." He extended his hand to the wolf as he would to a man to confirm a pact, and the wolf stood up, lifted his right hind paw and gently placed it in the hand of the saint, like a well-trained dog. The saint shook it in a friendly way and then said:

"Brother Wolf, I command you in the name of Jesus Christ to come with me, without fear, to sign this peace." So saying, the saint set out in the direction of the city and the wolf followed like a lamb, to the stupor of the crowd. Meanwhile, the news spread like wildfire and men, women, adults and tots, came running from all sides to see the defenseless man and the beast he had tamed by his words.

That human flock, which a few moments before had let itself be conquered by brute force, now was conquered by the force of the spirit. Francis preached to men in the same way he had talked to the wolf; he reproved them for being even more cruel than wolves and therefore of meriting God's punishment. He threatened them with the jaws of hell. And he invited them to do penance. Then he told them about the pact concluded between him and the wolf, provided that the people promised to give him the daily sustenance he required. In one voice the people responded, "We promise!"

"And you, Brother Wolf," said Francis then, "do you promise to observe the conditions of this peace, and never again to injure man or animals, or any living creature?"

Immediately the wolf knelt down and bowed its head, wagging its tail. Then at the saint's behest, the wolf confirmed the pledge by placing its right paw in the saint's right hand. The people on the square were delirious with joy and admiration for the miracle.

The wolf died of old age two years later, a grievous day for the citizens of Gubbio who in that domesticated beast which came into their houses and went from door to door, fed courteously by all, still felt the supernatural influence of the man of God.

THE MURDEROUS ROBBERS

Some say now that the wolf of Gubbio was not a wolf, but a highwayman who attacked travellers, robbing and killing them; others that he was a ferocious feudal lord of the kind who flogged his serfs until the blood ran, who gouged out the eyes of prisoners, set mastiffs against importunate visitors and who tied his enemies by the feet to the tail of a galloping horse. Even if this were the case, St. Francis tamed wolf-men no less than real wolves and the method was the same: courageous and humble charity. He maintained that one was not truly good if one does not love the wicked.

One day three famous brigands, looking for something to eat, knocked on the gates of the friary of Mount Casale near Borgo San Sepolcro. The warden, Friar Angelo, who belonged to the great and noble family of the Tarlati of Pietramala and of Biturgia, and who had passed from worldly chivalry to the Round Table of Poverty in 1213, sent them packing after delivering a long sermon to them on their misdeeds. And he told St. Francis about their visit when he returned from his tour of begging with his wallet filled with bread and a small vessel of wine which he and his companion had begged. Another person would have said, "You did well to chase those assassins away," Instead St. Francis chided him and reminded him of the example of Jesus who was so gentle with sinners. So he gave him the wallet of bread and the small vessel of wine and commanded him by holy obedience: "Go follow them and give them all this bread and wine from me, and then kneel before them and humbly confess your fault of cruelty. And then beseech them for my sake to do evil no more, but to fear God, and offend not their neighbor. And if they promise to do this, I promise to provide for their needs and to give them food and drink continually."

Friar Angelo set out quickly, and Francis betook himself to prayer, beseeching God to soften the hearts of the miscreants. As he was praying, the obedient warden found the murderous robbers; he presented them with the bread and wine of charity, and asked for their forgiveness on bended knee. What were the three assassins supposed to do before such a superhuman goodness? They became friars, and Francis recived them into the Order.

Many men, like wolves, take to crime either because they are hungry or ill-treated. Before reproaching or correcting others, St. Francis examined his own conduct and that of his friars, and where he may have been guilty of a shortcoming he accused himself almost as if to put himself on a level with the guilty one. He lowered himself in order to elevate others, finding the way of understanding only in humility, and in order to reduce the rebellious will to his will which conformed itself to the will of God. Then he went to the natural cause of the fault and sought to remove it. He provided for the needs of the body in order to arrive at the soul, and at the same time he prayed because only grace renews hearts. He never separated correction and preaching, that which is called the direct apostolate, from the work of corporal mercy and of prayer. And he never stopped halfway in the work of redemption, but continued it after forgiveness was granted, by harmonizing that which the world gives only with the greatest difficulty and which therefore constitutes the tremendous difficulty of all efforts at rehabilitation: full trust in the penitent.

Thus there is a program for preventive penal foresight and reform in the episode of the three murderous robbers. Indeed, for this reason alone would St. Francis deserve a place in judicial chambers and prison chapels.

MAJORS AND MINORS

Among the two-legged wolves the worst were not the brigands hidden in the hills and valleys. The worst were those who committed wicked acts among the human flocks. They were the proud nobles, the powerful rich cliques, the old people and the new people, the so-called "majors" who wanted to dominate and the so-called "minors" who did not want to be dominated. Murders and street battles took place in the cities divided by the factions and parties, the houses of enemies were attacked or set afire. Assaults and fires were common occurrences. The winning party drove the other into exile and confiscated the goods and properties of the exiled; but then the exiled would unite, conspire, and re-enter the city with force, allying themselves with enemies in nearby cities, and pitilessly put the houses of their adversaries to fire and sword.

Francis, who suffered at the thought of hatreds, went from town to town preaching love. "The Lord grant you peace!" he said at the beginning of every sermon, as Jesus had taught the Apostles. The Lord grant you peace! This was the greeting that every friar had to give to whomever he met. At first, the greeting annoyed people because peace is like salt which we think we can do without as long as it is within hand's reach. "Peace?" replied the riotous peasants and the arrogant citizens, "Peace is for the dead! Vengeance and victory, rather than peace!" But when boiling oil and blood coursed through the streets, when their houses went up in flames and the towers came crashing down and all trade was halted, and when the Germans levelled the castles and scattered salt on the villages razed to the ground, while hordes of refugees roamed through the countryside on which tribute was levied amid the shame imposed on the women and the wails of children, then the greeting of St. Francis was shouted like an invocation: *Peace!*

The effects of his word were immediately felt, beginning with his native city. In November 1210, a memorable pact was signed between the *majores* and the *minores* of Assisi. This peace treaty established a perpetual agreement between the majors and the minors. According to it, no pact could be made with the Pope or with the emperor, or with cities and castles without the consent of the two parties who then later, still in common accord, had to do what would best suit the honor, health and wealth of the Commune of Assisi. Neither the majors nor the minors were henceforth to create any divisions among the men of the city or outside, but they were to remain in a state and spirit of community, under the penalty of exile and confiscation of property, left to the discretion of the consul who ruled the city.

This was followed by many articles concerning the liberation of serfs, the extension of citizenship to the towns in Assisi's jurisdiction, the protection of foreigners, the amnesty granted to the conspirators involved in the betrayal of 1202. These were all laws of a most humane character with which little Assisi, through the influence of its saint, became a precursor to the other Italian communes in the taming of the wolfish instincts of the Middle Ages.

TEMPESTS, TUMULTS AND DEMONS

When Francis saw a city scourged by misfortunes, he did not seek the reasons in external facts, in natural or historical circumstances, but straightway in the wickedness of the inhabitants. Just as at Gubbio where, before entering into an agreement with the wolf, he had preached repentance, so in another town in Greccio, which was also tormented by a pack of hungry wolves and destructive hailstorms, he promised the end of these scourges on condition that the men of that town would sincerely repent and live like Christians.

The people hearkened to him, the wolves disappeared, and the hailstorms ended.

But he did not always find the people so docile. Once he went to Perugia where the Assisians, because of an ancient grudge, were suffered like smoke in the eyes. And while he was preaching on the square some men-at-arms, in the pay of the local nobles, began to joust and make a noise that drowned out Francis' voice. The listeners protested and the men-at-arms made even more noise by running up and down the square on horseback. Then the saint, in a prophetic tone, said, "Hear ye people, hear and understand what the Lord announces to you through me, His most unworthy servant. The Lord has exalted you above all your neighbors, but instead of being grateful and humiliating yourselves to Him, exercising your lordship in goodness, you are lifted up in pride and lay waste your neighbors and slay them. Wherefore I say to you that unless you are converted to God, making amends, the just Lord, who leaves nothing unpunished, will cause you to rise one against the other for your punishment and shame. And when war breaks out between yourselves, you will suffer more tribulations than all your neighbors together could visit upon you."

And so it happened. A few days later the people drove the mercenary bands out of the city. In revenge, the mercenaries ravaged the fields, the vineyards and trees around the city and the people in order to make up for their losses sacked and set afire the houses of the knights who had hired the mercenaries. Thus, tower-studded and rapacious Perugia, which had not heeded the word of *Il Poverello*, was severely punished.

But these failures were rare. In most cases, his words softened hearts, at least for a short time. Once, being unable to enter Arezzo because the opposing factions were fighting a desperate battle in the streets and boiling oil was pouring down in torrents from the windows, Francis stopped in a field near the city and his eyes, which, because they were pure, glimpsed the invisible, saw exultant demons inciting the citizens against each other. Then he said to Friar Silvester who was accompanying him:

"Go forward to the gate of the city, and in the name of the Most High God order the demons to leave the city immediately."

Friar Silvester obeyed simply, shouting in front of the gates of the bedeviled city:

"In the name of God and our Father Francis, O demons, depart!"

Then the blessed Francis saw the evil spirits pour out of towers and chimneys like a flock of bats and immediately the anger in the city subsided, the souls of men were calmed, and peace returned to the community.

Were those who were tormenting Arezzo really demons? Certainly they were diabolical instruments, and prayer, even before the sermon of a saint, had the power to disperse them.

COUNT ROLAND

Often, unfortunately, the effect of his work on crowds was impressive, but also fleeting. Once the deep emotion of the moment ceased, the city returned to its crimes and punishments. But this was not the case with his individual work. When a man of good will met Francis, he generally changed his way of life, since Francis had the secret of reading consciences and of indicating to each one his way.

One day Francis and one of his companions were passing by the castle of Montefeltro in Romagna, now called St. Leo. A festival was going on within and the banners were unfurled on the towers to the blare of trumpets and the ringing of bells. Knights and their ladies riding palfreys with embroidered saddle-cloths arrived at the drawbridge, and there was a constant going and coming of squires and men-at-arms, because one of the youngest sons of the count was being knighted. After having passed the whole night in vigil in the church of the castle, the young man had heard Mass and received the habits and arms and the ritual slap on the face. Now a great cortege was being prepared in his honor and a banquet was to be given attended by all his kinfolk, the lords of the castles of Romagna, of Tuscany and of Umbria because the Montefeltri were a powerful family. Ladies in velvet robes, and knights in armor rendered honors to the new knight with that encouraging smile of pleasure and of hope which even the most sceptical have for daring youth. The pages brought refreshments in ancient vases of silver and a jongleur hurled his witticisms from group to group waiting the hour of song that was to come after the banquet. Suddenly, two figures looking like something between peasants and hermits, barefoot, shorn, and girded with ropes, appeared in the court of honor of the castle. They passed through the elegant crowd with a humble nonchalance, and one of them took his place under an elm tree in the courtyard and began to speak in the manner of jongleurs and minstrels:

"Who is he?" asked the ladies, bitten with curiosity.

"Who is he?" asked the noblemen.

"Don't you know?" explained someone. "He's Friar Francis of Assisi, who was formerly a merchant and a very liberal spender, who stripped himself bare for the love of God. Now he goes from town to town preaching penance."

"Alas," sighed a lady, "now we're going to hear a sermon." But Francis in a voice clear as the horizon against which his gray small figure was etched, began with the couplet of a love ballad known to all:

> So great is the good that I await
> That every pain is a joyful fate.

And he continued in a fervor of spirit, talking not about the sorrows and joys of courtly love, but of the trials and tribulations the Apostles, martyrs, confessors, and virgins endured for eternal glory, for eternal love. The lords listened, merely curious at first, then attentively. What the marvelous preacher was expounding was not theology, for each one it was the dream of his heart, which was seeking a frivolous gratification in that festival and which suddenly, with the appearance of Francis, found the true solution. At the end of the sermon, everybody gathered around him to kiss his hand, the cowl, the rope, to ask his blessing and his prayers. When finally he was able to free himself somewhat, a rich Tuscan nobleman, Messer Roland of Chiusi of Casentino, who for a long time had desired to talk with him, now took him to one side and said, "Father, I would take counsel with you on the salvation of my soul."

St. Francis, who was impulsive but not precipitous, and who moreover could never neglect the duties of courtesy, replied,

"I am most pleased by your desire; but go this morning and honor the friends who have invited you to the festival and after you have dined we will talk together for as long as you please."

Messer Roland returned after dining and opened his soul fully and calmly to St. Francis from whom he received the rules of a new life according to God.

Then, still deeply moved by the gift of grace that *Il Poverello* communicated to him, he too offered a gift on his part. He spoke about a very solitary and wild mountain well adapted for anyone wishing to do penance and to give himself to contemplation. The mountain was in Casentino. St. Francis accepted it as a gift and promised to send some of his friars to visit the mountain which was called Mount La Verna. Thus, the two friends separated, the one to return to Chiusi, the other to St. Mary of the Angels. After some time two friars presented themselves to Count Roland in accordance with the promise, and accompanied by fifty men-at-arms who defended them against wolves, they climbed Mount La Verna. They searched it until they came to where it leveled into a plain, where, with the help of Count Orlando's men-at-arms, they built some small cells out of the branches of trees in order to prepare a little hermitage for the teacher. Little did they know that they were preparing the place of his martyrdom and of his sublimation.

"FRIAR" JACQUELINE

At the crossroads of Rome, when people gathered around this new jongleur who spoke about the feats of Christ rather than the feats of Roland, a lady had also stopped to listen and she had returned to her magnificent palace on the Esqueline hill with her mind in a turmoil. In 1215, when Francis, now famous, returned to Rome, the same lady entreated him to come to her residence. The saint looked into her eyes and immediately accepted since Lady Jacqueline of Settesoli had one of those rare womanly faces which inspired one to say, "Here is a friend!" She was the young widow of a Roman prince, Gratian of Frangipani, and she lived in a marble palace reconstructed on the ruins of the Septizonium of Settimius

Severus. It was one of those palaces that only Rome had in the Middle Ages, when the marble of the emperors served as the steps of churches and as building blocks for the new people who had come to the fore.

St. Francis entered the palace barefoot. The knight of Christ could not deny his help to a widow who asked to serve the Lord. He not only suggested a Rule to her, but took her under his direction and extended her his friendship, by returning to her house, by treating her as an equal, like a man, and by calling her "Friar" Jacqueline.

Friar and not lady, because Jacqueline had a virile temper; when she said something, so it had to be. She set her hand to rough tasks and knew how to make herself obeyed, even by St. Francis. In fact, with that brotherly bearing of hers, which hid a great maternal heart, she was the only person who ever succeeded in making the saint take some rest and some refreshment, making him eat "mostaccioli," a certain kind of Roman sweetcake made of almonds which she was very good at baking. She even made him wear a less worn and tattered tunic. Francis gladly wore his poverty in the palace of the Settesoli as at St. Damian. If Clare was his Mary, Lady Jacqueline was his Martha; if Clare was his daughter and disciple, Jacqueline was a sister; if with Clare it was sweet to meditate and sing praises to the Lord, gazing at the native horizon, with Jacqueline it was useful and good to talk about the kingdom of God in the world, gazing at the windows of the Colosseum reduced to a fortress; if Clare was a model of a cloistered virgin, Jacqueline was a model of a Franciscan woman living in the world; if few women would have been able to follow Clare, many would have been able to emulate Jacqueline. Therefore, the saint loved her frankly and confided his thoughts to her. In 1223, he came to the Settesoli palace with a lambkin bleating like a new-born babe. He had rescued it from the slaughter-house and thought to give it to "Friar" Jacqueline who understood the gift, since she knew about her great friend's love for baby lambs as a symbol of Jesus. The lambkin followed her everywhere, accompanying her on her visits to the poor, in the work of charity, and awakened her by bleating so that she could get to Mass on time. With the wool of the lamb, "Friar" Jacqueline wove a beautiful fabric with which to make a tunic for St. Francis. But instead of a tunic it became his funereal shroud.

THE LITTLE BLACK HEN

That movement of consciences toward God which St. Francis aroused everywhere he went was spreading. As a result he, with his soul of a dreaming saint, could no longer manage to keep it within bounds by himself. Many desired to become friars minor, but not all of them could live up to the Rule, not all of them had the tact of appearing before the people and the ec- clesiastical authorities. Hence, at times defects discredited the new Order and here and there were incomprehension, mistreat- ment, persecution. St. Francis grew sorrowful because the over- abundant haul of fish was tearing the net apart.

As he was pondering this problem, he had a dream. He saw a little black hen with hairy legs and the feet of a dove exerting and straining herself to gather her too numerous brood under her wings, although chicks were escaping hither and thither into possible dangers.

As soon as he awakened, Francis, ruminating on his dream, observed, "I am the little black hen, small and black by nature, and I must be as simple as the dove flying to God with affections feathered with virtue. But the Lord through His mercy has given me and will give me many children whom I shall not be able to protect with my virtue. It is needful that I commend them to the Holy Church, who will protect and govern them in the shadow of her wings." St. Francis perceived the necessity of entrusting to Rome a movement which was going beyond the authority of one man and which, if left to itself, could stray from the main road. Although he was one of the greatest cap- tain of souls, Francis did not have the imperiousness of the captain. Among the thousands of his followers he remained the nobleman of instinct rather than lineage, the nurse of the lepers, the solitary worker of St. Damian, the penitent of the prisons, the pitiless critic of himself, so humble that he saw in each man a brother. Others before him, like Pietro Valdo, had also wanted to return to the evangelical life, but by think-ing of reforming others, more than themselves; by not accept-ing the authority of the Church they had fallen into heresy, and their doctrine and their work, cut off from the divine trunk, withered like a dead branch. Humility, which assimilates and treasures the wisdom of others, saved St. Francis. The little hen went looking without fear for the wings of the eagle and thereby became powerful.

CARDINAL UGOLINO

To stop the irregularities of the friars, as in the disputes with the bishop, it was necessary to have recourse to the Roman curia. But to get to the Pontiff was a serious matter, especially in those days and for those poor ones of God who journeyed on foot and knew no way of pushing themselves upon authority. If Francis had enjoyed easy access to Innocent III it had been through the merit of Bishop Guido and of Cardinal Colonna. Now Giovanni Colonna was dead and, needing a protector, Francis commended himself to a cardinal who had shown sym-pathy for his work—Ugolino, Count of Anagni, Bishop of Ostia and of Velletti. He was a man of seventy, forceful yet of genial disposition, who had studied at Bologna and Paris, and he was a friend and adviser of the new Pope, Honorius III.

Delighted with the preference Francis had shown for him, Cardinal Ugolino immediately took his concern to heart and suggested that Francis himself request the Pope to recognize the confirmation of his protection. Then he asked Francis to prepare a beautiful speech to defend his Order at the pontifical court. Francis prepared himself studiously for this task but when he stood before the Pope he could not remember a word of his speech, and he said so. But immediately he lifted his eyes to heaven, invoking the Holy Ghost, and abandoned himself to his inspiration. As he spoke, Cardinal Ugolino was on pins and needles for fear that Francis might break into a phrase or gesture not according to protocol and which would not be understood by the prelates. But, Francis said marvelous things, and even though in his fervor he moved up and down like a dancer and almost jumped in front of the cardinals, nobody laughed because all understood that a divine fire burned within him. The Pope gladly granted the protectorate of the Order to Cardinal Ugolino, and henceforth this cardinal became the intimate counselor to Francis in all his acts.

There is something moving about the friendship between Cardinal Ugolino and Francis. Francis loved him as a son loves a father. And he needed him. To Francis who had undergone the sorrow of a father who did not understand him, to him who had chosen a beggar as a surrogate father who with his blessings was to protect him against the maledictions of his natural father, God now sent a father invested with the authority of the Church.

St. Francis needed that secure pulse, that eye at once human and supernatural which did not only look on high as he did, but also around and below; he needed that guidance which did not mortify his inspiration, but bent it to historical exigencies. Although he was the teacher and the leader, Francis nonetheless had an intimate need to feel himself loved and protected. As for the cardinal, for all his nobility, his experience, culture, and his white beard, he felt like a poor man near this man of God. And though loving him like a son, he venerated him as teacher, listened to him like a friend, and wanted him beside him because his presence was enough to bring him serenity. He tried to imitate his life and when his high post permitted him to, he dressed and ate like a friar minor.

When he could, Cardinal Ugolino attended the chapters of the friars of Porziuncola. He would arrive on horseback with his court, and the friars would come toward him in procession. Francis held his stirrup and helped him to dismount, as a squire performed this duty for his knightly lord. Then the cardinal celebrated Mass in the little rustic chapel of St. Mary of the Angels with more feeling than in the Lateran Basilica. And Francis, dressed as a deacon, intoned the Gospel with his musical voice. Then the cardinal would roam through the forest, among the hovels of the friars, and beholding them in such poverty, he wept, edified. "How shall we save ourselves, if the servants of God live in this way."

The Franciscan dream appeared as something ultra-terrestrial to him and he wanted to mitigate it, but Francis showed such passion for his Lady Poverty, that the cardinal bowed his head in submission. There was no sight more beautiful than to see them together: Ugolino with his flowing beard and his cardinal's purple and Francis, lean in his patched and tattered tunic, his bare feet in the dust, looking up at heaven.

"Francis, my most simple brother, you will be venerated on the altars," said the cardinal.

"Messer Cardinal and my father, you will be the vicar of Christ and father of all the world," replied Francis. He addressed letters to him as follows: "To the venerable in Christ, father of all the world."

Both were prophets.

LUCCHESIO AND BUONADONNA

As the number of Francis' admirers and faithful increased, how, he asked himself, could he neglect all this good will reaching out toward him? It was time to keep the promise of creating a new group of lay brothers which he had made at Cannara. . . .

Once, while stopping over at Poggibonsi, near Siena, he had encountered a singular couple: The man was called Lucchesio, the woman Buonadonna. He was a merchant, but for some time now he had given himself to God and instead of obtaining gain for himself, he obtained it for the poor. At first she, who lived a life of comfort, had been unable to adjust herself to that waste of alms, to that voluntary mortification, in short to her husband's new ideal, and she committed many wicked actions against the poor man. One day the cupboard was empty, when other poor folk knocked on the door.

"Go and get something for these creatures of God," he said to his wife.

"Fool!" the woman burst out. "Obviously your fasts have driven you out of your mind. Don't you know that the bread-bin is bare? When will you begin to attend to your affairs?"

"Go," replied Lucchesio mildly, "because Providence never fails."

Buonadonna rudely opened the bread-bin, to say "See, I told you!" but stood there in amazement. The bread-bin was full of bread. After this miracle she also was converted and competed with her husband in performing works of mercy.

As the fame of the blessed Francis spread, the couple pined to talk with him. When he came to Poggibonsi they asked him how they could arrive at perfection, although living in the world. Francis replied that he had conceived the idea of a new Order which would also take in marriage couples. And he explained to them how he understood the Order and the duties that it would impose. Lucchesio and Buonadonna beseeched him to receive them. So Francis dressed them in a poor gray frock almost like that of the minors, he girded them with knotted ropes and after about a month sent them a Rule which was that of the tertiaries.

From then on the couple dedicated themselves to succoring the poor, nursing the infirm, and lodging pilgrims, satisfying their own needs with the fruits of the kitchen garden which they cultivated with their own hands. And when they didn't have enough, they begged for alms. They went as far as the swampy seacoast to bring medicines to the fever-ridden. After many years of labor, Buonadonna died on an April day. Lucchesio, on his knees beside her, prayed to the blessed Francis who had joined them in a love higher than the human, to unite them also in death. And his prayer was granted. He died a few minutes later. From the monk's girdle of the Third Order the sanctity of marriage received a second link of purity and faithfulness.

BROTHERS AND SISTERS OF PENANCE

The Rule which St. Francis had given to Lucchesio and Buonadonna around 1218 and which in part had already been followed by Count Roland, "Friar" Jacqueline, Cardinal Ugolino and by many others, brought closely together and disciplined all the followers of St. Francis, living among the occupations of the world, into a Third Order (after that of the Order of Friars Minor and of the Poor Ladies) which Cardinal Ugolino, now become Pope Gregory IX, called the Association of the Penitents and the Order of the Brothers and Sisters of Penance.

The name was austere, and the Rule was difficult for those times. Everyone could become a tertiary: priests, laymen, virgins, widows, married couples, provided they were Catholics devoted to the Church. And they could continue to live in their own homes, but in a Christian manner, occupying themselves with works of piety and charity, dressing themselves in a special coarse gray frock, with a rope hanging from the side. In short, they exerted themselves to bring the Franciscan ideal to their daily life.

Anyone who enlisted in the Order of Penance pledged himself to make peace with his enemies, to make restitution of ill-gotten gains, to pay his tithes to the Church punctually, to write his own last will and testament in accordance with the precepts of justice so as not to give rise to quarrels among his heirs, never to bear arms, never to take oaths, except in cases permitted by the Church (i.e., in order to defend the faith, to preserve peace, to testify to the truth in courts), and never to accept public honors. The tertiaries had to meet monthly to hear Mass and a sermon and to deliberate on common works. They were to take Communion at least three times a year: Christmas, Easter and Pentecost. They had to visit their sick brothers, pray for the dead and pay a monthly quota, proportional to their property, to succor the poor and to help those struck by misfortune. Poverty was not obligatory as in the other two Orders, but implicit in the detachment of the heart from terrestrial goods of which they made sober use as a means and never as an end. The name Order of Penance, given to the whole congregation, was an indication of its spirit.

This Rule, which appears excessively severe to us, was almost revolutionary seven hundred years ago and it would have been revolutionary in a total sense of the word, like that of some heretical sects, if it had not tied itself to the pillars of Rome.

It was going against the current, not only as Christianity always goes against the current insofar as it opposes the instinct, but it was going against the structure of society in Italy in the thirteenth century, which was feudal in its residues, and communal in the new societal forms that were slowly emerging.

The obligation to return properties acquired through deceit and violence could wipe out an inheritance, arousing resentment in a family group, but it re-established justice, it appeased the rancor of the ones who had fallen low in social state, it prevented fiscal oppression, and by its example, it was an admonition to money-lenders and perjurers. The same effect was achieved by the obligation to testify according to one's conscience.

The obligation not to bear witness except as a moral duty broke the feudal net of factions by which its powerful families linked themselves to one another and also linked the minors who were in need of protection, subjecting the will of their dependents to their own interests as over against those of the commonweal. On the other hand, this obligation withdrew the tertiaries from another enmeshment which was more communal than feudal, that of the factions which divided the citizens into groups barricaded one against the other. Forbidden to take oaths, the Tertiaries could not link themselves to a party or to a lord. Thus, they escaped personal as well as collective tyranny, in order, of their own free will, to be part of the militia of the spirit.

The obligation not to bear arms was a serious novelty in those days when the most peaceful nobleman never left his house without at least a dagger hanging from his belt. "They'll kill you," said their friends. And the tertiaries answered, "If God is with us, who is against us?"

"You are weak-livered cowards," said their enemies, insultingly. But the tertiaries showed that they were not afraid because, thus unarmed, they hurled themselves into street brawls at the cost of their lives. And in the struggles between the citizens these men of pure hands still fundamentally pledged themselves to placate hatreds, reconcile enemies and restore concord to the country. This obligation along with that of forgiveness reduced the danger of civil war, eliminating the temptation of the unarmed person to provoke others, and smothering in the others who were armed the will to strike at a defenceless person.

The obligation of the monthly quota offered an early example of the savings bank and the mutual aid society. That communal fund gleaned from knights, artisans and peasants took welfare aid away from the humiliating monopoly of the rich, from the monasteries which did not always use their privilege in an exemplary manner, from the arbitrariness of partisan authorities, from the disjointed and desultory uncertainty of personal initiatives, to make of it a work of foresight and assistance due only to the charity of the faithful, regardless of social class. Thus, the rich man could not boast that he was the only one who gave, nor could the poor man do without the rich. And the humble Franciscan girdle held both the rich and the poor in a tie of Christian love which anticipates, sustains, and repairs, even better than a belt of gold.

The Third Order gives as the measure of the social greatness of St. Francis. If he had stopped with the first two he would have been a great founder, but not a reformer, not an *emendator* as the holy Pope Pius XI called him, with a title that was daringly new in the history of the Church. The Third Order can invest the whole of life and all lives, resolving economies and social problems there where alone they can be resolved: in the conscience of individuals, and by letting the spirit of the other two orders reach every class of persons, in any field of work.

The Militia of Penance which had the girdle as its sword, the Cross as its banner, blessed Francis as its captain, was preparing the future by leading minds back to evangelical charity. Today, when history has made some principles, then required only by religious perfection, a matter of common ownership and when the diversity of life itself has mitigated the penances, the Third Order seems like a very innocuous institution. But for anyone who wants to follow it in the spirit of the founder, it is still the Militia of Penance. The Rule is like the girdle: very loose or very tight according as to whether one girds it tightly or not. And this too conforms with the pedagogy of St. Francis, who commanded little and demanded all.

THE GREAT PARDON

To lead man back to the Lord, to help them to live by teaching them the secret of virtue and gladness was not enough for Francis. The most serious problem of life was eternal salvation, and he understood that if he could not assure this in some way to his fellow men, he would have done nothing for them. He thought that the forgiveness of sins which for many years had been the incubus of his life, to the point where it was an interior assurance of God, was the incubus of all others too, even of those who forgot it. Oh, to be able to go toward death with the certainty of paradise! He had to wrest this from the great King for everybody.

One starry night in July, Francis was praying in the little church of St. Mary of the Angels when the Lord Jesus and Mary, His Mother, appeared to him in a nimbus of light. "What do you wish, Francis?" asked the Lord in His voice without words. The saint, still in the rapture of his ecstasy, remembered the souls of the brothers and expounded his old desire:

"Most Holy Father, although I am a most wretched sinner, I bessech Thee to grant full forgiveness and a complete remission of all their sins to all those repentant and confessed who will come to visit this church."

Said the Lord Jesus: "Francis, you ask much, but you are worthy of greater things and greater things will you have."

And He consented to his prayer, commanding him to ask the Pope to grant this extraordinary indulgence in His name. Pope Honorius III happened to be in Perugia and next morning at dawn Francis climbed up to the turreted city. He presented himself with the usual simplicity, unintimidated as one who lives in secret with God. For at that moment Francis truly felt himself to be the herald of the great King.

"Holy Father, I beseech you to impose a plenary indulgence, without the obligation of oblation, on the little church of St. Mary of the Angels."

Honorius III marvelled at the extraordinary request because an indulgence of this kind was granted only to pilgrims bound for the Holy Land, to those of St. James of Campostella, to those who came to Rome for some special solemnity, and never without receiving an alms from them in exchange. Yet, he could not reply with a dry "no" to this little friar kneeling at his feet, with such humility and sureness. Certain requests can only be made by children and saints.

"Very well," Honorius consented. "For how many years do you want this indulgence?"

"Holy Father, I do not ask years, but souls."

"What do you mean?"

"Good Father, I would like all those who will go to Porziuncola confessed and contrite to obtain the remission of all their sins both on earth and in heaven, from the day of their baptism to the day and the hour of their entry to that church of Mary."

The church of Mary: St. Francis did not say this casually. It seemed to him that every authority should bow before that regal and maternal name.

Again the Pope marvelled. St. Francis was asking for a regenerative pardon like a second baptism, on no other condition but the pilgrimage to his little church, made with a deep repentance and a sincere confession. It was the greatest privilege, but *Il Poverello* insisted, with the insistence of the poor, and the pontiff gave in.

"I also in the name of God accord you this indulgence," he said to him three times.

The cardinals who were present protested: such an extraordinary favor to a little unknown church, where no miracles had ever taken place save those revealed to a man who could be a saint, but who could also be crazy, since nobody swears to the sanctity of the living! If indulgences began to be handed out so generously, the smallest parish would claim an indulgence equal to that of the Holy Sepulchre. The cardinals, who were conservative men, held to the strictness of the Church.

But the Vicar of Christ sensed the new spirit of mercy which the saint of Assisi was bringing in the name of the great King, and he answered the cardinals:

"Now that we have promised, we shall not go back. Only we shall limit the time useful to acquire the indulgence to the duration of one day."

And he fixed the day for August 2, beginning with the vespers of the preceding day.

Full of bliss, Francis left Perugia without asking for any document certifying to the pontifical concession. He never bothered about written documents since he knew that faith dwells in the heart and if it is missing in the heart, documents become scraps of paper even if they are signed by sovereigns. That evening, when he stopped to rest at a leper hospital near Colle, while praying, he was assured by a voice from heaven that the indulgence granted by the Pope had been confirmed by the King of Kings. He had the word of God and the word of His Vicar, what more did he need?

On August 2 of that same year, 1216, the Bishops of Assisi, Perugia, Todi, Spoleto, Nocera, Gubbio and Foligno convened at Porziuncola to consecrate the little church of St. Mary of the Angels. And before them and the assembled people Francis proclaimed:

"I want to send you all to paradise. Our Lord Pope Honorius has granted me this indulgence, on that account you who are present here, as well as those who will come here on this day in the years to come with a heart well disposed and truly contrite, will have forgiveness for all sins."

I want to send you all to paradise. This was the goal of the charity of Francis. The great pardon of Porziuncola crowned the work of the three Orders, opening the portals of grace to all penitents and preparing them for a life of virtue on earth and a life of glory in heaven. The little church of Mary, hidden in the valley between Perugia and Assisi, as poor as the stable in Bethlehem, was to become one of the greatest hearths of christianity, a pilgrimage for souls. And justly so. Had not the Franciscan ideal been born there in the benediction of the Mother of God? Even among the ancients the sources of great rivers merited a privileged cult. And Francis in spirit already heard the trampling of footsteps lost in the parade of centuries and a sound of diverse tongues, Slav, French, German, Spanish, and he saw streets of people hastening to Porziuncola. Another saintly friar saw this same multitude which never ceased coming from the most remote lands, he saw it kneeling around St. Mary of the Angels with its arms stretched and its eyes blind, invoking mercy, until a great light shone from above, enveloping the little church and the crowd in a single effulgence. Millions of people would find salvation through the prayer of a saint and through the intercession of the Virgin.

7

FEATS IN
DISTANT LANDS

WHEN FRANCIS was a child, admiring the jongleurs who celebrated the feats of Roland and Oliver in song and the knights
who rode through the city on horseback—no knight was considered a perfect knight who had not first gone to the Holy
Land, and if he had not acquired the right to place a Cross on
his coat of arms by fighting to liberate the sepulchre of Christ.
True nobility was the nobility of the Crusade, there seemed to
be something lacking in any other.

But in recent years the Crusades had lost their value as an
ideal and had been transformed into business, for the nobility
as well as for the bourgeoisie. In theory, one left on a Crusade
and one fought to liberate the holy places from the Moslem but,
in fact, the great feudal lords, especially the French and
Provençals, who had been more or less courteously sent packing by the king and emperor, tried to recoup in the Orient the
domination they had lost in the West. And the Italian maritime
republics, by lending ships to the Crusades with a calculated
generosity, availed themselves of their arms to occupy the best
ports of the Aegean, the Black Sea and the Mediterranean; and
Italian merchants, by opening the ports of the Levant, took
over all the trans-European trade. The label remained the same,
but the contents changed. The effects achieved conformed to
the content, that is, all were of political and economic advantage

only and not at all advantageous in a religious sense. The scimitars of Mohamet flashed brightly around the Holy Sepulchre, and the horses of the Cadi grazed on the hills where the Saviour had prayed.

Francis suffered from this annihilation of the religious idea which had been the great soul of the Crusades. But as a weaponless knight, he maintained that the Cross is brought far with the Cross and not with the sword, and that before conquering places it was necessary to conquer hearts. Finally, rather than kill infidels it was needful to convert them. Furthermore, by converting them, the liberation of the Holy Sepulchre in consequence would take place of itself.

Having posed the problem solely from a religious point of view, Francis thought that a band of preachers ready not to deal out death, but to die for the faith, would be of more use than a whole army, and that he and his fellow friars should be the first in this ideal band.

But the Saracens were cruel and acquired merit with Allah by slitting the throats of Christians! All the better, for this was precisely Francis' most ardent desire, to shed blood for Jesus Christ just as Jesus Christ had shed it for him. For him, the Crusade had to be a martyrdom and the Cross was to be emblazoned not on the coat of arms, but on his body, and death was to find him on the field, fighting with faith and acts. This was the dream of the knight of Christ.

LIKE THE BIRDS

What he dreamed, Francis did. In order to actualize the dream of a spiritual crusade in the Holy Land and of implicit martyrdom, two things were necessary: the permission of the Holy See, and the consensus of his friars. Not that this consensus was absolutely required but because he, as a teacher, wanted to persuade them of the supernatural reasonableness of his undertakings.

At that time—toward the end of 1212—Innocent III was preparing another Crusade directed against Egypt, the center of

Moslem power. Francis set out for Rome to ask for permission to go crusading, as an unarmed standard-bearer of Christ. Upon arriving at Bevagna, a castle between Assisi and Todi, his attention was drawn by some trees filled with birds. Even the adjoining fields were thick with them: it was probably a migration flight of birds of passage, as took place in Autumn. Gladdened at the sight of these winged little creatures and in a fervor of spirit, Francis said to his companions: "Wait for me on the road, and I will go and preach to my brother birds."

Then he went toward them and greeted them as if they were persons:

"My brother birds, you are much beholden to God your creator and you must always praise Him because He preserved your seed in Noah's Ark and has given you the freedom to fly where you please, and a dwelling in the purity of the air all for you."

The birds, fixing their eyes on him, listened attentively. They craned their necks and bowed their heads.

"My brother birds," continued the holy man, "praise God because you neither sow nor reap, and the Lord gives you rivers and springs for your drink, tall trees for your nests and mountains and valleys for your refuge. You neither weave nor spin and the Lord dresses you and your children in feather raiments, doubled and tripled, for summer and the winter. Behold, then, how the Lord loves you and yet, my brothers, guard yourselves against the sin of ingratitude and be ever heedful to praise God." And the birds responded, opening their beaks, spreading their wings, twittering discreetly at first, then chirping in chorus. St. Francis rejoiced and watched them with wondrous delight, marvelling that none became frightened or flew away as he walked among them, grazing them with his tunic, until raising his hand in blessing he gave them leave to depart. Then the birds rose in flight and separated into four bands, according to the cross traced by the blessing of Francis which corresponded to the four cardinal points, and each band flew off singing marvelous songs.

The friars, their noses in the air, were sure that their teacher was really a saint if he could speak to animals. "What a beautiful sermon you delivered to the birds!" said Friar Masseo.

"Rather," replied the blessed Francis, "what a beautiful sermon they delivered to us! For we must bring the preaching of the Cross to the four parts of the world, living in the manner of birds, possessing nothing of this world, and committing our lives solely to the providence of God."

The friars understood.

SLAVONIA AND NOT BEYOND

But St. Francis wanted to be the first to set the example of the Crusade of penitence and martyrdom for his friars. Therefore, upon receiving permission from the Pope, he named Pietro Cattani, the canon, as his vicar in Italy, and with a single companion he embarked for Syria in early October, 1212. But a tempest ran the ship aground on the coasts of Slavonia, preventing all the passengers from continuing the journey. Francis knew that another ship would not set sail for the Orient for at least another year, because in those times boats navigated slowly by means of oars and sails. So he beseeched the owner of a boat bound for Ancona to take him and his companion aboard.

"I don't want any extra mouths to feed," replied the seawolf. "We barely have enough provisions for the trip."

But the two friars were not men to be frightened by the spectre of hunger. That evening, they stowed away in the hold. Meanwhile, a good man, a native of the coastal city, consigned a supply of victuals to another good man of the crew for the poor friars who, when the ship was far out to sea, were able to emerge from their hiding place.

The owner at first grumbled, but later he had to bless those unwanted pilgrims because during the crossing, which took a longer time than had been calculated because of a storm, the sailors ate all the rations and it was the provisions of St. Francis (who always ate so little) which saved the crew from starving. Those provisions seem to be touched with magic; no matter

how many were distributed, they sufficed each day: the Lord
multiplied them for love of Francis.

ON THE ROAD TO MOROCCO

A good knight does not fear failures. Francis was not discouraged over the failure of his first Crusade. Instead, he returned to his country with a greater ardor for martyrdom, with
a greater desire to carry the Gospel to where it was unknown
and hated. Therefore he chose Morocco, another great Saracen
center, where the Arabs, repulsed by Spain, had grouped themselves for reinforcement around their Sultan, Mohammed-Ben-
Naser, called "The Mill Watcher."

In June 1213, Francis left with a few companions among
whom was Friar Bernard. His enthusiasm was so great that he
always walked ahead of the others and at a faster pace. He did
not feel well, but he walked anyway. He wanted to get to
Morocco by going through Spain, and he and his friars were
much pleased at the thought of stopping at the shrine of
St. James of Compostella, the most venerated shrine in the
Middle Ages, after Rome and Jerusalem. On a lap of their
journey they found a sick man abandoned on the road, and
Francis was so moved that he said to Friar Bernard:

"Son, I want you to remain here and nurse this sick man."

Friar Bernard, verging on tears but fighting them off, knelt
humbly, received the obedience and remained to perform the
duties of a nurse while St. Francis and the others proceeded
to St. James' shrine.

But the saint was unable to reach Morocco; he became
gravely ill and once more he was forced to return to Italy. On
the way back he found Friar Bernard with his patient perfectly
healed, and he promised his first-born knight to send him to
St. James' shrine in the following year. Meanwhile he returned
with him to Porziuncola, in the valley of Spoleto, which for
St. Francis was the finest and most joyous spot on earth.

Once again the will of God had halted him on the road of the
Crusades. And still the thirst for martyrdom grew in his heart.

THE KNIGHTS GO FORTH

If the first two missions had no practical result, they did have the advantage of teaching the friars about the ways of the world and of conferring on Francis the right to say to his ideal crusaders, "Arm yourselves and go forth," because he would have never commanded what he himself had not done first. Moreover, the journeys, and especially the one in Galicia, skirting southern France, which gave him a knowledge of the heretics and an experience of other countries, suggested to him the idea of preaching the Gospel not only among the Saracens, but among Christians in Europe. His adventurous spirit, his consciousness of the importance of his work, the unexpressed but implicit criticism of the violent and incoherent religiosity of his contemporaries, contributed to convincing him that it would be useful to launch the knights of poverty on a conquest of the world.

The pontifical approval and the attempt which he had personally lived through gave him wings. Yet when he was on the point of expounding his grandiose design to the friars assembled for the first general chapter of Pentecost 1217, his humility, delicate to the point of timidity, made him hesitate. There were already too many convents and too many learned and theologians in the barely born Order! How would his simple words be greeted? Anyone else would have overcome his inhibition, by recalling his own authority as founder. "After all, if these fellows want to wear my habit they must pay heed to me." Instead, St. Francis demeaned himself.

He set out for the chapter ready to receive criticism and instead, as always happened, he received an ovation. His simplicity transported the most astute, the most refined. Encouraged, he spoke about the missions not only in the Holy Land, but in all parts of the world. And the chapter decided to divide the then known world into provinces to be visited and evangelized, as had been done in Italy. They discussed the provinces of Germany, Hungary, France and Spain, and a group

St. Francis in Ecstasy
El Greco (1542-1614)

St. Francis Embracing Christ on the Cross
Attributed to Murillo

of friars was assigned to each one. Francis chose France, toward which he was drawn unwittingly by his mother's blood and wittingly by his devotion to the Blessed Sacrament, which French Catholics cultivated with a particular piety.

Then the teacher bade leave to the new missionaries, counseling them, "In the name of God go forth to all lands. And on the road walk two by two in all humility and modesty, especially keeping silence from dawn until after the hour of terce, praying to God in your hearts. And speak no idle or useless words. Even on the road speak always with humility and honesty as if you were in a hermitage or a cell. Indeed, wherever we are and go, we always have a cell with us. The friar's body is the cell and the soul is the hermit who dwells therein to pray to the Lord. And if the soul is restless in the cell that God has given to it, it will find meditation in the cell of no convent, made with the hands of men."

The first band of the Knights of Poverty sent to Germany were under John of Penna; to France under Friar Pacifico, to Tunis under Friar Giles; to Portugal under Friar Zacharias and Friar Gualtheri; and to Spain under Giovanni Parenti. All, except the last two, had catastrophic adventures. Foreigners, poor, ignorant of the language, if they were maltreated in their own country, abroad they were actually persecuted. This was especially the case in Germany where with their reply *"Ja, Ja"*— the only German they knew—to any question addressed to them, they exposed themselves to the dangers of death.

"Are you Catholics?" asked the Germans; the friars answered *"Ja, ja"* and all went well. But, then others asked, "Are you Catholics, Waldensians, Albigensians, heretics?" *"Ja, ja!"* responded those simple men in the same way and then they were beaten, exposed to ridicule, imprisoned and tortured until the misunderstanding was cleared. In Hungary things were even worse. Gypsy and semi-barbarians insulted them fiercely. The friars, thinking they wanted the rags they were wearing, gave them their tunics, their leggings and remained half-naked, but their bearing excited the contempt of the Hungarians all the more. Yet this persecution did not discourage the Knights of

Christ, instead it enflamed them like a proof of the protection of God. "Whether these coarse and harsh Hungarians understand us or not matters little," they thought. "We die to save their souls and that's enough. God will do the rest."

The mission to Tunis finished before it really began because the Christian inhabitants, not at all pleased with those street preachers who disturbed their peaceful relations with the Moslem authorities, put Friar Giles and his companions on the first boat sailing for Italy. But a young lay person remained on land, because he recalled the admonitions of St. Francis and sought martyrdom. The Saracens discovered him and sentenced him to death. The little friar fell to his knees, his face radiant, clutching the Rule of the teacher against his heart, asking forgiveness of God if he had at any time failed to follow it. Then he bowed his young head under the scimitar of the executioner and his blood consecrated the Rule.

More fortunate were the expeditions in Spain and Portugal. In Spain, Giovanni Parenti, a man of God, made the burgeoning Order known and loved and formed an important Franciscan center at Saragossa. In Portugal, Friar Zacharias and his seven companions, after some persecution on the part of the inhabitants, were well received and protected by the Princess Sancha, sister of King Alfonso II and of Queen Urraca.

In France, however, Friar Pacifico ran against the opposition of the clergy, who mistrusted their vagabond preaching, which was too much like that of the Albigensians. St. Francis, too, set out for France, but upon arriving at Florence, was dissuaded from continuing further by Cardinal Ugolino. He employed the only argument, among many, which could overcome Francis' desire to conduct an apostolate, stressing the necessity for Francis to remain in Italy to defend the Order now misled by laymen and clerics. After presenting his friend to Honorarius III, Cardinal Ugolino requested and obtained a pontifical Brief which commended the Friars Minor to the bishops and pastors. With these authoritative letters of presentation which they always carried on their persons, the new knights errant could find a friend in every priest, a shelter in every parish.

FAREWELL TO THE KNIGHTS OF MOROCCO

The sufferings of the companions only further inflamed those who had remained behind to imitate them, and to vindicate them with the sublime vengeance of the Gospel. At the chapter of Pentecost of 1219, at which Cardinal Ugolino was present, there was an air of excitement characteristic of a new army that has had its baptism of fire in vanguard skirmishes and is impatient of a great victory.

St. Francis wanted to try the road to Morocco again, which he had given up about a year before, and therefore he summoned six young friars, Vitale, Bernardo, Pietro, Adinto, Accursio and Otho, and said, "My sons, God has commanded me to send you among the Saracens to preach his faith and to fight the law of Mohamet. Prepare yourselves to fulfill the will of the Lord."

The chosen six, in the fervor of their singular election, responded spiritedly, "We are ready, father, to obey you in all."

"My beloved sons," continued Francis, moved by this obedience, "preserve peace among yourselves, love one another, dispel envy, be patient in tribulations and humble in prosperity, imitate Jesus Christ in poverty and chastity, in obedience. Trust only in the Lord who will be your guide and your help. Carry the Rule and the breviary with you, and always recite the office with great devotion. Give obedience to the oldest among you, Friar Vitale."

Suddenly, the exhortation was interrupted, like a string suddenly slackened. Francis' voice trembled, he bowed his head, and changed his tone—the man, with his inmate tragic delicacy, shone through the teacher and the saint.

"My sons, although I enjoy your good will, my heart can do no less than to suffer over your departure, because I love you, but I must put divine commands ahead of our desires." The sadness of St. Francis was communicated to the departing young friars like a presentiment of death.

"Father," said Friar Vitale for all, "send us wherever you please, because we are ready to carry out your will, but you, father, keep us with your prayers to fulfill your commands. Because we are young, and we have never once been out of Italy, and that people is unknown to us, and we know that they hate Christians. Nor do we know the language of the people. Certainly when they see us so wretchedly dressed and girded with a rope, they will despise us as madmen and as incapable of pronouncing words of life. This is why we have such great need of your prayers. Oh, sweet father, how can we separate ourselves from you? In what way can we, miserable and orphaned, accomplish the will of God without you, if He does not keep us with grace?"

Something struggled through their words: youth was in rebellion against death. Meanwhile, May smiled on the blessed valley of Spoleto, and all the forest around Porziuncola looked so fair, fragrant with its golden broom.

At once Francis conquered himself, shaking off the spell of discouragement.

"My sons, surrender yourselves to God, since He who sends you will give you all the aid needful to fulfill His will."

Thus did the crusaders of Morocco leave, their shaven heads bared to the sun, their bare feet in the dust, holding the Rule against their breasts and the crucifix in their hearts.

Before them stood dark Africa.

FRANCIS IN LANDS BEYOND THE SEAS

If Francis commanded his brethren to leave, it was because he had already decided to leave himself. The Fifth Crusade, desired by Innocent III and announced by Honorius, was being conducted wearily because of the dissolution of the Christian army, while the united Moslems defended themselves fiercely. In 1219 St. Francis, followed by several companions went to Ancona to embark on a crusade ship sailing for St. John of Acre, capital of the Latin kingdom of Syria. But, since there was no place for all the friars, St. Francis entrusted the fate of those to leave or remain behind to a child's choice.

"Tell me, little one, is it the will of God that all these friars come with me to Egypt?"

"No," replied the child.

"Which ones then?"

"This one and that one, and this one," the child pointed to twelve of them, among whom were Pietro Cattani and Friar Illuminato of Rieti who was indeed a man of great illumination and virtue.

After a crossing that took one month, they landed at St. John of Acre, where they found a group of brothers who had preceded them the year before and where, according to their custom, they divided two by two to evangelize the countryside. Francis, with Friar Illuminato, chose Damietta in Egypt, which at that time was a rallying center for the Crusade because for more than a year, the Christians had been besieging the city which the Moslems were defending with a kindred doggedness. Francis arrived in August when an assault of the crusaders against the fortress had been repulsed with heavy losses by the Saracens, who were led by two courageous and skillful chieftains: Melek-el-Kamil, the Sultan of Egypt, and his brother Melek-el-Mohammed, the Sultan of Damascus.

St. Francis found the camp in a deplorable moral state: hatreds, envy, ambitions for power, revelries, vice of all kinds; it was an outrage to keep the Cross in the camp.

"This is why we are not winning."

The saint felt the wrath of the Lord, and one day while the crusaders were preparing for a new assault, he said to Friar Illuminato:

"The Lord tells me that if we come to blows today we shall not have victory. Yet if I warn them, they will think me crazy, and if I keep silent I will not have easy conscience. What should I do?"

Even this time the great Francis doubted himself and asked counsel of a disciple. Like a true Franciscan, Friar Illuminato replied, "You, of all people, worry about the judgment of men? It is not the first time that you will have been thought crazy. Act according to your conscience and fear God rather than men."

So the blessed Francis warned the leaders not to give battle because they would get the worst of it, but he was ridiculed as a fanatic. Events proved him right, however, because on that nineteenth day of August the crusaders suffered a defeat in which they lost about 6,000 men. This beating humiliated them, disposing them to listen to the despised Italian pilgrim who now understood how much more urgent his mission was among the crusaders than it was among the Saracens. And speaking to the knights and warriors in French and Italian, with the very language of chivalry and of arms, he converted them to the Lord and rekindled in them enthusiasm for the almost forgotten purpose of the holy war.

His preaching, his example, his charm, spread throughout the Christian camp, arousing the Franciscan vocation among the best elements. Jacques de Vittry, the French bishop of St. John of Acre, who was present at the siege of Damietta, saw his own zealous priests, his own secretary, who was an Englishman, enter the Order of St. Francis. And he had to work hard to dissuade others from imitating them.

IN THE PRESENCE OF THE SULTAN

But Francis could not content himself with these victories, which were not the purpose of his journey. Nothing more remained for him to do except to hurl himself into the mouth of the wolf. But he wanted the authorization of the Church. So he asked Cardinal Pelagio Galvani, the papal legate in the Holy Land, for leave to preach to the sultan. The cardinal legate denied it in order not to be responsible for their deaths, but, overcome by Francis' insistence, he allowed him to cross the lines, saying to him and his companion, "Take heed to have your heart and mind always turned to God, who alone can save you. And remember that it is not I who am sending you."

There were frightening rumors about the hatred of the Saracens against Christians. "Don't go, don't go," said the crusaders. "There's a reward of a golden ducat for the head of every Christian."

Francis made the sign of the Cross, as when he had set forth

on the encounter with the wolf of Gubbio. And with Friar
Illuminato he entered the enemy territory singing the versicle
from David, "For though I should walk in the midst of the
shadow of death, I will fear no evils, for Thou art with me."

Along the way two lambs came toward them, a sight which
encouraged St. Francis. "Friar," he said to his companion, "let
us trust in God because the Gospel says 'Behold, I send you
forth as sheep among wolves.' "

When they arrived at the camp they were seized, bound and
roughly handled while the blessed Francis, entirely happy,
thought: "This is a beautiful beginning."

But since he wanted to try to convert Melek-el-Kemil he
began to shout, "Sultan! Sultan!", and the Saracens, though
doubting that he had a message or a revelation for their lord,
nonetheless led him to the sultan's camp.

"Have you come as messengers of peace, or to become wor-
shippers of Allah?" asked the sultan, carefully scrutinizing the
two bizarre figures.

The man of God replied with great assurance, "I am sent
by the Most High and by no man of the world to teach the
way of salvation to you and your people, and to announce the
truth of the Gospel of Christ." And he preached with such
fervor that the sultan, an intelligent and cultured Arab, marvelled and judged the poor little Christian not unworthy to
figure among the wise men of his court.

And he answered, "Stay here with me."

Inspired by God, Francis replied, "I will stay willingly with
you if you and your people will be converted to Christ. If you
have doubts about leaving the faith of Mohamet for that of
Christ, command that a great fire be lighted and let me and the
priest of Mohamet enter the flames and then believe in the faith
of the one of us who emerges from the pyre."

If the sultan had been a tyrant in the ancient manner he
would have amused himself by ordering the ordeal by fire. But,
because he was a wise man and had noted that some among his
learned men had slipped away upon hearing that proposal, he
said:

"I feel that not even one of the priests of Allah wants to expose himself to that risk to defend our faith."

St. Francis made a last attempt.

"Then if you will believe, I will throw myself into the fire, and if I am burnt impute the reason to my sins, but if I come out alive, acknowledge Christ as the true God and Saviour of the world."

The sultan, who had never found a man ready to throw himself into the fire for his soul, presented him with gold, silver, silk cloths, precious objects, commanding him to take what he wished. St. Francis naturally refused, to the growing astonishment of the sultan who, in order to test him fundamentally, offered him all sorts of honors and pleasures and Francis firmly replied no to all the flatteries and blandishments.

Then Melek-el-Kamil convoked the more authoritative and religious personages of the encampment to get their opinion of the two prisoners. And the opinion was that they be beheaded without mercy, because they preached against the law of Mahomet and he, as a custodian of the law, ought not permit such sacrilege.

"Christians," said the Sultan of Egypt to the two friars, "My doctors counsel me to have your heads cut off, but I will never send to his death one who would give his life for my salvation." He let them go free then with a decree permitting Francis and his fellow friars to roam undisturbed through the Saracen lands, including Palestine, and go to the Holy Sepulchre without paying tribute.

St. Francis took advantage of this and, always trying to evangelize enroute, he visited Bethlehem, Jerusalem and Mount Calvary, visits which were destined to bring most important fruits to the Catholic Church. But since the purposes of his crusade (conversion of the infidels and martyrdom) were not being realized, and from Italy disturbing news arrived soliciting his presence, he decided to return to his native land.

Before leaving, he again went to see Melek-el-Kemil who said to him, "Friar Francis, willingly would I be converted to the faith of Christ but I fear to do so because if my Saracens knew it, they would kill me, you and all the friars. Since you can do much good and I must settle some important questions, I do not wish to provoke your death and mine, but do teach me how I can be saved and I will do it."

"Lord," replied St. Francis, "I am returning to my country, but after my death I will send you two of my friars from whom you will receive the baptism of Christ. Meanwhile, release yourself from every impediment so that the grace of God may find you prepared for faith and devotion."

Francis promised this because he felt most deeply grateful to him. Seven years later, Francis died on the bare ground. Another twelve years went by, and the sultan fell ill in his royal palace and, suffering on his rugs and pillows, he waited for the fulfillment of the promise made to him by the Italian pilgrim. His border guards were ordered to be on the lookout for two friars dressed in the habit of St. Francis. And one day two brothers did come from the sea, because St. Francis had inspired them in a dream, and the guards immediately sent them to the dying sultan who rejoiced as if the countenance of the saint whom he had benefited stood once more before him. He was baptized and died as Christian among the Saracens, because the Lord has promised that there is no sinner so great who will not be saved if he truly love the Order of St. Francis with all his heart. So say the "Little Flowers."

Apparently this crusade of St. Francis had also failed. He had sought martyrdom and, instead, found honors; he had dreamed of an evangelical preaching tour among the Saracens and accomplished little more than a pilgrimage. He was returning, therefore, with an increasing ardor to crusade for that Lord Jesus whose birth, life and passion he had reconstructed in His natural setting, and with the certainty that God had denied him the beautiful death of the martyr. Instead He was preparing an even more beautiful one for him.

As for its religious and social importance, his crusade surpassed anything he and his contemporaries could have hoped for. Francis had been the first to go into the very tents of the Saracens, to show what the infidels had never seen: an authentic Christian, a living replica of Christ, a man ready to die to save the soul of another, unknown to him and a sinner. And he restored the apostolic spirit among the crusaders, the immediacy of the Gospel among the Italians, and among Europeans in general, an ancient and new sense of the civilizing mission which the conquests beyond the seas had all but lost.

By virtue of St. Francis, sanctity, the Franciscan idea developed with greater vigor where he personally initiated the missions. The custody of the Holy Land has always remained Franciscan. What is best in Palestine even to this day is Franciscan and Italian; even today the Franciscans are the most effective defenders and propagators of the Roman spirit among the Slav populations—mystical natures who would not understand an over-reasoned and too formalistic religiosity. St. Francis opened the borders of all countries to his Order and taught its members how to establish advance guardposts, how to make impetuous and brave assaults leading to conquest without victory, and victory without a crown.

THE MOROCCO ENTERPRISE

While Francis was carrying out his crusade in the Holy Land, his little Moroccan expedition was crossing Spain where it halted at Seville, the last bulwark of Arab rule in Europe. Unfortunately, the head of the band, Friar Vitale, had to stop at Aragon because of illness, and the five youths, who had more fervor than expert knowledge, were left without a guide save for the Rule of St. Francis. This Rule counselled the friars who were going among the Saracens and other infidels to conduct themselves in two ways: to engage in no strife or contention but to subject themselves to every creature for the love of God and to confess to being Christians; and to preach the word of God openly and frankly. Of the two ways the little band stressed the second: overt propaganda for the faith.

And they began preaching in a strange Italo-Arab-Spanish *patois* in front of the mosque of Seville. They were immediately arrested and sent to Sultan Abu-Jacub, "The Mill Watcher," and son of the other "Mill Watcher" under whom Francis had attempted his crusade.

Abu-Jacub, who took up residence in Morocco after the defeat suffered by his father at Toulouse in 1212, entertained no bellicose plans against Christians, indeed he entrusted the command of his army to a Christian prince, Don Pedro Infante of Portugal, who because of quarrels with the king, his brother, had unblushingly passed over to the service of the Mohammedans. Instead of imprisoning the five missionaries, Abu-Jacub entrusted them to Don Pedro who received them most respectfully in his palace. The friars took advantage of their freedom to preach the Gospel publicly, and one day the sultan ran into Friar Bernardo who, standing on a cart, was inveighing against Mohamet. The sultan ordered the five missionaries to be seized and expelled from the country. Don Pedro put them aboard a ship leaving for Ceuta, warning them to sail for Italy from there. Instead, a short time later, they were once more seen preaching on the roads of Morocco and the sultan had them imprisoned, and then dispatched to Ceuta. But the heroic band, vowed to martyrdom, returned to Morocco. Once more, Don Pedro took them in tow and for fear that their stubborn resistance might prejudice the native Christians, he had them interned on Moroccan territory under close guard. The five, however, managed to escape surveillance and re-entered the city. One Friday—the Mohammedan Sabbath—they began to preach on the public square through which the sultan was bound to pass. This repeated and open defiance infuriated the sultan; he had the missionaries arrested and submitted them to an interrogation to which the heroic youths responded with the steadfastness of the ancient martyrs. Then he tortured them, making them roll on a carpet of broken glass and finally, driven to ferocity by their very patience, he lopped off the heads of all five with his scimitar.

Don Pedro composed the bodies of the martyrs and sent them to Coimbra. The pious procession accompanied them to the church of Santa Croce, where they were buried with the reverence of the people.

Thus ended the Moroccan mission which had been vowed to death from the moment of its departure from Porziuncola in that fragrant month of May, a memorable Spring in the annals of Franciscan chivalry. When the teacher heard this news, he exclaimed, weeping for sorrow, consolation and envy, "Now I can say I have five brothers" for in them he found fulfilled his own ungratified thirst for martyrdom. But since the brothers all gloried in the honor accruing to the Order born of that crown of blood, Francis immediately admonished them, "It is needful to extol one's own martyrdom not that of others."

For he feared collective pride as much as individual pride, and he wanted his fellow friars to consider themselves minors even in matters of superiority.

THE PURPLE SEED

If among the two roads of the apostolate indicated by the blessed Francis, the five knights of Morocco chose the most perilous, it was also because it was the shortest one to martyrdom and the most effective one for converting the infields. If they took to this road with a fury so desperate as to seem madness, it was under the pressure of the circumstances amid which they found themselves. The Saracens, who did not understand their words, understood their blood, they believed in their death if not in their sermons.

Nonetheless, that blood seemed lost on the Saracens. But the purple seed, fallen in Morocco, sprouted in Portugal and bloomed in Italy in prodigious flower which makes us marvel even today: St. Anthony of Padua. He was an Augustinian student in the monastery of Coimbra when the bodies of the five martyrs were brought to his country. So deeply was he moved by their sight and the story behind them that he fled his native country, his studies and prelatic honors to wear the habit of those sublime madmen who followed *Il Poverello*.

Most people know the miracles that St. Anthony performed on earth and which he continues to perform in heaven. But few realize that this great saint was a gift showered upon the world, especially upon Italy, because of the first spilled blood of the Franciscans.

THE TWO CAPTAINS

At the time when Francis was launching his Knights of Poverty, another great person, born in Spain, St. Dominic was founding another militia which was to defend the Church of Christ with doctrine and zeal.

Dominic and Francis met in 1220 in Rome, to which city both always turned for the seal of approval on their works: Dominic, the older of the two, looked graceful and gentle in his tunic, black and white like the swallows; Francis, the younger, but already worn out, was dressed in his tunic which was the color of larks. They did not know each other, but Dominic had seen Francis in a dream as the man destined by God to revise the destinies of Christianity and at their first encounter they understood each other without saying a word. They were standing on the Aventine hill where Dominic founded the two first great convents of his Order, and Rome was spread out before them in its arches, columns, blackish ruins, campaniles, towers, façades shining with mosaics and marble, the whole panorama here and there dotted with meadows and woods, among which the Aurelian walls stood out like an enclosure of bronze beyond which imperial Rome faded away in the deserted countryside. Under the bridges, the Tiber flowed like time.

The two great reconstructors confided their lives and ideals to each other before that cyclopic disorder of a fallen world and a world once more on the rise.

"I come from Spain," said Dominic. "I have been studying since my childhood; the University of Salamanca unveiled to me the verities of theology and the beauty of science, the sister of faith. I spent ten years among the worst heretics of Provence. I have known the evils of error, the danger of knowledge without God. I stood at the side of Simon of Montfort, like a priest at the side of a knight; I fought with the word of the Gospel before the soldiers fought with the sword; I prayed and fasted while the inevitable battle raged. From my knowledge of the heretics I have learned that the evils of the century stem from the pride of intellect which is blindness and servitude. Only the truth will make us free. What can you tell me of yourself, brother?"

"I was a merchant, a man of the world and a sinner: I studied little and I read little save for the ledgers of the shop and songs of love and chivalry and ballads and other vanities until the merciful Lord touched my heart, and gave me the Cross to read. I knew no heretics, I came to know lepers. And then when the Lord entrusted the friars to me, no one showed me what to do but the Most High Himself revealed to me that I should live according to the Holy Gospel."

"My holy friars also live according to the Holy Gospel and they pray and study in order to combat the astuteness of the world."

"Mine are simpletons and unlettered and have no book but the crucifix."

"Mine must possess nothing save the common cloister and the cell which is theirs today and no longer theirs tomorrow."

"My friars have no place on which to lay their heads, and their cell is my heart."

"My most simple brother, how can a community sustain itself without having care and solicitude for the things needful to the body?"

"O Father Dominic, the Lord has revealed to me that if we will tightly embrace holy poverty, the world will follow us and will nourish us copiously since God has placed this pact between us and the world: that we set a good example to the world, and God will provide for our necessities."

"We too are poor: we are naught but the dogs of the Lord and with the lighted torch of the faith we sow terror among packs of heretic wolves, scattering them."

"We are the jongleurs of God and we wish to keep Him happy with our praises, with our countenances happy even in tribulations, and thereby we wish to make men understand that to serve God is to reign, and that to serve Him is needful, but in gladness."

"We strike the roots of heresy and extirpate the weeds that poison."

"We have no valor for cutting others down but only to let ourselves be cut down willingly, for if the seed die not the earth brings forth no fruit."

"God is truth and sin is born of our ignorance."

"God is love and ignorance is born of our want of love."

"I would fain, O Friar Francis, that your Order and mine should become one, and that we live in the Church with the same Rule."

"We are two wheels of the same cart, and mine is always the smaller."

"Brother," said the blessed Dominic with great reverence, "deign to give me the rope with which you are girded."

Francis refused out of humility, but St. Dominic insisted with so much charity that he won, and placing his hands in the hands of the other, he commended himself to his prayers.

Thus, the Spanish saint and the Italian saint embraced under the great sky of Rome.

8

The Perfect Joy

When St. Francis returned from the Orient, he landed on a little island in the lagoon of Venice and rested there to meditate. The island, crowned with poplars and girded by waters the color of mother-of-pearl, was deserted but not quiet: the waves beating on the shore, the wind murmuring through the poplars, the birds, singing in the branches and on the meadows, made a great orchestra. St. Francis, although his heart was troubled by many adversities, was gladdened and said to his companion.

"Listen to our brother birds who praise the Lord. Let us go among them and sing our canonical hours."

They went, and the little winged creatures continued their song but so loudly that the two friars could not hear each other as they took turns reciting the versicles of the Divine Office. The blessed Francis was forced to say:

"Brother birds, refrain from singing until we are finished with our hours."

The birds were still until he blessed them and gave them leave to resume their song. It was not the first time that such a thing had occurred, nor was it only birds that understood Francis. Almost all the animals on which he turned his eyes understood him. One day at Greccio they brought him a little

176

live hare, the kind that dashes away at the slightest footstep. Francis admonished the hare never to let itself be caught again and set it free, but instead of running away the little hare leaped into his lap and crouched there. Every time the saint set him down the hare returned to his lap. Finally, in order to separate the hare from the saint, it was necessary to take it back to the forest.

The same happened with a rabbit near Trasimeno, and with a water-fowl and a fish from the lake of Rieti, with a pheasant presented as a gift by a nobleman of Siena. The pheasant would not eat when it was away from its great friend. Hearing a cicada chirping on a fig tree near his cell in Porziuncola, Francis, instead of consigning the cicada to the devil, as an irritated person would have done, said to the cicada,

"You do well, praise the Lord." And then he called it to him and the cicada flew into his hand like a well-trained bird, and the saint said to it, "Sing, my sister!" And the cicada sang more loudly. Then he said to it, "Sing no more!" And the cicada was silent, and flew off to a more distant tree and it resumed its song eight days in a row, until the saint said, "Let us give leave to our sister cicada which has greatly delighted us." And the cicada flew away forever as if it dared not disobey.

But Francis had a special tenderness for birds and for lambs: for birds because they had drawn the attention of Jesus, who had cited them as testimony of the providence of the Heavenly Father, and because as free, winged and singing creatures they resembled his ideal of the friar minor. And for lambs because the lamb was the symbol of Jesus. With animals his sympathy did not stop with words. One day, meeting a boy who was bringing turtle-doves to market, he was moved to think how they would end up on a spit. He beseeched the boy to give them to him. The boy handed them over quickly, and the saint rested them in his lap and caressed them gently.

"O my little sisters, you simple turtle-doves, innocent and chaste, why did you let yourselves be caught? Now I will rescue you from death, and make nests for you."

He made nests for them all and the turtle-doves, now no longer wild, lived with the friars as though they were pigeons.

He preferred cowled larks among birds, because they resembled friar minors with their cowls of feathers. And he said that if he could he would beseech the emperor, for the love of his God, to make a special law prohibiting the hunting of larks, and another law obliging all the rectors of the cities and the lords of the castles to go out on Christmas day to scatter grains on the roads so that the sister larks and other birds might eat during so great a solemnity. In his feeling of brotherhood for all creatures he did not at all consider the idea that the emperor might act on behalf of small animals a strange one.

Sheep engaged his tender feelings in a particular manner. To him (as to Dante) they did not seem to be stupid creatures; in them rather, he saw the humility and mildness of Christ the Lord among the Pharisees. And when he met one being led to slaughter, he did everything he could to ransom it, even at the price of giving up his cloak or tunic. Then he would tranquilly show up with the rescued little beast among his friends.

One day, in the March of Ancona, he met a tough-looking man who was carrying two lambs, tied together by their feet. The lambs were bleating desperately. Francis approached them and caressed them like a mother caresses a weeping child, and he inquired of the owner, "Why do you torment my little brother lambs, tying them up and letting them hang in such a fashion."

"I am taking them to market because I need money."

"What will happen to them?"

The man laughed. "What a silly question! They'll have their throats slit and be eaten."

In order to ransom the lambs, Francis offered his mantle which was brand new, since he had received it to protect himself against the cold. The merchant could hardly believe what he heard, since the mantle was worth much more than lambs would fetch at the market. And the deal turned out to be even more advantageous to him. For the blessed Francis, not knowing to whom to entrust the beasts, gave them back to him, ordering him neither to sell them, nor kill them, nor to do them any harm but to nourish and keep them with care.

THE BEAUTY OF CREATURES

Francis knew how to see goodness and beauty in all creatures, even in earth-worms which he picked up from the ground so that they would not be crushed by the feet of passers-by. He loved flowers. And he insisted upon the luxury of a garden near the habitations of the friars, and in the kitchen garden he charitably set aside a strip of uncultivated terrain so that grass and wild flowers might grow in freedom. He had such a respect for life, even in plants, that he prohibited his friars to cut trees to their roots. For him a tree was a living organism which breathes, nourishes and reproduces itself; it was not to be killed but the stump should be left to it so that it might sprout new shoots.

He loved water which runs and leaps, which quenches thirst and washes, and he looked for places where it was most limpid to immerse his hands in it. He loved neat, shining stones and walked over them lightly; he loved the sky in its alternating moods of smiling serenity and foreboding cloudiness, and the earth in her providential fruitfulness. But what attracted him most, like an ever new miracle, was light, the light of the sun, the light of fire. Once he said that every morning, at sunrise, all creatures should praise God who created them for our use, and at every eventide they should thank them for the fire that illumines us in the night. He felt the beauty of fire as no poet has felt it, because a poet limits himself to singing the beautiful flame in verses, but St. Francis loved it to the point where he never wanted to put it out, not even when it was about to burn him alive, or to burn down his cell. One day when he was seated beside the fireplace, the fire caught his clothes and a companion ran toward him to put it out. St. Francis forbade him, saying, "No, dearest brother, harm not the fire!"

Harm not the fire! As if it were a sentient creature. But in reality Francis, a poet among saints, considered that no other element better rendered the image of the ardent spirit. Hence, to put it out seemed to him equivalent to suffocating life itself.

On another occasion on Mount La Verna the little cell in which he was eating caught on fire. While his friend, frightened and shaking, tried to put it out, St. Francis did not even want to help him. Instead he picked up a skin which he used as a covering, and tranquilly retired to the forest. The fire had been put out by the time he returned, and he said to his companion, "I don't want to keep the skin anymore, since by reason of my avarice I did not allow Friar Fire to eat it."

He spoke thus because in the flame he saw not only life, but the love of God which invests and devours all, and from which nothing may be withdrawn, not even a coverlet, under penalty of being misers, that is to say, very poor in a false richness.

St. Francis was born with the gift of gathering beauty like a flower, and he enjoyed it exquisitely even when he lived according to the ways of the world. But at that time elegant and precious things distracted him. Only after the great renunciation did he begin to penetrate into the beauty of nature, which at first he admired superficially as an illiterate admires the illustrations in a book. When he had thrown away the luxury of house, table and garments, he learned to know the luxury which the Lord showers so prodigally on life and he sought to surround himself with it and enjoy it, as though he were doing a wrong to the Creator by not recognizing the wealth of His gifts.

It was neither novel nor meritorious to know how to enjoy beautiful things, but what was new and meritorious was the way in which St. Francis enjoyed them. After his conversion his eyes were opened, like those of an illiterate who learns to read, and in everything he discovered the seal of God, the creator and redeemer. Thus to him wood meant the Cross; stone, Jesus Christ, who is called the corner-stone in Scripture; flowers signified Our Lord, called the lily of the valley; water signified Our Lord, the source of eternal life, and signified also pure and penitent souls; and finally the sun, God, signified the sun of justice. This symbolic vision in no way altered the real vision of things, indeed it rendered it perfect because it was more spiritual and more profound, not stopping at appearances but going forward to their origins. This brought important consequences.

For him, creatures were neither a temptation nor a distraction, as they were for so many ascetics before him, but a continuous reminder of the Creator, just as the work recalls the artisan, and a motive for loving Him the more. Another consequence was that Francis, seeing in all things, in animals, plants and rocks, the work of the Father, never treated inferior creatures as a master but always as a brother and with a very great affection, with a deferential delicacy which probably no man in the world has ever shown since. For this reason, things, knowing themselves loved, loved him in turn. It is not known whether it was Francis who opened the intelligence of beasts, or whether it was the beasts who understood Francis. They loved him by giving themselves to him, as the hare, the pheasant, the wolf, the falcon and the birds did visibly, and as all the creatures, flowers and grass, water and sun, did invisibly as they discoursed with him about the Most High and responded with their praises to his. Since he wished to do no harm to things, things wished to do no harm to him. His soul, purified by penance and trans-humanized by love, again acquired that mastery over nature that Adam had enjoyed in the terrestrial paradise, and which he had lost by sinning. To the man, returned to innocence, all things responded with innocence.

In the last years of his life when he suffered from an agonizing eye ailment, Francis was commanded by Cardinal Ugolino to go to Rieti to be treated by a famous physician. This doctor suggested a frightful remedy, of the kind so common in the barbaric therapy of the Middle Ages. It consisted of opening all the veins from the ear to the eyebrow of the diseased eye with a red hot iron. Although he was used to sufferings, Francis shuddered when he saw the iron glowing red on the coals. But even at that moment he was comforted by his love for creatures, and he spoke to the fire as to a friend:

"O my noble and useful Brother Fire! Do not hurt me too much, just as I have never hurt you. Indeed I have always loved you for love of that Lord who created you."

He retired to meditate and pray, and then he made the sign of the Cross on the coals. The surgeon withdrew the irons, and brought them close to Francis' temple. Francis stood, calmly waiting. Then he pressed them against the flesh which crackled as it burned, while the friars fled in horror. But they were immediately recalled by the voice of the teacher:

"O brethren of little faith, why do you flee? Friar Fire has not hurt me at all: Indeed I beseech him to burn me again if it be needful."

"In truth this is a miracle!" said the surgeon. "The strongest man would not have endured this operation."

By living thus in communication with creatures, the saint received a great joy from them; he possessed them with love and they were his. He who wanted nothing for himself, actually had everything. And since he possessed things without desiring them, without fear of losing them, in short without selfishness, he enjoyed them infinitely with the freedom of one who has abolished the ego and its duplicate the possessive pronoun "mine," and with the humility of one who never feels himself to be the master but always the depository, never a host but always a guest, thereby arriving at the contemplation of beauty which is a joy only when it is disinterested. And he gave vent to this joy by singing in French and making believe that he was accompanying himself with a viol, which was really only a piece of wood supported on his arm, over which he ran a kind of bow bent with thread. Nobody who heard him laughed because music does not come out of the instrument but out of the heart of the player, and the heart of Francis, like that of a true master-singer, drew harmony from all things.

TALKS WITH MEN

This harmony was drawn less from things than from men. Francis was not a hermit by nature. From his early youth he loved fellowship, and almost had a greater feeling for friendship than for family. Involuntarily he became the leader of his friends because of the loftiness of his spirit. When he was converted he could not remain in solitude as he would have desired.

The man of old remained even in his later years and the more he was followed the more he withdrew, clearly seeing the goal and the way in himself. The King of Festivals became a captain of souls, but without the gestures of a conqueror. Like the Lord Jesus he began with a few friends. And he again found that delicate pleasure of friendship, which he knew how to gather amid the boisterousness of the brigades, at his Round Table, where he cultivated it with a more elevated spirituality, and where friendship was purified and guaranteed by poverty. He was most sensible to the least courtesy that he received, and just as at one time he would have requited it with munificent gifts, now he requited it with prayers. One evening at Cortona he and one of his companions were the guests of a nobleman of the city, who went to great lengths to do him honor. He embraced him, he washed, dried and kissed his feet, lit a fire, prepared an excellent table, at which he served him with great ceremony, and at the end, not knowing how further to show his devotion, he offered to pay all the expenses of their needs.

Francis, deeply grateful, began to love him as only he knew how to love. And when they resumed their journey he told his companion that the nobleman deserved to become a knight of Lady Poverty because of his courtesy. "Courtesy," observed the saint, elevating what seems to be a human virtue to a divine level with his superatural glimpse into things, "is one of the properties of God, Who of His courtesy gives sun and rain to the just and the unjust, and courtesy is the sister of charity by which hatred is extinguished and love is preserved." From that moment he confirmed his intention of giving that good man the greatest good that he could, a perfect life. He said many prayers for him, and one day he returned to Cortona but he did not go to talk with him because he knew that words represent the last cartridges in the conquest of souls. When he was near the residence of his courteous host, he knelt down to pray in a quiet place to one side. He prayed so much that the nobleman, as if summoned, went to a window and saw him. Francis looked like an other-world creature to him. Immediately, the nobleman left his palace, ran over to St. Francis and knelt at his feet, beseeching him to receive him among the penitents. The saint opened his arms, thanking the Lord. The courtesy had been requited for eternity.

When he was greatly troubled with his eyes at the hermitage of Fonte Colombo, near Rieti, desiring to be courteous to the doctor who visited him every day by order of Cardinal Ugolino, he said to the warden in the manner of a man of the world, "Invite the doctor to stay for dinner and prepare a goodly table for him."

The warden hesitated. "We are ashamed to invite him. We are so poor!"

"O friars of little faith! Don't make me repeat things!"

"Indeed, indeed," said the doctor courteously, "I will the more willingly eat in your poverty, dearest brothers."

Somewhat confused the friars set the table as best they could with bread, cooked grass, lots of water and a little wine, when there was a knock at the door. It was the maidservant of a lady of a castle seven miles away who was sending the blessed Francis a basket full of white bread, fish, crayfish patties, honey and eggs.

"I told you that the poor have God as a servitor. And that the table of the poor is richer than a king's as God is more generous than man," observed St. Francis.

The doctor, deeply moved, said, "Neither you friars nor we lay-people know as we ought the holiness of this man."

And they ate little, since wonder conquered the appetite and the sense of the divine made them forget the present.

Of penetrating insight, Francis discerned the desire of men at a distance, and he responded with an immediate readiness to those who loved him. Once he was at the hermitage of Greccio and spent whole days in contemplation, appearing among his fellows only occasionally at meal-time, when two friars came from far away with the long-nourished hope of seeing him and receiving his blessing. But his companions at Greccio did not want to disturb the blessed Francis, and with that little touch of jealous selfishness which distinguishes the guardians of a great man, they escorted the two strangers to the door, recommending resignation to them. The two friars left disconsolately, heads bowed, accusing themselves of not being worthy of that grace because of their sins. Suddenly the voice of the saint called them to the threshold of the cell and he blessed them so affectionately that the two friars left in a happy frame of mind, praising the Lord.

Just as St. Francis understood creatures who do not talk, so did he understand the thoughts that men do not express. Among his friars there was a youth of noble lineage and customs, Friar Rinieri, who was determined to conquer the affection of the teacher, but the poor youth pined away with his secret torment and every time he ran into St. Francis he would think to himself, "If he smiles at me, God too smiles at me. If he does not look at me, God too is angry with me."

One day he was passing near the cell of the teacher, feeling very forsaken. Francis called out to him. "Son," he said to him, "let not yourself be conquered by temptations and doubts. You are most dear to me and among those most worthy of my affection and of my friendship. Come to me without fear whenever you wish, and talk with me as with a friend."

Friar Rinieri did not puff with pride. Instead he became more respectful because he was more trusting, and more virtuous, because the security of being loved gave him new heart.

Another time Francis approached a friar who for long had been troubled by temptations and who could not find a confessor to restore his peace. Softly, Francis said to him,

"Courage, dearest brother, fear not and do not distress yourself over those temptations which do no harm to your soul, but with my leave recite seven Our Fathers every time you are tormented by them." And the friar comforted, marvelled at these unexpected words. Thus did Francis speak to the heart, because love sees invisible things, and by giving gladness to others he luminously increased what he bore in himself.

FRIAR LEO

Among the knights of the Round Table, St. Francis had a most faithful one who was called Friar Leo. This ferocious name contrasted greatly with the dove-like timidity of his soul for which reason the teacher, who had the felicitous gift of defining a character with a single image, called him the "little lamb of God," requiting his devotion with a paternal tenderness as well as with the confidences of a friend. Friar Leo was one of those men who, though simple and inconspicuous themselves, in the company of a great man are totally invested by His light, which they reflect. Permeated by the charm of the teacher, he almost always went along with him during his journeys, and intimately clung to all of his ideals. He had been with him at Monte Feltro, at Fonte Colombo, at Siena, at Mount La Verna, and was especially close to him in the last years of his life, during his illness and at his death. His company had a soothing effect on the saint who spent hours of painful forsakeness and hours of great jocundity with him. One of these hours was spent together in Porziuncola. Friar Leo had prepared dinner in the shade of a hedge, when a nightingale, on the other side, began to sing. Francis, who was never in a hurry to eat, said, "Let us too go and praise the Lord with our brother bird." For among all beautiful things, it was music that transported him most. When they were near the tree on which the little musician was perched, the saint said, "Come, Friar Little Lamb, sing!"

"I have no good voice, father. It is meet that you who have a seemly voice and mastery in the art of singing compete with the nightingale."

Then Francis began to sing and the nightingale stopped, then Francis stopped singing and the nightingale resumed its song. Thus alternatingly Francis improvised the praises of God in new verses for His creatures, and the nightingale trilled its unconscious thankfulness. It seemed as though the man were giving words to the bird, and the bird were giving the theme to the man. Thus the voice of the one and the other, in a musical dialogue, was raised in the valley until vespers. Finally St. Francis turned to his companion and said, "Verily, Friar Little Lamb, the nightingale has surpassed me in singing the praises of the Lord. Let us eat now."

They had hardly seated themselves on the ground when the nightingale flew to the hand of the saint, who greeted it with great festivity. "Let us feed our little brother bird who merits it

more than I." The nightingale pecked at the crumbs in Francis'
hand and did not fly away until it received his blessing.

At another time the two friends were in the countryside, and
not having books for the office of dawn, St. Francis proposed
that they sing the matins without a breviary, one reciting the
praises of God and the other responding as the heart dictated.
More than singing lauds, the saint's intention was to conduct
a dialogued meditation for his own self-clarification. "I will
begin and you will answer and beware not to change the words.
I will say thus: 'O Friar Francis, you have committed so many
evils and so many sins that you are deserving of hell.' And you,
Friar Leo, will respond, 'Truly you do deserve the deepest hell.'
Have you understood?"

To which Friar Leo, with dove-like simplicity, replied,
"Willingly father, begin then in the name of God."

And St. Francis began, "O Friar Francis, you have committed so many evil deeds and sins in the world that you are
deserving of hell."

And Friar Leo replied, "God will perform so many good
works through you that you will go to paradise."

"Friar Leo, don't say that!" exclaimed St. Francis. "Answer
as I have taught you." And he repeated the lesson. But when,
sighing and beating his breast, he wept, "O Lord of heaven
and earth, I have committed so many sins against Thee that I
am deserving of being cursed by Thee," instead of answering
as he had been instructed Friar Leo answered, "O Friar Francis,
God will make you singularly blessed among the blessed."

Again the teacher marvelled over this because he had never
encountered resistance in Friar Leo.

"Why have you had the presumption to act counter to
obedience, and answered the contrary of what I have imposed
on you."

"God knows, my father, for every time I purposed in my
heart to answer as you commanded, God makes me speak as
pleases Him and not as it pleases me."

St. Francis, who could not doubt the sincerity of his faithful
friend, began to think that that candid soul might be truly
inspired by God, and he wanted to try a question that had been

oppressing his heart for years. But first he made Friar Leo promise to respond in the way he had taught him. Then weeping Francis said, "O Friar Francis, little wretch, do you think that God will have mercy on you?"

And Friar Leo answered, "Indeed, you will receive a great grace from God, and God will exalt and glorify you in eternity for he that humbles himself will be exalted. And I can say naught else since God speaks through my mouth."

Then Francis wept, but for joy, and this was one of the most beautiful matins of his life.

But despite the honor of the confidence, the soul of Francis remained in part a mystery to his humble friend, who did his best, through observation and prayer to penetrate its most jealous and incommunicable secret, the intimacy with God. He spied on his anxieties, he was afraid of being separated from his teacher, he was afraid of losing him, of being forgotten, of going astray without him. Friar Leo, who was the confessor, secretary and confidant of St. Francis, was in reality his penitent and he would have been unable to move without thought of his teacher, just as he would have been unable to live without his love. St. Francis, who knew him better than he knew himself, wrote him the following letter, a masterpiece of tenderness, to guard him from discouragement and dejection:

"Thus I tell you this as a mother, my son, and I gather up all the words we said along the road in this one word and counsel. And if after this you find it needful to come to me, come, because I counsel you as follows: In whatever manner that best seems to you to please the Lord God in order to follow His example and His poverty, do it with the blessing of the Lord and with my obedience. And if it is needful for the good of your soul and for your consolation and if you wish to come to me, Leo, come."

FRIAR JUNIPER

Before his conversion, the blessed Francis preferred the company of nobles; after it he preferred that of the poor. At first

he admired chivalrous elegance in manners, later he admired
the spontaneity of the heart, however rough, awkward or naive.
Men who were naturally frank delighted him as did the flowers
of the field, the berries of the woods, the birds of passage.

Among his knights was an original character named Juniper
who surpassed them all in simplicity, generosity and gaiety,
three gifts which when combined can either make a saint or a
buffoon of a man, and a farce or a feast of life. His escapades
were famous at the Round Table of Porziuncola.

Once, upon hearing that a sick fellow-friar was yearning to
eat a boiled pig's foot, Friar Juniper said, "Let me get you one."
So saying he took a kitchen knife, and stealthily proceeded to
a wood where a herd of pigs was pasturing. Here he grabbed
a pig, cut off a foot, and ran away leaving the animal screaming.
Upon returning to the kitchen, he washed, dressed, cooked
the foot, and then triumphantly brought it to the infirm friar.
And to entertain the friar as he ate it, he told him about his
struggle with the pig.

Meanwhile the swineherd came running up to Porziuncola
and denounced the deed to St. Francis. "It's not possible," replied the saint, meekly trying to pacify the peasant by promising to make amends. When the swineherd left, he thought,
"Can Friar Juniper have been up to one of his escapades?" So
he sent for him.

"Indeed," replied the candid Friar Juniper, "indeed it was
I. And if I tell you the consolation and comfort he took from
that foot, had I cut off the feet of a hundred pigs, I certainly
believe that God would have been content."

But these reasons did not make Francis content. And making
him understand that he had robbed, albeit with good intent,
he ordered the friar in holy obedience to ask pardon on his
knees from the legitimate owner. Friar Juniper humbled himself before the pig's owner and so embraced the man as he told
him what great good had been done by that foot, that the man
ended up almost asking the friar's pardon. He slit the throat
of the pig, roasted it in the oven and brought it to Porziuncola
to eat it with the friars.

Friar Juniper was the buffoon of the Round Table not by

intention but by nature. And like the buffoons at court, every act of buffoonery hid an admonition, but it was born of something quite different from the jongleuresque spirit; it was born of charity. Thus once, having been severely rebuked by the superior for having given some little silver bells to a poor woman, he thought that his superior had become hoarse because he had raised his voice so high and that he might make amends for the harm done by preparing a good dish of porridge and butter. Late at night, he knocked on the cell of the minister-general, holding a dish of porridge in one hand and a candle in the other.

"What is this?" asked the general.

Father Juniper answered, "Father, today when you chided me for my defects I perceived that your voice was growing hoarse, from overfatigue, I think. Therefore I thought of a remedy and made this porridge for you. I beseech you to eat it because it will ease your chest and throat."

The superior became furious at this new roguish act and sent him to the devil. But Friar Juniper, seeing that neither prayers nor coaxing were of avail, said candidly, "Father, since you do not want to eat this porridge and since it was made for you at least do me the favor of holding the candle for me, and I will eat it."

This burlesque twist to the matter which was still a salty lesson would have angered anyone else, but the general took it as befitted a good Franciscan, and said, "Look now, since you wish it so, let us both eat it together." And they ate, refreshed as much by the devotion as by the food.

When the blessed Francis heard about this exploit, he smiled, saying, "I would like to have a whole forest of such junipers!" And he was right, because Friar Juniper was of jongleur stamp with the heart of a hero as he demonstrated several years later. After being mistaken for a rebel who had made an attempt on the life of a tyrant lord of Viterbo, he was arrested and tortured. Since at every interrogation, instead of clearing himself by declaring his true identity, he answered that he was a wicked sinner deserving of death, he was condemned to be tied to the tail of a horse and dragged to the gallows. Fortunately, as they were tying him, the warden of a nearby convent arrived and recognizing his voice which was sighing, "Don't, don't, you wicked men, you're hurting my legs!" the warden shouted to them to free the innocent man. And he removed his own tunic with which to clothe the naked Juniper. Friar Juniper, still jocose, said to him with a happy countenance, almost laughing, "O warden, you are too fat and it were an ill-sight to see your nakedness. I won't have it!"

This roguish spirit, peppered with humor and strong in virtue, pleased Francis. He thought that if life were all heroic it would be a heavy burden indeed, and if it were all comic it would be stupid. But it is needful to moderate effort with laughter and to take temporal things comically, and eternal things heroically. And this thought gave him open-hearted, if not perfect, joy.

BEAUTY OF THE SPIRIT

Francis was also much pleased by the simplicity of a certain Friar John who in secular life had been a peasant near Assisi. He came to know the saint when he saw Francis one day humbly sweeping out the church of his village. For St. Francis, out of reverence to the Body of Christ, could not suffer churches to be ill-kept. And when he saw them in a state of neglect he took a broom and set them in order. John left his fields, his oxen, and his cottage, and while his parents and brothers consoled themselves over his departure with the ox he had given to them, instead of to the poor, he was quickly clothed with the habit of the order by St. Francis, the knight of the Round Table, and admitted to his intimate friendship. John observed his teacher night and day in order to copy him faithfully. When Francis kneeled, he kneeled, when Francis lifted his hands to heaven, he lifted his hands to heaven, when Francis sighed, he sighed. Upon noticing this the saint cheerfully rebuked him. "My father," replied the little friar, "I promised to do everything that you do. Therefore I must conform myself to everything you do." They called him John the simple, but he progressed so rapidly in virtue that Francis called him John the saint.

Francis preferred humility and simplicity in his knights, perhaps because these virtues had been more costly to his princely spirit. He knew, however, how to enjoy every trace of goodness that he perceived in his friars and he rejoiced in it intimately for the glory of God and theirs. When he saw Friar Rufino, who was a descendant of one of the greatest noble families of Assisi, at his harsh command preach in his breeches in a church of his native city, and when he saw him enter into a forest and remain there in a state of contemplation for two whole days, he said that his soul was one of the holiest in the world. When Friar Bernard of Quintavalle, his first-born son, as it were, appeared empty-handed before him after a tour for alms because, being himself starved to death, he had eaten the crusts of bread and left-overs on the way for which he accused himself as of a sin, St. Francis wept and embraced him as a perfect follower of the Gospel which commands us not to accumulate things and not to be solicitous of the morrow. And when he met one of his friars who returned from a tour for alms singing and bent under the weight of his sack, he kissed his shoulders, relieved him of the load and thanked God for having given him brothers. But he also knew how to admire the virtues of genius subjected to the faith, and he wanted the friars to remain and to advance in their vocations. He wanted Guglielmo Divini, a troubador crowned by Frederick II who later became Friar Pacifico—through Francis—to continue to be the King of Verses for the joy of the highest Emperor; and that Friar Anthony, born in Lisbon and formerly an Augustinian theologian, who had revealed himself to be a stupendous orator in an impromptu speech at Forli, should teach theology, and he was so pleased with his merit that he called him his bishop. Even in dealing with his knights he had a special regard for birth, culture, tastes, and the state of mind of each one. In each he saw some virtue which gave him joy and he developed that in order to have all the other virtues follow in its train.

From his observation of personal merits he began to fashion an ideal friar minor who, according to him, should possess the

St. Francis Feeding the Birds
Giotto (1266-1336)

St. Francis of Assisi
Artist Unknown

most perfect faith and love of poverty of Friar Bernard; the simplicity, candor, and purity of Friar Leo; the contemplative spirit of Friar Giles; the union with God of Friar Rufino, who prayed even when sleeping; the patience and love of the Cross of Friar Lucido, who was unwilling to remain for more than one month in one place for fear of getting to like it there. Besides the virtues of the soul, the ideal friar minor would have to have the gifts of the body and of genius: the bull strength of Friar John of the Lauds, the handsome appearance, the noble bearing, the fruitful and ornate speech of Friar Masseo; the humanity of Friar Angelo Tancredi, who was the first knight to enter the Order, adorned with every courtesy and benignity. Thus the blessed Francis, stroke by stroke, etched his ideal knight, neglecting neither the human nor superhuman nuances of perfection. And within himself he admired this imaginary masterpiece of spiritual beauty, without perceiving that his life was the masterpiece, and that he, the divine, poor, little man, was the ideal friar minor.

TALKS WITH GOD

It was the beginning of the night and the friars, each in his place, were in their first deep sleep, stretched on the ground, their heads on a stone or a piece of wood. But two were keeping vigil: a boy, most pure and innocent, received young because of his precocious devotion, and Francis who had gone to his place to make the friars think that he was likewise retiring. In truth however, he was waiting until they all fell asleep in order to go alone to the forest to pray. The boy friar, who wanted to wrest the secret of holiness from the teacher and who had noticed his nocturnal flights, had set his heart on spying upon him. So that night he tied his cord to the cord of Francis so that he might hear him when he rose. Then he too fell asleep, and only Francis remained awake with his heart beating the minutes for his encounter with God. When the noisy breathing of the friars assured him that all were asleep, Francis rose, but something held him: his cord tied to that of the boy.

Smiling, he loosened it gently, went out, and entered into a little cell in the wood. In a little while the boy friar awakened also, and finding the cord loosened and Francis' place empty and the door opened toward the wood, he went to look for him. He was guided by the sound of voices that came from the little cell where the teacher was praying. He drew closer and, in a wondrous light, he saw the Lord Jesus, the Virgin, St. John the Baptist and St. John the Evangelist, and a multitude of angels who were talking with Francis. At the vision the boy friar fell to the ground in a faint. When the saint emerged from his ecstasy to return to the hut, he stumbled against the boy's body. He bent over and recognized him in the first light of dawn, lifted him in his arms without awakening him, and carried him back to his cot. But upon learning how he had seen the wondrous vision he commanded him to tell it to no person so long as he, Francis, should live.

The boy friar was not the only one desiring to know the mystery of St. Francis's interior life. One friar claimed to have seen the teacher lifted in the air, another in a chariot of fire, another in a wondrous cloud, and still another in conversation with angels and saints. Another more indiscreet friar who, like the Bishop of Assisi, dared to stick his head inside the door of the cell where the saint was praying, was pushed outside by a mysterious force and remained as if paralyzed.

There was one thing that was noticed by all the friars: that Francis lived in constant prayer, and however he exerted himself to hide his colloquy with God in order to listen to all, his eyes now and then betrayed his desire to enter within himself. At such times he would break off superfluous speeches, hiding his face in his hand as if to withdraw himself from an importunate distraction. When he prayed in public he did nothing that was singular, and was distinguished only by his most devout bearing, rigorously correct, the bearing of a soldier before a general, a vassal before his prince, standing erect, without leaning on anything for support even when he was very sick, without his cowl, without turning his eyes, without distractions of any kind. When he had to recite the Divine Office on a journey, he always stopped if he were on foot, and alighted from his donkey if he were riding. He prayed standing erect and bareheaded even under the rain, as happened to him once upon his return from Rome, when he was soaked to the bone. In explanation he said to his companions: "If the body wishes to eat its food in peace and quietness, with how much more peace and quiet should the soul receive that food which is God Himself."

His concrete reality was God, his thought never strayed from Him, it lived in Him. Francis passed through the world like one absent-minded; not so withdrawn, however, as not to know how to see God in things. He immediately did what he felt he should do, passing over from prayer to action almost without distinguishing the two moments, for action was either an inspiration or a conclusion, or a continuation of prayer. It was a prayer of deed. Hence, having had its remote preparation in the colloquy with God, it sprang forth as if suddenly, rapidly, coherent, without hesitation or remorse. And he did not distinguish it from God, just as creatures did not distinguish him from the Creator.

Sometimes, it is true, the ecstasy seized him while he was working, rendering him insensible to the variety of the places he was in and to people who came toward him, as happened when he went through Borgo San Sepolcro, without noticing the clamorous crowd that surged around him. For him ecstasy was a more intimate penetration of that reality which he always lived within himself and which is veiled to us by the distraction of sensible things. This veil which is sundered for men only at death, did not exist for St. Francis; his eyes already saw the celestial spirits the way we see the persons who talk to us. For him it was as natural to find himself suddenly with angels as with his friars. Ecstasy was merely a change of company. When it was over, he would make an effort to return among his companions in a composed, indifferent state of mind, and to talk about common things as if nothing had happened.

But this domination of himself in order to hide grace cost him much. And the more he grew in perfection the more he felt the need to abandon himself without reserve to his God, in solitude.

SOLITUDE

One year at the beginning of Lent, finding himself near Trasimene, Francis beseeched one of his devotees to accompany him secretly in a boat to Isola Maggiore. The faithful friend obeyed and on the evening of Ash Wednesday the little boat pulled away from the bank and carried the two men to the wild little island. "You will come to fetch me on the evening of Holy Thursday, and you will tell no man I am here," Francis ordered his companion.

"And how about food?" asked the faithful friend.

"I have two little rolls. They will suffice."

The boat returned, and the saint remained alone, with the birds, the thick plants luxuriating in their freedom, and the lake lapping the silent shores. It was a vast and melancholy lake. In stormy weather the lake flashed tongues of foam in a leaden-gray light, spreading among the reeds of the plain, and insinuating itself among the hills like one seeking an embrace.

The devout admirer of St. Francis returned to the little island on Holy Thursday with a certain trepidation. He found the saint in prayer in the hollow of a hedge which formed a kind of large nest, well adapted to a man-lark like Francis. He looked a little leaner, a little paler and still had one of his two small rolls. But he was in good condition, nonetheless, as if he had found his natural food in contemplation. The lake seemed to reflect the light of his countenance. Content because he had imitated the Lord Jesus, fasting forty days and forty nights, but less than the Lord because he had eaten a roll, St. Francis returned among men and nobody ever learned what happened during those weeks between him and the Infinite.

It was generally known that when he was alone he wept, prayed out loud, beat his breast, and threw himself on the ground. Sometimes he stood still and motionless, completely outside himself, for hours at a time. But he did not like a closed-off solitude, he sought the sky, the hills, the uncultivated woods, primitive creatures unmodified by man. And on his journeys he always found one of these natural cloisters in which reposed his Lord: he found such cloisters on the lagoon of Venice, in the little island that still bears his name, and found them especially in Tuscany and Unbrin: at Carceri near Assisi, Saint Urbano near Narni, Fonte Colombo, Poggio Bustone, Greccio, in the green irrigated valley of Rieti, Monteluco above Spoleto, the Isola Maggiore on Lake Trasimene, and Mount La Verna in Casentino.

Today each of these places is a convent or a sanctuary, an admonition and a lyric poem. For the saint at that time each of these places was a prayer, a state of ecstasy, the sublime moment of life. Who would get an idea of his way of praying must re-read the few written prayers he has left behind: the commentary on the Our Father, the praises of God, the salute to the Virgin, the prayerbook of the Passion, the invocation of the Almighty for light and the strength to do His will. They are short, concise prayers, inspired by the Holy Books from which emerges a concept of the Most High God which might be defined as severe were it not tempered by an immense trust. Every word is simple and profound. So much so as to serve for a year's meditation. Among all the prayers the most expressive is the following which summarizes the interior flame of the saint, and the reason of his whole life.

"Lord, I beseech Thee, let the ardent and sweet strength of Thy love carry my mind away from all terrestrial things, so that I may die for the love of Thy love, as Thou didst deign to die for love of me."

To make no effort to understand this desire to be intimately united with God, and to die of love for His love, not to understand this passion of gratitude toward the Creator and Redeemer, is not to understand St. Francis.

THE CRIB OF GRECCIO

Francis understood that if all men had had the image of the Saviour as clearly present and concrete in their minds as he, they would have loved God with deeds not words. Therefore, upon returning from the Crusades, with his mind lit up by remembrances of the holy places, he thought of a way of re-awakening the faith not only through preaching, but through the dramatic re-evocation of a scene from the life of Jesus. This re-evocation, besides serving the purposes of an apostolate, responded to an exigency of his own soul. Francis did not feel that thinking and loving were genuine until he translated his thoughts into deeds.

Christmas day of 1223 was approaching. St. Francis had always most venerated the mystery of the Infant Jesus, which recalled Bethlehem. Finding himself at this time in the hermitage of Fonte Colombo, he said to Giovanni Vellita, a nobleman who belonged to the Third Order, and who was a friend and admirer of the saint:

"Messer Giovanni, if you will help me we can celebrate this year the most beautiful Christmas that has even been seen."

"Certainly I will, father."

"In one of your forests around the hermitage of Greccio there is a cave similar to that in Bethlehem. I would like to symbolize the Nativity scene and see with bodily eyes the poverty in which the Infant Jesus came into the world, and how He was placed in a manger and how He lay there between an ox and an ass. I have leave from the Holy Father to make this memorial of the Nativity of Christ."

"I understand. Let me take care of it, Father Francis."

On Christmas Eve all the bells of the valley of Rieti rang out in celebration of the double festival. Having been advised of the new celebration the inhabitants came from their villages, the castles, and most distant cottages. They came running along stony paths, under the stars, in the cold clear night, bringing offerings, like the shepherds of Judea. Meanwhile from the hermitages of Fonte Colombo and Poggio Bustone and from other places came a torch-lit procession of friars intoning litanies; they had mixed feelings of devotion and curiosity about this great novelty. But when they entered the grotto which had been carefully prepared by Messer Giovanni Vellita, under the fervid inspiration of St. Francis, they were transfixed. There stood the manger with the hay, and above it a rock on which to celebrate Mass. The ox and the ass were there. The Infant was not there but at the Consecration would invisibly descend into the Host. What was missing, the vision of the Virgin, of St. Joseph, and the Angels, was supplied by St. Francis who, dressed as a deacon, sang the Gospel with a voice so musical as to rouse thoughts of the celestial Glory, singing hosannahs on the hills of Judea. Then he spoke about the nativity of the poor King with such deep emotion that upon uttering the word Bethlehem his voice trembled. He spoke with such fervor that the rapt throng believed it was living thirteen centuries earlier in time at the beginning of salvation. The night was passed in festivity, the whole forest was resplendent and it seemed as though the Infant Jesus had returned to earth.

Someone did see Him. On the empty hay which to the eyes of all the others lacked its flower of flesh, the blessed Francis saw a new-born babe, pale and cold as a little corpse. He took Him in his arms, pressed Him to his heart, and warmed Him with a moving paternal affection that revived and reanimated the child who opened its eyes and caressed the emaciated face of His *Poverello* with His little hands. If St. Francis spoke in a way that made everybody weep, if his voice trembled and his words made the Infant Jesus live again in the imaginations as though He were present, this was because his arms held Him tight, his eyes saw Him, and his heart melted with love and gratitude.

St. Francis found the source of joy in himself with prayer, and from its luminous font he aroused joy from creatures and circumstances as light arouses colors. But what merit is it to know how to enjoy beautiful creatures, virtuous men, and the revelations of God? Ever since the time that he had been living mundanely, Francis never conceived real joy without an overcoming of himself. This was all the more so after he became a Knight of Christ and Lady Poverty, taking the Cross as his emblem. For love of the Cross he began to draw gladness from the persons who caused him displeasure, and such persons became his friends and afforded him satisfactions.

Once while passing through Imola he asked the bishop for permission to preach. The bishop, distrustful of the mendicant, brusquely replied, "It suffices that I preach to my people!" St. Francis bowed his head and left, but he came back one minute later. Impatiently, the bishop asked, "What do you want, Friar?"

"Father," replied the Saint, "when a son is driven out of one door he comes back through another." The exploit was in the manner of Friar Juniper, but it was done with such child-like simplicity that the bishop, overcome, opened his arms and granted Francis and his friars full permission to preach, feeling that men so humble must be saints.

Another bishop, some say he was the Bishop of Terni, others the Bishop of Rieti, after hearing St. Francis preach turned to the people and said: "Let us thank God that He has served Himself of this poor ignorant and despised man to illustrate the Church, thereby revealing His mercy on us."

His serenity was not even disturbed when the insults came from his social inferiors. St. Francis accepted counsels and admonitions from all, in a gladness of spirit. Once when he was riding a donkey toward Mount La Verna, because he was too feeble and infirm to go afoot, the peasant who owned the donkey asked him, "Tell me, are you that Friar Francis of Assisi of whom so much good is spoken?"

"I am," replied the saint.

"Then strive to be as good as you are held to be by all folk, for many have great faith in you and you must not deceive the faith of the people."

St. Francis was not angered by the admonition of a peasant. Instead he alighted from the donkey, and knelt before the rustic, kissing his feet and thanking him for his charitable admonition. He could not have been happier had he received an eulogy.

THE LEPROUS BROTHERS

Francis did not seek the joys of friendship and prayer: he enjoyed them by thanking the Lord, but for love of Him he sought rather the company of lepers, from whom everybody fled and whom the disease often maddened like dogs. He preferred them because above all in their poor martyred flesh, in their abject humanity, he saw, much more than in healthy people, the humiliated Lord Jesus reputed leprous for love of us.

Once in a leper-hospital served by his friars there was a patient so wretched from his disease that he beat his nurses and cursed like one possessed of the devil. The friars humbly endured the personal insults and injuries in payment for their sins, but they could not stand the curses. And after having preached to him many times they said, "Let us give him up. He has the devil in the flesh." However they could make no decision about this without the permission of the teacher who at that moment was living nearby. They informed him about the case and Friar Francis came.

"May the Lord grant you peace, my dearest brother," said the saint immediately, giving him his customary greeting.

But the envenomed leper replied, "What peace can I have if God has reduced me to stinking, rotten flesh?"

"Patience, son," the saint tried again, lovingly. "The infirmities of the body are the salvation of the soul when they are endured patiently."

"Patience! Patience! The head of the one who counsels does not ache! How can I patiently endure the pain that afflicts me day and night? Not only am I tormented by my sickness, but so are your friars who do not serve me as they ought."

Francis knew there was no reasoning with the man, and he had recourse to his greatest strength, prayer. Then he returned:

"My son, I will serve you since you are not content with the others."

"Very well, but what more for me can you do than the others?"

"Whatever you wish," replied the saint humbly.

"Then I want you to bathe me all over, for I stink so foully I cannot abide myself!"

St. Francis ordered water heated with sweet-smelling herbs, and undressed the leper. Then he began to bathe him gently, while another friar helped him, pouring the warm and perfumed water.

The saint continued to bathe him and, to overcome his nausea, he thought of Jesus Christ. He touched the loathsome sores as if he were touching the five wounds, and he prayed, "Heal him in body and soul, Lord!"

The leper felt a new surge of life at the contact of hands which caressed more than bathed, and his heart melted before a holiness which humiliated itself without humiliating him, because Francis loved him. For the first time in his life the leper felt himself loved, and he no longer suffered. He forgot his disease, and instead of the wounds of his body he saw the wounds of his soul, anger, rebellion against God, the sins of his youth from which his leprosy came, and he wept. His tears, falling into the fragrant water, healed his body and soul.

Miracle! Miracle! The news spread throughout the hospital. Friar Francis had healed and converted the possessed of the devil! The saint left immediately and went into the mountains to thank God, because he sought the glory of God, not his own.

A month went by and a white shade appeared to Francis who was praying among the trees. "Do you know me?"

"Who are you?" asked the saint.

"I am the leper whom the blessed Christ healed through your merits. On this day I am going to life everlasting for which I render thanks to God and to you. Blessed be your soul and your body, blessed your works and your words, and blessed be your Order!"

THE PERFECT JOY

The weather was bad, the evening biting cold, and the road from Perugia to Porziuncola seemed endless. Friar Leo walked ahead, and Francis behind, lashed by the north-wind in his tattered tunic, with a fatigue and hunger which the bitter cold increased. In such tribulations even the hovels of St. Mary of the Angels seemed like a palace, and the only relief that presented itself to the two pilgrims was the thought of the brethren who were waiting for them, saving dinner for them, and being sparing of the wood so as to make a good fire when they returned, saying, "Poor fellows, with such weather! When will they come? Can you see them on the horizon?" And the brothers would welcome them with that special tenderness which those without families feel for their companions of destiny or election.

This was the way Father Francis desired his knights to love each other, but it did not seem to him perfect to lose the merit of that journey of tribulations with thoughts of human comfort. On the other hand fearing that Friar Leo, the "little lamb" might be suffering too much, he began one of those dialogued meditations with him which were at once instruction and prayer.

"Friar Leo."

"Here I am."

"Write down what is perfect joy." (He usually said "write" because Friar Leo was his secretary, but in that moment he said "write" because he was about to dictate something that was worthy of being recorded, and in reality it was his doctrine.)

"Although friars minor in every land give a great example of sanctity and good edification, write it down and note it well that nevertheless perfect joy is not therein."

They continued their journey further in silence, and then once more St. Francis called out to him:

"Friar Leo, although the friar minor receives so much grace as to heal the sick and perform many miracles, and even resuscitate those who have lain four days dead, write down that perfect joy is not therein."

They journeyed farther in silence. Then St. Francis called out again, "Friar Leo, although the friars minor know all tongues, and all the sciences and all the Scriptures, and can foretell and reveal future things and the secrets of consciences, write down that perfect joy is not therein."

Silence. Friar Leo began to forget the cold, losing himself in the thought of the teacher and asking himself where he was to find this perfect joy, when St. Francis continued: "Friar Leo, although the friar minor can preach so skillfully that he may convert all infidels to the faith of Christ, write down that perfect joy is not therein. And if a messenger should arrive from Paris announcing that all the teachers of Paris have come into the Order, write down: This is not true joy. And if further there should come all the prelates from beyond the Alps, archbishops and bishops and even the King of France and even the King of England, write down: This is not true joy."

During this talk which went on for two miles, Friar Leo did not know what else to think, so he asked, "Father, in God's name tell me where this perfect joy is to be found."

Francis explained: "When we shall have come to St. Mary of the Angels, soaked as we are, frozen and cold, hungry, with icicles on the hem of our tunic which strike against our legs and draw blood from the sores, and when we shall have knocked at the door and called out for a long time, and the doorkeeper comes and says, 'Who are you?' and I answer, 'Friar Francis.' And he says, 'Begone! This is not the hour for travelling, you may not enter!' And when I persevere in knocking on the door, he rushes out in a rage and drives me away with abusive language and blows, saying, 'Begone! You are a simpleton and a fool, you shall not come among us now. We are just so many and have no need of you.' And if I suffer this patiently and with gladness and love, Friar Leo write down that this is perfect joy."

Friar Leo so marvelled that he no longer felt hunger, cold or fatigue.

St. Francis continued, "And then compelled by hunger, by cold and by night, with many tears I insist, 'For the love of God, shelter me this night.' And he replies, 'I will not. Go to the hospital of the Cruciferi.' And then coming out with a big knotted stick he grabs me by the cowl, flings me to the ground, rolls me in the snow, and beats every bone in my body, and I endure all these things patiently and gladly recalling the sufferings of the blessed Christ. Friar Leo, write down that this is perfect joy! Yet, hear now the conclusion. Above all the gifts of the Holy Ghost the greatest one indeed is the overcoming of self, and willingly for the love of Christ to endure pain, injuries, abuse, and discomforts, for we may not glory in all the other gifts of God since they are not ours but of God. But we may glory in the cross of tribulation because this is ours."

This dialogue, in the profundity of its Christian philosophy, presupposes a very advanced disciple, for in the enumeration of the benefits of joy, St. Francis never alluded to those most commonly desired and positively appreciated boons like riches, health, pleasure, glory. Instead he passed in review the most elect gifts of grace: sanctity, wisdom, miracles, the conversion of infidels. Then rising even higher he reviewed the impersonal gifts, the triumph of the Order and of the idea, yet he excluded them all as imperfect, and went in search of gladness by different degrees of suffering, beginning with physical sufferings like cold, hunger, the fatigue of a winter night, to the details of the legs bloodied by icicles, and then proceeding to the cruelest suffering which is the repudiation of him by his brethren, the non-recognition of his own work, the conscious contempt of persons whom he had benefited and loved. St. Francis' imagination internalized itself in this situation and he learned that whosoever can surmount it with love and patience must be perfectly joyous because he possesses the greatest gift of God, which is to overcome oneself.

This thought would have been subscribed to as a celebration of man by the ancient sages who taught that true joy is something severe. But St. Francis, the Christian, added that an innocent person who suffers so atrociously and gladly, has a reason for joy not from his strength but from the imitation of Jesus Crucified, and the triumph of grace over nature.

A man who disposes himself to be happier the more he is buffeted by earthly fate has naught to fear from life. This is one of the greatest teachings of St. Francis.

9

THE PERFECT
SUFFERING

IN THE DIALOGUE on perfect joy, St. Francis had imagined the worst that could happen to make him suffer pain and sorrow. And he surmounted it with his will. But by so doing he did not destroy his capacity for suffering, which in him was as acute and ever-ready as the capacity for enjoyment. If a nightingale invited him to sing, a lamb being led to slaughter made him cry; if courtesy from a stranger moved him to the point where he wanted to obtain sanctity for him as compensation, a hostile thought from one of his friars pierced his heart like a dagger, so much so that he instinctively preferred the company of those most delicate of soul and education. Even that exceptional penetration which invested him with the feeling of another and made him weep with one who wept was a singular suffering, just as that joy which the beauty of creatures gave him reduced itself to suffering, and which began with a song only to end in tears of anxiety.

The price of everything was an act of violence against his nature: preaching in public, reprimanding his friars, making a show of severity and hardness for the sake of justice. By intimately sensing the soul of whosoever approached him, which is a poet's gift, he transmuted himself entirely into all others. And since he combined the exquisite taste and the courteous ambition of a gentleman, incapable even of a vocal inflection which might displease others, he experienced difficulty and distress in the dissension, in the discussion, and contradiction inevitably imposed by the apostolate.

In fact when a Dominican theologian asked him whether he should or should not admonish certain sinners, since Ezekiel says that whosoever does not reveal that one's wickedness to a wicked person is responsible for his soul, St. Francis, after having humbly excused himself as a simpleton, replied as follows: "If the text is to be understood generally I understand thereby that the servant of God should so burn and shine forth with life and holiness in himself that he should reprove all the wicked by the light of his example and by the words of a holy conversation. Thus, I say, that his splendor and his fame will unveil to all their iniquities."

This bespeaks the humanity of the saint who subjected himself to everybody and who preferred deeds to words. But it also bespeaks the gentleman who finds everything that might shock or offend others repugnant.

He had the same bearing toward anyone who contradicted his preaching, he never wanted to assert authority. He demeaned himself without words. One day some friars said to him, "Father, you know that sometimes the bishops do not permit us to preach, and sometimes make us stand idle for days in a town before we can announce the word of the Lord. It were better if you obtained a concession from the Pope concerning this matter as it would mean the salvation of souls."

St. Francis replied that his friars had not understood him:

"I wish by perfect humility and reverence first to convert the prelates who, once seeing our holy life and our humble reverence toward them, will beseech you to preach and to convert the people. And they will call them to the preaching better than your privileges which would lead you into pride."

It was not only toward his superiors and peers that he bore himself with the delicacy of the knight in the humble charity of the saint, but also toward sinners, the poor, the infirm.

One evening, returning to Porziuncola, he met one of the friar nurses of the leper hospital with a leper who was plagued by the most revolting sores. Friar James was calmly taking him for a walk as if he were his companion, while people fled from them in horror, holding their noses. St. Francis was the friend and the doctor of the lepers and he called them his Christian brothers. But he also remembered the repugnance which they had aroused in him as a youth, and how by embracing a leper he had died to the world and undergone an almost complete change of character. Therefore, out of regard for others, he rebuked the overly simple Friar James, "You should not lead these brother Christians abroad, because it is not seemly for you or for them."

But he immediately repented of these words because they might have humiliated the leper, so he imposed on himself the penance of eating out of the same dish with him, and he ate with a smile on his face, while a sweetness of peace rose to his heart.

Even with such a sensibility St. Francis succeeded in casting out all feelings of sadness as though they were demons: regrets, nostalgia, melancholy, worries, uncertainties, all the innumerable troubles in which the ego is constantly involved, which men and women dramatize, and of which they make a cult to vaunt with pride. He succeeded in extirpating not only the sorrows that derive from the passions, the stupid sorrows, but also the complaisant acceptance of sorrow, that caressing self-pity by which the one who suffers thinks he is the only person to suffer and therefor entitled to everybody's condolences. Francis succeeded in extracting gladness from sorrow.

But he did not do this to avoid suffering. He did it because the sentimental sorrows of the ego do not merit the honor of tears. He saved his suffering for others so that he could understand and have compassion for them.

HIS INFIRMITIES

Nonetheless suffering pursued him. The penances, the discomforts, the poverty-stricken life he led, the exertions of preaching, during which he visited from four to five villages a day, the sleeping on the ground and the poor eating ruined his health. In Egypt his infirmities became even more serious.

His eyes, the gentle black eyes that discoursed of God, were rimmed with blood because of an incurable oriental disease. His friars and the cardinal forced him to take treatment, reminding him of his duty toward his body. So Francis docilely submitted to cauterization by hot irons, a treatment a hundred times more painful than the disease. Yet he never complained. Instead, in his last years, reduced as he was to skin and bones, crucified by the stigmata and destroyed by liver, splenic and stomach disorders, which produced whole days of bleeding, he called his infirmities his sisters. One of his simple friars said to him, "Father, pray to the Lord that He lift these unbearable pains and suffering from you." But St. Francis was annoyed by this advice, and he said to the brother, "If I did not know that you are of a good and pure simplicity I would hate you and I would no longer want to see you because you have dared to judge God, by saying that He sends me sufferings greater than my powers to endure them."

However sick he was he would throw himself from the bed, kiss the ground and exclaim, "I thank Thee, my Lord God, for all my sufferings; and give me even ten more if it pleases Thee for this would please me much, since to do Thy will is my eternal consolation."

The infirmities, coming directly from God, were a good suffering for St. Francis but not the perfect suffering: the will accepts it and transforms it into patience, but a base of materiality remains in it, of carnal opaqueness common to brutes.

THE TEMPTATIONS

St. Francis was familiar with those spiritual battles that are called temptations. His soul, glad with the gladness of the pure, which rebounded from sorrow to joy like a sunbeam rebounds from a mirror, for two years experienced the incubus of a thought that made him fear that he was distant from God. This thought assailed him so much that it altered his customary serenity. In order to free himself from it the saint wept, prayed, scourged himself, fasted, and hid from his companions. What afflicted him most was that he was no longer able to show himself with a gladsome countenance as he so firmly required of himself and his fellow-friars.

Finally the Lord consoled him: "If you had as much faith as a grain of mustard seed," said an inner voice to him once, as he was praying in the little Church of St. Mary of the Angels, "and you told that mountain to remove itself to another place it would thus remove itself."

"What is that mountain, Lord?" thought St. Francis. "That mountain is your temptation!" continued the inner voice. Then the saint, reviving his spirits like one who thinks he is sick but who leaps out of bed at the word of an esteemed doctor, exclaimed, "Therefore, Lord, be it as Thou hast said."

Sometimes the devil tempted him with the memory of his past life, with the desire of the life of the world. One winter night in the hermitage of Sarteano, as he was trying to fall asleep with his head on a stone and the wintry blasts blowing in through the cracks between the cells, the devil assailed him with the nostalgic yearning for a family, presenting his fantasy with a vivid image of a beautiful room, a fireplace, a woman who smiled lovingly at him, and children who called him papa.

"There's still time for these joys, if you want them, only hurry. You are still young!" insinuated the evil one. Francis fell to his knees; he removed his habit and began to scourge himself with the rope.

But the devil persisted. "You can belong to God, without doing such crazy things. A good father of a family is worth more than you!"

"I'll give you your family!" thought St. Francis to himself. Immediately he rushed out half-naked into the snow where with that remnant of boyish playfulness which had been left to him he began to make snowmen. He made seven. "Do you want a wife? There, the biggest one is your wife. Do you want children? Here are four of them, two boys and two girls. But to take care of them you will need at least two servants: Here then is the manservant and the maidservant!" And in the light of the moon Francis, now warmed by his exertions, stopped, distractedly, to look at his family of snow-figures. Then internalizing himself with his fantasy in the crude part of the reality which the temptations concealed, he continued talking to himself, "Now, my dear, make haste to clothe them, for they are dying of cold. And if the care of them weighs heavily on you, dedicate yourself to serving God only."

The devil had taken to his heels. So the saint returned happily to his cell, when he noticed a fellow friar observing him in great wonderment. Francis blushed and then, simple as always, he explained the secret of the seven figures in the snow.

But the devil, chased out the door, came back through a window.

One evening at Trevi Francis entered an abandoned church to spend the night there, and he beseeched Friar Pacifico, who was accompanying him, to leave him alone. He commanded Friar Pacifico to return to the leper-hospital and to come back for him early next morning.

St. Francis was jealous of his freedom and of his nights, sacred to his colloquies with the Most High. But that night, in the abandoned church, the devil assailed him with every kind of perverse suggestion. Francis went outside to free himself from these diabolical urgings, making the sign of the Cross and commanding the devil to leave him in peace. At dawn Friar Pacifico came and found him in prayer in front of the altar and while he was waiting for him, praying likewise but outside the choir, he had a vision. He saw a sphere of paradise and among many shining seats he saw one higher than the others, scintillating with every kind of precious stone.

"Friar Pacifico, Friar Pacifico," said a voice, "this was once the seat of Lucifer, but in his place will be the humble Francis."

The vision vanished and the dumbfounded friar presented himself to his teacher, falling at his feet with his arms folded on his chest in the shape of a Cross, as before a saint, "Father, father, forgive me and pray to the Lord for me."

St. Francis raised him benignly and gently, and Friar Pacifico, who was still under the spell of the vision, asked him in a voice as if from afar, "What do you think of yourself, brother?"

"Oh," replied Francis immediately, "it seems to me that I am the greatest sinner in the whole world."

And immediately the inner voice revealed to Friar Pacifico, "Here is the confirmation of the vision. The place which Lucifer lost because of his pride will belong to this man because of his humility."

But the struggle was a harsh and continuous one while he waited for paradise. The demons inflicted other great torments, one night in Rome beating him sorely. There he was living as the guest of Cardinal Leone of Santa Croce, who was very happy to have him so near, in the little room of a solitary tower that had been placed at his disposal. At this time he said to Friar Angelo Tancredi who accompanied him, "Perhaps the Lord punishes me by means of the demons who are His sergeants because I accept the hospitality of my lord cardinal for the relief of my body, while my brethren go through the world enduring hunger and tribulations, and others live in ruined hermitages and hovels. Let us leave here as I want to give them a good example. The others bear their tribulations more patiently when they know that I bear the same and more." So they left the cardinal's residence.

Whenever he was literally undone by his infirmities, the devil whispered to him, "Francis, Francis, the Lord forgives all sinners who are converted, but whosoever kills himself with overharsh penances will never find mercy in eternity."

Thus in different ways, by moral disturbances and by physical sufferings, by fantasies, doubts, disquietudes, his lower will rose up against his holy will. Francis suffered, but once the storm was over he recognized the benefits of it. Indeed he observed that temptation tests the valor and the loyalty of a soul as war tests the soldier. Whoever does not have temptation is an incompetent, like one rejected for military service, one who is conquered before fighting and whom the Lord preserves in order not to expose to death. And he said something that was even more profound: he said that temptation was the nuptial ring between the soul and God. In fact the union with the Most High does not occur in peace, but in struggle, not when we think of ourselves as good, but when under the impact of the instincts we savor our misery and overcome it, when we prefer duty to any pleasure, and the approval of the Invisible to any tangible satisfaction.

THE TABLE NO LONGER ROUND

If the interior battle between the terrestrial ego and the divine ego was a rough one, another one which was even rougher for so gentle a soul as St. Francis was the external one for the defense of his ideal. The original twelve Knights of Poverty at Rivo Torto had become several thousands and they could not all have the same spirit. Quantity is almost always injurious to quality, and numbers weaken an idea rather than strengthen it. St. Francis knew this. He was still in the Orient with Pietro Cattani when a lay friar, who had come especially from Italy without the knowledge of his direct superiors, brought him disturbing news about the Order. The two vicars whom he had left behind had permitted themselves to modify his Rule in regard to fasts. Friar Philip had requested Rome for letters of protection for the Poor Ladies, and Friar John de Compello was about to found a new Order with a group of friars and lay-people who did not entirely approve of Francis' directives.

The saint received this sheaf of disturbing news just as he was about to sit at table. And since a victual of meat was being served which was contrary to the new regulations of his vicars, he asked Friar Pietro with a humility that might have appeared as irony to others, "Messer Pietro, what shall we do?"

"Oh, father," replied the good canon, "we shall do what pleases you since you alone have the authority to command, you alone are the founder of the Order."

"Then let us obey the Holy Gospel and eat what is set before us," replied Francis tranquilly.

He returned to Italy with Friar Pietro and Friar Elias and learned that several friars had truly betrayed Lady Poverty. In Bologna where Friar Bernard had left behind the good seed of his humility, another friar, Pietro of Stacia, in consideration of the fact that even a friar minor had to study, had accepted as a gift a house for students of theology. When he learned about this St. Francis ordered all the friars, including the infirm, to leave it forthwith and he allowed them to return only when Cardinal Ugolino publicly announced that the house belonged to him.

A vicar had begun to build a little house in which to assemble the friars to recite the divine office near Porziuncola. Hearing the picks of the workmen from his little cell, Francis ordered the vicar to demolish the construction because he could not permit the very palace of poverty, the first community of the Order, to be built in stone and lime, whereas all the other dwellings of the friars were required to be of wood, clay and reeds.

Many friars opposed these deliberations of the teacher, and they defended themselves by saying that it was not even economical to construct huts of wood or wattle where stones might be purchased more cheaply. In order to avoid contention, St. Francis reminded them at least to limit themselves to accepting the churches and dwellings built for them only as loans, and that they sojourn therein only as guests, pilgrims and strangers.

He did not even approve of a certain largesse in the meals of the friars. One day at the hermitage of Greccio a relatively sumptuous table was being prepared in celebration of Easter, and also of the visit of the friar minister. When St. Francis came down from his cell later than the others, he saw the table set with a white tablecloth and glasses. He did not enter the room, but a little while later the friars seated around the table heard a lamenting voice from the half-opened door, entreating them, "For the love of the Lord God, give an alms to this poor and infirm pilgrim."

"Brother," replied the minister, "we too are poor, and we are many, and we live from alms. But for the love of that God whom you have invoked we shall give you part of the charity that has been given to us."

The pilgrim entered the room after this little speech and immediately the friars recognized their teacher under his cloak.

The embarrassed minister offered him his plate and some

bread. Francis sat down on a step of the fireplace, put the plate on the ashes and between spoonfuls he talked as though to himself, while the friars did not dare to open their mouths, not even to eat.

"Now," he was saying, "now I sit as a friar minor! But seeing a table so sumptuously set and adorned I did not recognize it as the table of the poor who go begging alms from door to door. Yet it behooves us to follow the example of the humility and the poverty of Christ because this is our vocation, this is what we profess before men and God. And even our tables should be such that if a poor man were invited by the friars, he should sit as their equal and near them, not the poor on the floor and the friars on high."

His attitude toward dissident friars always reflected humility, good example, sermonizing through deeds and suffering. He saw abuses but did not know how to fight them except by redoubling his austerity toward himself. With his mystic and adventurous soul, with his thirst for dedication and his secret desire for consensus, with his poetry that liberated and that contemplation that enchained, he could not be a systematic disciplinarian of the very energies that he aroused. He had the genius of the poet but not the ability of an organizer, the suggestive intuition of the teacher and not the pulse of the rector and abbot. This practical fundamental incapacity was increased by his gentlemanly education and his most profound humility which always prescribed the last position to him along with an excessive distrust of himself, and finally by his infirmities ever more frequent and serious. It was for these reasons that he resigned from the post of general of the Order at the chapter of San Michele in 1220, appointing Pietro of Catania in his place. On this occasion he said to the assembled friars, "From henceforth I am dear to you, but behold Friar Pietro of Catania, whom we must all obey."

He was the first to kneel before him, promising him obedience and reverence. Then he rose and commended his religious family to the Lord. The friars began to weep as though that abdication were a pre-announcement of death. In fact St. Francis intended to die, as a living person, to his authority. But in this voluntary death there was a part determined by the dissension among the friars and which constituted its intimate drama.

"My son," he said to one who was lamenting his separation from them, "I love the brethren as I am able, but if they would follow me I would love them still more, nor would I make myself strange to them."

Never, however, was he troubled by those who contradicted him or offended him. Sometimes the consciousness of his value and the devotion of the many who had remained faithful to Lady Poverty found expression in an impetuous outburst of strength, "If I so wished it, the Lord would make me to be so feared by my friars as no superior in the world is feared."

If I so wished it! But he did not wish this. He preferred to be a friar minor. Humanity and holiness competed in this desire of his to be minor, giving him cruel torment on the one hand, and a great gladness on the other.

Meanwhile his Round Table divided into two wings, a right and a left, lying somewhere between the broken lances of Lady Poverty and the fallacies of common sense, between the madmen and the wise. In the depths of his heart, the blessed Francis favored the madmen.

THE KNIGHTS OF COMMON SENSE

His friars were not all lions and at the same time lambs of God. Francis liked to conciliate the highest strength with the highest gentleness in his ideal knight, but reality surrounded him with men of quite a different stamp.

Friar Elias Bombarone of Beviglio, near Assisi, had been notable among his friars since 1212. He was the son of a Bolognese merchant. Thanks to his talents he succeeded in studying at Bologna, after having been a mattress-maker and a teacher of the psalter to children, before he joined the Order. Here he quickly revealed an energy, a practical sense, and a broad and constructive judgment that pleased Francis. Therefore in 1217 he was nominated head of the expedition to the Holy Land. And in 1221, upon the death of Pietro of Catania, the excellent and faithful knight of the first hour, the aged canon whom St. Francis always called *Messere* out of respect and who in turn bore himself with the devotion of a son towards his young teacher, Elias was elected general of the Order, because Francis recognized his gifts of command.

Friar Elias loved the teacher very much, but near him he was like all men in the proximity of a saint. Francis lived of faith, Elias of reason. Francis wanted to conquer men only with love, Elias with grandiose gestures and magnificent ceremonies that struck the imagination. Francis depended only upon Providence, Elias upon his own forces. Francis had an interior vision of souls and events and he resolved all questions with the eternal principles without concerning himself about the earthly result, as was apparent in the first foreign missions which ended so disastrously, however extraordinarily ingenious they had been in conception. Elias viewed men and facts in the reality of the moment and did not resign himself to purely supernatural solutions. His good sense immediately understood the difficulties which the absolute poverty, desired by St. Francis, would run into. Therefore he sided with the dissident friars.

The two wings of the Round Table had champions in every friary. It was not exactly easy to achieve an accord between them since the zealous ones vaunted their virtues with a jealous intransigence, which did not shrink from rebellion against the wardens. Friar Elias asked St. Francis how he was to conduct himself toward the insubordinate friars. St. Francis replied with a letter that cannot be read again without a deep emotion.

After telling Friar Elias that he should rejoice over the contrarieties and praise God for the beatings from whatever quarter they might come, as a signal favor, he added:

"Love whosoever treats you thus and wish for them only what the Lord will give to you, and love them precisely with the wish that they might become better Christians. Take this more to heart than the hermit's life itself. And it is precisely from this sign that I wish to recognize whether you love the Lord and me, who is His and your servant, that is to say, you will deport yourself in such a way that there will be no friar in all the world who has sinned more than he could sin, or who after having seen your eyes should depart without having obtained your forgiveness if he asked it of you. Indeed were he not to ask for mercy, you yourself must ask him whether he wishes to be forgiven. And if he should then present himself a thousand times before you, love him more than you love me, so as to draw him to the Lord and always have compassion for him."

There is no page more profound than this in the pedagogy of punishment. Yet despite this sublime goodness, despite this love which shone in the pupils of his eyes to espy penance, and which opened his arms to offer pardon to the guilty for which they did not ask, his Rule seemed harsh to many. And when it was learned that he had retired to the hermitage of Fonte Colombo with Friar Leo and Friar Boniface to compile a new Rule, many ministers went to Friar Elias, the vicar general, and said,

"We hear that Father Francis is making a new Rule. We fear he will make it too harsh so that we shall not be able to observe it. Therefore we wish you to go to him and say that we do not wish to be bound to that Rule. Let him make it for himself and not for us."

Friar Elias replied that he would not go alone, so they all left for Fonte Colombo together.

"What do these brethren want?" asked Francis when they called out to him. And Friar Elias, standing on no ceremony, said, "These ministers, hearing that you are making a new Rule and fearing that you might make it too harsh, protest that they do not wish to be bound to observe it. And that you make it for yourself and not for them."

St. Francis was humility personified, but under such attack an inspiration rose in him. Raising his eyes to heaven, he invoked his Inspirer and Defender with a cry that also revealed all his suffering at not being believed, "Lord, did I not justly say to Thee that they would not believe me?"

It seemed that a voice replied from heaven, "Naught in the

Rule is yours, Francis, but all is Mine. And I will that it be observed to the letter."

The knights of common sense understood that one does not discuss with heroism, and that the Rule was divinely heroic. Either follow it, or leave the Order!

They understood this then and there, under the personal influence of St. Francis. But as soon as they were far away, human weakness overcame them in the face of practical difficulties. The Rule, dictated by the hermit between prayers, while he fasted on bread and water, was entrusted to Friar Elias for safekeeping. Several days later when St. Francis asked him to return it the vicar candidly replied that he had lost it in a moment of carelessness.

Common sense indulges in such acts of negligence.

THE WILL'S MARTYRDOM

The opposition in the Order was represented by the most learned friars who, reasoning on the basis of logic, were more inclined to see the human shortcomings in the Franciscan conception. But they did not perceive that by continuing along that road they would arrive at a complete denial of it, because in the eyes of the world it was thoroughly illogical. These learned friars had been beseeching Cardinal Ugolino to persuade Francis to follow their advice ever since the Chapter of the Mats, to let himself be guided, and to study the Rule of St. Benedict and of St. Augustine. Was it not presumption to place so much trust in personal inspiration?

The cardinal tactfully delivered this message to his protegé. Francis, without replying, took his hand, impulsively, led him before the friars assembled in chapter, and spoke:

"My brethren! The Lord has called me by the way of simplicity and humility, and He pointed out this way to me in truth for myself and for them who are willing to believe me and imitate me. Speak to me not of any other Rule, neither of St. Bernard, nor of St. Augustine, nor any other way and manner of life beside that which the Lord has mercifully shown and given me. And the Lord told me that He willed me to be poor and foolish in this world, and He did not wish to lead us by any way save by that knowledge."

Beneath the delicacy of the gentleman and the humility of the saint, the certainty of his mission was forming with the hardness and splendor of a diamond. He would have never surrendered an inch of the rights of Lady Poverty to men, but when the Church through Cardinal Ugolino made him understand the reasonableness of mitigation of the severity of the Rule, he bowed agreement that the versicle from the Gospel, which had been the revelation, the foundation, the support of his life, "Do not keep gold, or silver . . . nor wallet for your journey, nor two tunics, nor sandals, nor staff" be cancelled from the definitive Rule, compiled in 1223 and approved by Honorius III.

The gospel of Porziuncola sounded like the voice of God in that distant February dawn! The Gospel drawn by chance in the Church of San Nicolo, between Bernard of Quintavalle and Pietro di Cattania in order to establish the bases of the Order! His first friars had followed it to the letter and nothing had ever been lacking at the little Round Table of Rivo Torto! Now the time of the heroes was past and his sons told him that such an ideal was madness. Never, perhaps, did the founder of an Order have to drink a chalice more bitter.

Father Francis took refuge in God, his fortress, and God assured him his sanctity, heavenly protection and the immortality of the Order. Now he considered that he was of no further use to his fellow-friars except through example and prayer, no longer was he of use through word or through immediate direction. The left wing of the Round Table chilled his intimacy with the friars, the dissension which he felt or saw in the assemblies increased that intimate tremor, that disposition to violent speech which he prepared to make despite his nature and humility. And he did not notice that his person was such as to dispel every opposition, and that secret fear of being badly received endowed his countenance with the gentle timid expression of a young girl, most rare even among the good, which rendered his perfection enchanting. But he was this for others: for him the suffering remained.

If some friar told him that he should intervene in the administration of the Order, Francis replied, "The friars have their Rule and they have sworn to observe it, and I have sworn to observe it likewise. Since they know what they must do and what they must avoid, naught else remains save that I teach them by good works."

Thus he separated himself from his work, and since his thought had crystallized in the Rule, he obeyed the Rule as though obeying a higher will, in which his will was of no matter.

On the other hand the ministers and the other dissidents were not wrong in supporting the rights of common sense. The opposition which broke the heart of St. Francis was necessary in order to give an historical substance to an ideal which otherwise would have passed on like a meteor. And if his ideal survived despite the opposition, if indeed it adapted itself to the opposition in order to compose that masterpiece of humanity and holiness which is the Rule of the Order of Friars Minor, it was by virtue of the martyrdom of will to which St. Francis subjected himself before meriting the stigmata.

THE SAINT'S SUFFERING

The dissension among his fellows and the ruin of the ideal caused suffering for St. Francis but he shook it off with trust in God. But the suffering which he endured indefatigably was the remorse for the sins that he had committed, and for all the least imperfections into which he seemed to fall. Disloyalty to his God made him desolate.

But remorse as remorse did not truly exhaust his capacity to suffer, because in the end Francis also threw his miseries in the lap of God's mercy. Nor did he have that selfish piety of one who when praying thinks always and only of himself, and eagerly desired to feel himself forgiven, pacified, and beloved by the Most High. Another suffering dominated him ever since the crucifix had spoken to him at St. Damian: the *suffering* of the Passion of Christ. The thought of the crucifix made him weep so that he emerged from his meditations with eyes swollen. When the doctor, treating him for the eye disease contracted in the Holy Land, forbade him to weep, St. Francis replied, "We must not lose the vision of the eternal light for the sake of the sight which we have in common with flies. Sight is not given to the spirit through remedy or through the merit of the body or through its usefulness. I would willingly prefer to lose the eyes of the body than to refrain from weeping because weeping purifies the eye of merit and renders it capable of beholding God."

They were tears for the love of God, it was suffering for the suffering of Jesus Christ. How had he arrived at this suffering, the idea of which we find so difficult to form for ourselves? By subjecting or almost nullifying all selfish feelings, however justifiable they might be, by convincing himself through creatures of the goodness of God and of His particular tenderness toward him, because beautiful things testified to him that "the Lord loves you." And the unpleasant things asked him, "Do you love the Lord? If you love Him, endure us; we come to test you." He wished and asked for the love of God. The love of God is a gift the entire greatness of which St. Francis had understood to the point that he changed color when he heard it mentioned. And he would do anything immediately if it were asked for in the name of that love. The torment of all men is that they may be pursuing a chimerical happiness, by seeking apparent good instead of the absolute good. The torment of poets is to feel more than can be expressed. The torment of saints is to pine in the desire for perfection and the possession of God. To love without being loved is the torment of Christ.

St. Francis, like a true lover, sought to suffer the same suffering as the beloved.

ON MOUNT LA VERNA

St. Francis had a particular devotion for St. Michael the Archangel and he kept a special Lent in his honor, consisting

of fasts and prayer, from August 15 to September 29, which is
the feast of St. Michael. In 1224 when he had arrived at such a
height of spirituality that his body and soul lived only for God;
when, cut off even from his own work, he thought only about
preparing himself for death, he decided to spend the feast of
the Assumption and the lent of St. Michael on Mount La Verna,
the wild mountain site of devotion, which had been presented
to him as a gift by Count Roland. He chose three companions,
Friar Masseo, Friar Angelo, Friar Leo. And after having named
Friar Masseo, who was the most skillful in practical matters,
their warden and superior, he said:

"On this journey we will observe our custom, that is, we will
say the Divine Office, or we will discourse of God, we will keep
silence, and we will think neither of eating, nor of sleeping.
And only when it is time to seek lodging will we beg for a crust
of bread, and we will stop and rest at the place that God will
prepare for us."

The three companions, used to this manner of travel, bowed
their heads, made the sign of the Cross and then set forth. All
went well on the first night because they stopped at a friary, but
on the second, caught by surprise by the rain and tired and
hungry, they took refuge in an abandoned church where the
three friars immediately fell asleep. But the teacher remained
awake. Devils assailed him with temptations and pains of all
kinds, yet he resisted and thanked God because he thought, It
is a sign of a great love when the Lord roundly punishes his
servant in this world, so that he may not be punished in the
other. Toward dawn he left the church, entered a nearby wood
and plunged deeply into prayer, discoursing with his Lord
Jesus from the intimate depth of his soul, now as a judge, now
as a father, now as a friend. When they awakened, the friends
heard him weep for the Passion of Jesus and pray for sinners
with such fervor, that they were more convinced than ever
that the teacher lived more with the invisible God than with
them.

But the climb up Mount La Verna was steep and tortuous, and
St. Francis was worn out from weakness. They got a donkey for
him, led by a mountaineer, who half-way up the mountain,

either because of the heat, or the toilsome ascent, began to rave
that he was dying of thirst. St. Francis immediately alighted from
the donkey, and knelt down to pray with his hands lifted to
heaven, not moving until he felt that the prayer had been
heard. Then he said to the mountaineer, "Run quickly over to
that rock and you will find running water that Jesus Christ in
His mercy has provided." The thirsty man ran to the spot and
as he lowered his lips into the spring, he felt another wave
water and refresh his soul. It was the grace of God and the goodness of Francis, that goodness which makes tears gush from
hearts of stone.

At a little distance from the summit St. Francis rested for a
while under a giant oak. As he was gazing at the landscape
below, a multitude of birds fluttered about him, some on his
head, some on his hands, some on his shoulders, some on his
chest, some on his feet, chirping, peeping, whistling, warbling,
as though to greet him. "Look! Look!" said the friars and the
guide, and St. Francis rejoicing at that manifestation of love of
his feathered friends, said:

"Dearest brothers, I believe that it is pleasing to our Lord
Jesus Christ that we dwell on this solitary mountain since our
brothers, the birds, show such gladness at our coming."

Someone else, in addition to the birds, came to welcome the
saint: Count Roland. As soon as he heard the good news that
his unforgettable Father Francis had climbed up Mount La
Verna with three companions, he set forth with squires and
highlanders of his castle, bringing with them victuals. At the
top of the mountain they found the friars in prayer. St. Francis
rose to meet the company, thanking the count again for the
mountain, so suitable for prayer, and for the visit and the
provisions. Count Roland asked to be permitted to do a favor
for his Father Francis, but the saint needed nothing. He asked
only that a little cell be built at the foot of a beautiful beech
tree, about a stone's throw from the friary, so that he could be
alone when he prayed.

The count's men immediately set up the cell under the beech
tree. Then since it was getting late, and it was time for the

group from the castle to depart, St. Francis preached to them and blessed them. Evening was near, the road back was long, but Messer Roland could not bear to separate himself from his friend. But when he left he said, "My dearest brothers, I do not wish you to have any material cares on this wild mountain top which may distract you from spiritual things. So once and for all again I say that you send to my house for all your needs, and if you do not I shall take it very ill of you."

While the group went down the mountain talking about the virtues of those friars, St. Francis gathered his companions together. Himself moved by the gifts of Providence, he admonished them never to betray Lady Poverty because the world showed itself generous only as a reward of their faith in poverty. Then he concluded, "Since I see myself drawing close to death, I purpose to withdraw to a solitary place and make my peace with God and weep for my sins, and Friar Leo, when it shall seem good to him, will bring me a little bread and water. Let no lay folk come to see me for any reason. Answer them for me."

Then he gave them his blessing and retired to his cell under the big beech.

THE LENT OF ST. MICHAEL

The feast of the Assumption being over, St. Francis had a presentiment of an intimacy with God which could not tolerate any distraction. So he looked for an even more solitary and secret place for the Lent of St. Michael, like a bird who instinctively finds the outermost eaves, the most remote holes, the thickest and highest branches for its love nest. He chose a point of the mountain, facing south, so far from the hut of the friars that even Friar Leo's voice, calling loudly, could not reach him. And it was so difficult of passage that in order to get there it was necessary to lay a log across a great chasm in the rocks. St. Francis had a little cell built in that solitude, where nobody would have seen or heard him, and then took leave of his friars, saying, "Do not come here, nor let any other person come here. But you, Friar Leo, you will come once a day with a little bread and water; and you will come once again, by night, at the hour of matins, and when you are at the foot of the bridge, you will say, *Domine, labia mea aperies,* and if I answer you with the other words of the psalm, you will pass the bridge, you will enter into my cell and we will say matins together. If I answer not, you will go back immediately."

He blessed them and remained alone. But there was no sweetness in the solitude. At first God did not make Himself felt, instead the devil made an appearance with frightening fantasies. Once, being in prayer near a frightful precipice, it seemed to him that he was being thrust down into the abyss. He did not know what to hang on to since the rock was smooth, but groping his way and commending himself to God he turned with hands and face and all his body close to the rock, and the rock, as though it were wax, hollowed itself out to the form of his body and received him into itself as though in a niche. Thus he was saved from the devil. But other sadnesses afflicted him. During the long hours in which the sweetness of prayer often converted itself into tedium, he reconsidered not so much the world of his youth as much as that religious world which he had awakened into being and had left, the Round Table no longer round, and the new knights who did not trust in Lady Poverty Finally he wondered what would become of the Order when his personal influence should cease to be a factor. "Lord God,' prayed Father Francis, "what will become of Thy poor little family? Who will comfort them? Who will protect them? Who will pray to Thee for them?"

The Lord sent an angel to comfort him with wondrous promises for the future of the Order, which would never fail or perish until Judgment Day, which would never be lacking in holy religious. Thus say "The Little Flowers."

With the passing of days, his body weakened by fasting and his soul weary of thinking and weeping, St. Francis began to meditate about paradise, the measureless glory and the eternal joy of the blessed, and he beseeched the Lord to send him some foretaste of that blessedness. Soon an angel appeared to him in an aureole of sun-like splendor, with a viol and a bow. And while St. Francis watched him in a great wonderment, the

angel drew his bow once across the viol; only one, a single note
but so divine that St. Francis was lifted beyond all bodily sense.
If the angel had drawn the bow again the soul of the saint might
have parted from his body.

THE THREE GIFTS

Stormy days and arid days went by in the search for the
Supreme Good, and then came the blessed moment in which
Francis again found the vein of gold of contemplation in a
double question that has assailed the philosophers of all the
world, that torments each reflective mind:
"Who art Thou, Lord, and who am I?"
On his knees among the rocks and the trees, with his face and
hands lifted up to heaven, St. Francis said,
"Who art Thou, my God most sweet? Who am I, the vilest of
worms and Thy unprofitable servant?"
And the Lord, Who does not reply to many proud philosophers, replied to humble St. Francis in the woodland silence of
Mount La Verna. He replied not by reasoning (for reasoning
belongs to man) but by illumination, showing him by means
of a most resplendent flaming torch the abyss of divine greatness and the tearful depths of human misery. Then the torch
halted, grew large and took the form of the burning bush that
had appeared to Moses, and from that flame the voice of the
Lord said to Francis, "I want three gifts from you."
Three gifts? Three things? Did he, the poor one, still possess
three things? Indeed, precisely three—but they were rags. What
would the Lord do with them? Nonetheless he answered with
the candor of a child:
"Lord God, I am wholly Thine. Thou knowest well that I
have naught else but tunic, rope, and breeches and even these
three things are Thine. What then can I offer or give to Thee?"
Francis did not know what riches he possessed. The divine
voice continued, "Search in your bosom and offer me what you
find."
The saint looked and found three balls of gold and one by

one he offered them to the Lord, Who made him understand that they signified three virtues: obedience, poverty, and chastity, and that he possessed them perfectly.

While St. Francis was discoursing with God, Friar Leo, the hour for saying the matins having drawn near, came to the foot of the bridge over the chasm and as usual he called out, *Domine, labia mea aperies*. The teacher, rapt in God, did not answer and Friar Leo, disobeying the order he had received, crossed the bridge because he feared St. Francis might be ailing or that an accident might have befallen him. He found his cell empty. He looked around for him cautiously, among the shrubs, in the light of the moon and finally he beheld him in his ecstatic state and he heard the question, "Who art Thou and who am I?" And he saw the resplendent torch over his head, witnessed that gesture of taking three things, unseen, from his bosom and handing them to some person unknown to him, after which the flaming torch returned to heaven. Beholding these marvels Friar Leo, rejoicing in his heart, was returning secretly to his cell when Francis, hearing the rustling of leaves, ordered him to stop. Friar Leo obeyed, but he would have preferred that the earth swallow him rather than await for St. Francis because he thought he would be angry on account of his disobedience.

"Who are you?" asked Francis, who could hardly see, partly because of the night, partly because of his tears, and partly because he was just emerging from his ecstasy.

Trembling all over, the little Friar answered, "I am Friar Leo, my father."

Having perceived the distress of his favorite from his voice, St. Francis heartened him immediately by calling him with the nickname that he had given to him. "Why did you come here, Friar Little Lamb? Did I not tell you not to spy on me? Tell me by holy obedience whether you saw or heard anything?"

Friar Leo told him about all that he had seen and heard. Then he fell to his knees and, weeping, he asked forgiveness for his disobedience, and finally he beseeched him to reveal the mystery of his vision. St. Francis, considering that God had deigned to reveal half of His secret to Friar Leo, confided the rest of it to him.

THE OMEN

From the first days of his sojourn on Mount La Verna St. Francis had been struck by the enormous fissures in the mountain. While praying he had learned that the clefts and caverns had been produced in the hour of the Passion of Christ, when, according to the Gospel, the rocks were rent asunder. Moved by this revelation, St. Francis without knowing that this mountain, rent asunder by the death of the Man-God, was to be the mountain of his own mystic crucifixion, the man favored by God, proposed a more rigorous solitude to himself because it appeared shameful to him that his heart should remain indifferent where the rocks had been cleft out of compassion for Jesus.

The thought of the Passion dominated him more as the feast of the Most Holy Cross neared, the fourteenth of September. He had a vague presentiment that some mystery was about to be accomplished, and he said to Friar Leo, "Have diligent care of me for in a few days God will work such great and wondrous things on this mountain that all the world will marvel."

Then he was seized by that presentiment of greatness that had made his dream as a youth, and that had driven him from the summits of nobility and festivals, to the summits of penance and the apostolate. And now where did the Lord want to lead him? What did he ask of him? What was he still to do? He felt himself prepared for any torture, as long as it accomplished the will of the heavenly Father. But what was this will? As he had interrogated the Gospel seventeen years before, now Francis interrogated the Gospel again. The saint knelt in the little cell where Friar Leo was saying the matins, amid the chirping of the birds, and charged his friend and confessor to open the Gospel with his priestly hands in the name of the Most Holy Trinity. The book fell open at the chapter of the Passion of Christ. They closed the book, and at the second time the book once more opened on the Passion. The same thing happened the third time. The heart of St. Francis trembled. The will of God was evident: After having followed Jesus in all the acts of

His life, he had to follow him to Calvary and conform himself to Him in his Passion, before dying. Therefore he should prepare himself for suffering. Here was the highest summit, the glory that surpasses all glory. The apparition of an angel, on the thirteenth of September, confirmed him in this thought. The angel, illuminating his cell, said to him:

"I am come to comfort and admonish you to receive with all patience that which God wills to work in you."

"I am ready," replied St. Francis.

THE PERFECT SUFFERING

It was the dawn of the fourteenth of September, feast of the Most Holy Cross, and St. Francis was praying with a new throb in his heart, as he had prayed as a young man waiting for some great thing.

"O my Lord Jesus Christ, I pray Thee to grant me two graces before I die: The first, that while I live I may feel in my body and in my soul, so far as is possible, that suffering, that Thou, sweet Lord, didst suffer in the hour of Thy bitterest Passion; the second is that I may feel in my heart, so far as is possible, that exceeding love wherewith Thou, O Son of God, wast enkindled to endure willingly for us sinners an agony so great."

St. Francis asked to love and to suffer like his Lord, and since he could not conceive of a love that did not express itself in action and suffering, all that remained to him was to renew the Crucifixion sensibly. He so ardently desired this, he was so burning with this desire that the Lord participated in all his love and suffering, as friend to friend: He crucified him as He was crucified.

In that dawn, alone on the mountain, St. Francis beheld a seraph with six resplendent and flaming wings come down from the profundity of the dazzling heaven. Two wings were extended over his head, two covered the whole of his body, two were spread out in flight. And Christ stood resplendently before him in that divine bird. While the saint beheld this extraordinary apparition, divided between the joy of beholding the

Lord and the suffering of seeing Him crucified, a wondrous
ardor invested him, ending with the spasmodic sensation of
wounds in his hands and sides, while a voice told him, "Do you
know what I have done to you? I have given you the stigmata
that are the marks of my Passion, in order that you may be My
standard-bearer."

The winged seraph vanished, the suffering ceased, and when
St. Francis returned to consciousness, he felt his hands wet and
a warm stream ran down his left side. He looked. The moisture
was blood. He tried to get up but his feet would not support
him. Seated on the ground under the trees, he looked at his
hands and feet and saw them transfixed by nails of flesh, black
as iron, their great round heads plain on the palms of his hands
and the soles of his feet. He opened his tunic where he felt
a pain that reached his heart. He noticed a wound as from a
lance, open, red and bleeding. These were the stigmata of which
the seraph had spoken. So his prayer had been answered! Love
had transformed him into the Beloved, as one becomes what
one loves.

While the seraph was appearing to Francis, a light enveloped
the summit of Mount La Verna in a aureole, illuminating the
surrounding hills and valleys. The shepherds minding their
flocks asked themselves in amazement what could be happening
up there in that brightness that was not a fire. Some travellers
who were going to Romagna and were spending the night in the
hovels along the coast, seeing the light in their windows and
believing it was already dawn, saddled and loaded their beasts.
But they marveled when on their way they saw the bright light
wane, and later the true dawn rise in the east, tinted a coral-red.

The mountain was spiritually aflame with a great miracle.

But St. Francis was not aware of it.

FRIAR LEO'S MELANCHOLY

St. Francis was annihilating and transhumanizing himself in
that test of love of his God, and he would have wanted to
conceal it because his humility almost feared to reveal the extraordinary miracle. But how could he if the wounds bled,

staining his tunic, and if his feet could endure neither the contact of the ground, nor the weight of his body?

He had to talk. He assembled his faithful and recounted the miracle to them, at first vaguely, as if it had happened to another person. Then, after reminding his friars that the Lord did not grant him special graces for himself alone, but also for the edification of others, he confided the prodigy of the fourteenth of September and a part of the revelation of the seraph: that is, the promise that after his death every year on the day of his death he would descend into purgatory, as Jesus descended into limbo, to liberate the filial souls of his three Orders and the souls of others who had a great devotion to him. The friars listened, and the veneration for the teacher knew no bounds.

Friar Leo, the pure, the simple, and the most faithful, had the honor and the happiness of attending to him. St. Francis wanted him only to see and swathe his wounds, only Friar Leo to wash away the blood, and change the bandages daily and to ease his pains.

From Thursday evening to Saturday morning, however, Francis did not want to mitigate the suffering with any human remedy. On Saturday, the bandage was so encrusted that when Friar Leo was loosening it, Francis had to lay his hand on Friar Leo's breast, suffocating a cry of pain.

At the touch of the holy hand of the teacher, Friar Leo felt such a sweetness he almost fainted. It seemed that the miracle of love was spreading from soul to soul, like a flame.

St. Francis was suffering, but he was happy. He adored, praised, gave thanks. And whereas he might have grown in self-esteem because of the privilege of crucifixion, which made him like another Christ, he humiliated himself to the point of immersing himself in God and completely forgetting himself. But if he forgot himself, he did not forget the others, and this was a most certain sign of his union with Jesus Christ. In fact in those days he noticed that Friar Leo wore a funereal expression. Sadness, which is the sickness of the devil, had seized the friar in the form of discouragement. Perhaps he felt too demeaned before the sanctity of the teacher, perhaps he feared that that unreachable sanctity would drive him farther away from him, perhaps he suffered the consuming jealousy of the humble when they see the creature of their cult become too great, too illustrious, too universal. And he thought that if he might obtain another proof of the teacher's affection, a special benediction, not those spoken and addressed to all and sundry, but a written one which could be preserved, read over and over again, and held close to his heart, the sadness would disappear. St. Francis divined his secret desire. So to satisfy the disciple of his soul, he said to Friar Leo a day before the feast of St. Michael the Archangel, "Bring me paper and pen and ink, because I want to write the praises of God which I have meditated in my heart."

And with a round and tremulous hand, because his nailed hand held the pen badly, he traced these words:

"Thou art the holy Lord God Who Alone worketh marvels. Thou art strong. Thou art great. Thou art most high. Thou art an almighty King. Thou holy Father, King of heaven and earth. Thou art Triune and one, Lord God. Thou art the good, every good, the highest good, the Lord God living and true; Thou art charity, love. Thou art wisdom. Thou art humility. Thou art patience. Thou art security, Thou art rest. Thou art joy and gladness. Thou art justice and temperance. Thou art all our wealth. Thou art beauty. Thou art gentleness. Thou art protector. Thou art keeper and defender. Thou art our refuge and strength. Thou art comfort. Thou art our hope. Thou art our faith. Thou art our great sweetness. Thou art our eternal life, great and wonderful Lord God Almighty, merciful Saviour."

Could he give a greater proof of his love to his disciple than by introducing him into the cell of his soul, confiding to him what his God said to him alone?

There are no expressions more jealousy modest than those of prayer. Did this supreme confidence, therefore, not suffice?

It did not suffice. St. Francis, who understood the hearts of men even more from the moment that he was carrying the same heart wound as Christ, reflected that Friar Leo wanted a word for himself, whereas that prayer addressed to the Lord only would have confirmed him in his thought. "See, he loves God so much that there is no more room for me."

Then St. Francis turned the parchment over and resumed writing with his wounded hand. "The Lord bless thee and keep thee. The Lord show His face to thee and have mercy on thee. The Lord turn His countenance to thee and give thee peace."

The ancient biblical blessing was also the best augury that Francis could note, it was a crescendo of a blessing invocation: custody, mercy, peace. And that the Lord show him His countenance, indeed that He look at him, by turning His face to him.

Could any more be said? Yes! The address and the signature were still lacking, otherwise that benediction could be sent by anybody to anybody! With the profound understanding of love, St. Francis intertwined the one with the other. He wrote his friend's name, but instead of his own name, he wrote a letter. After dipping the ostrich feather in his blood at the end of the letter he traced a big "T" (*TAU*), an ancient letter which is the last letter of the Hebrew alphabet and means sign, and which for the ancient sacred writers signified the Cross. Under the "T" he sketched a kind of profile of the mountain. And that kind of decapitated bloody cross, expressed him, Francis, crucified like our Lord and reborn to spiritual life after having cut off the head, that is, his worldly dreams, and having buried it under the Cross, on the rock of penance. Then in black ink he wrote:

"May the Lord, Friar Leo, bless thee."

This time there was no doubt as to the dedication of the missive and that final *thee* alluded to the intention of the writer. Not only that. The word Leo was divided in the middle between the *e* and the *o* by the red trunk of the *Tau*, almost to indicate that Francis wanted to live in the soul of his friend, but not so much through his world as a man, as through the new life to which the Lord had elevated him by imprinting the stigmata upon him. Now the signature of the saint was the Cross, but the mutilated cross, because he did not dare to identify himself with the Cross of Christ. And he traced that Cross as a seal of the immortality of their friendship.

PERFECT LOVE
IN PERFECT SUFFERING

After the thirtieth of September St. Francis arranged to return to St. Mary of the Angels with Friar Leo, leaving Friar Angelo and Friar Masseo on Mount La Verna. The separation was painful. The saint suffered at the thought of leaving the mountain which had been his Calvary, he felt that he would never again return there. The two friars who were to remain up there, weeping, beseeched him to bless them and to show them his blessed wounds. The teacher consented, and he bid them farewell one by one by name, with an infinite tenderness. "Goodbye, goodbye, Friar Masseo; Goodbye, goodbye, Friar Angelo. Rest in peace, my dearest sons! May God bless you, my dearest sons! Goodbye, I take my leave from you with my person but I leave you my heart. I am going to St. Mary of the Angels with Friar Little Lamb of God, and will no longer return here. Goodbye mountain, goodbye Mount La Verna! Goodbye mount of the angels! Goodbye dearest Brother Falcon, I thank you for your charity. Goodbye rock, which received me inside your entrails, thereby making mock of the devil; goodbye Saint Mary of the Angels (this was also the name of a little church on Mount La Verna), I commend these my sons to Thee, mother of the Eternal Word!"

While St. Francis was taking his leave with tears in his eyes from men and things, one by one, the friars wept, their hearts wrenched as though they would become orphans.

The saint descended the mountain on a little donkey, passing again by Chiusi to say farewell to his dear Count Roland, and set out for Borgo San Sepolcro. But when he arrived at a summit from where he could see Mount La Verna for the last time, he ordered the donkey to halt, alighted, and knelt on the road, his eyes fixed on the summit of his crucifixion and he again greeted it with the words of the psalm:

"Good-bye, rich mountain, mountain on which it has pleased

God to dwell. May God the Father, God the Son, God the Holy Ghost bless you. Rest in peace, for we will see you no more."

Thus ended that extraordinary lent of St. Michael of 1224 which marked a dizzying ascent for him. From the humble question of the first days, "Who art Thou and who am I?" He rose to the intimate question which tends to level differences, "Grant me to love as Thou hast loved and to suffer as Thou hast suffered!" After obtaining this the man did not swell with pride, but disappeared in an adoration of gratitude letting God alone triumph, and breaking forth in that song of praise which is a perfect prayer, without no shadow of a thought for himself. Having arrived at this religious height, it seemed that no earthly suffering could reach St. Francis. Instead, upon leaving Mount La Verna, he wept as though his heart had embraced all creatures, men, beasts, plants, rocks, and that it could not console itself over the separation except by finding them again in God.

IO

PRAISES OF LIFE
AND DEATH

THE NEARER the goal the swifter the race. In the last years of his life, St. Francis felt the desire to send the invitation to love and penance far and wide; yet he also felt the decline of his powers. So he had recourse to paper, pen and ink, and wrote several letters which are reminiscent of the Epistles. The certainty of a universal mission asserted itself in him, rising above his humility, and he dictated words of warning not only for his friars, but for all the faithful, for rulers and for ecclesiastics themselves. Nonetheless St. Francis remained so humble as not to use his own words, but those of the Gospel as much as possible as though he were prescribing to himself the task of the spokesman, of the herald who announces the will of his sovereign and nothing else.

When he addressed himself "to all religious Christian clerics and lay-people, living in the entire world," as the servant and subject of all, sending his reverent homage, and auguring "true peace and the secure charity of the Lord" from heaven, he was recalling the fundamental points of the faith and the Gospel. Only the selection was his own, but this selection revealed the characteristics of his piety which revolved entirely around the two mysteries of divine love: creation and Redemption.

Here Redemption predominated, and the saint again evoked the birth of Christ, the Blessed Sacrament, the duty of confes-

237

sion, of communion, of penance, of praise to God, and of charity toward one's neighbor.

His spiritual preferences burst forth in the brief comments where he despised "wisdom according to the flesh" and recommended simplicity, humility, purity; where he insisted that those in authority be like those who obey, and urged those who were considered the greater to be as the lesser; where he humbly advised, "Let us love our neighbor as ourselves but if anyone will not or cannot love him as himself, at least let him bring upon him no evil but rather let him do him good," which is a moving concession to natural selfishness. Finally he recalls the poverty of spirit with a vivid description of an impenitent sinner. In the other letters, two to his friars, one to ecclesiastics, one to the rulers of peoples, the dominant counsel is to praise and thank God publicly, and to love and venerate the sacrament of the Holy Eucharist with a most singular cult. This preoccupied him above all: "In all your preaching remember that no one can be saved, except by receiving the most holy Body and Blood of the Lord," he said to his friars. "I counsel you, my lords, to postpone every other care and solicitude and to receive willingly the most holy Body and the Blood of Our Lord Jesus Christ," he said to the governors. His delicacy of love led him to a respect for words, because it is by means of the word that bread and wine are transformed in the Body and Blood of Christ, and it filled him with sorrow that writings which bore the words of the Gospel often fell to the ground, and were crushed under foot. Enamored of poverty, he said to the clerics who bordered on being unscrupulous:

"Consider how poor are the chalices, the corporals and the linens in which the Body and the Blood of our Lord Jesus Christ is sacrificed." And to his friars, "Humbly beseech the clerics to adore the Blessed Sacrament above all things. The chalices, the corporals and everything needful for the sacrifice must be kept like precious things. And if in some place the most holy Body of the Lord be conserved too poorly, when you replace it in a precious place, keep good watch over it, carry it with great reverence, and give it to others with discretion."

His passion for Jesus Christ increased after the stigmata. Now that he suffered like his Lord, he understood the nature of Redemption—a mystery of suffering and of justice in the felicity of a God-Man—the value of individual souls, and what a suffering it was for Jesus Christ to lose them despite His sacrifice. And he burned with the desire to serve Him as though he were just then beginning his imitation of Christ.

So upon returning to St. Mary of the Angels, he resumed taking care of the lepers and preaching in the nearby villages, and he resumed his penances even though he was reduced to a mere shadow.

Yet his poor body did not rebel, instead it was in such concord with the spirit that it seemed to him that he could do everything, now that he was honored with the banner of Christ. And like a captain, inflamed by a reward of his lord, every day he proposed to himself greater things than he had done in the past.

The news of the miracle of the stigmata spread among the people, who came streaming in from distant places to see the saint. But he concealed the wounds from view as much as possible, by drawing his sleeves over the tips of his fingers, by avoiding walking, and by never talking about them. He also concealed the revelations that the Lord had made to him, because he understood that it is bad to confide things to everybody, and that one is very poor when in the depth of the soul one does not possess a good much more profound than that which is revealed at the surface. He had entrusted the care of his person to four especially beloved friars: Leo, Angelo Tancredi, Ruffino and Bernard. These four took care of him also at the express command of Friar Elias, the vicar general, and of Cardinal Ugolino, by providing for anything he might need, and by trying to mitigate his penances and by protecting him from the indiscreet devotion of the crowds.

But despite his extraordinary energy of spirit, the body was wearing out. Friar Elias realized this during their meeting at Foligno, and, perhaps because of the shattering impression the sight of his teacher in such a state made upon him, he had a dream of an old priest, clothed in white, who announced, "Rise and tell Friar Francis that the eighteen years since he renounced the world to follow Christ are now past, and that he will remain in this life two years more after which he will pass on to the other life."

PRAISE OF LIFE

There was one person who merited to participate in the dolorous glory of the teacher, a person who said nothing, and asked for nothing. Indeed this person was hardly ever seen but nonetheless was ever present in the mind of St. Francis, even more than Friar Leo and the others around him constantly. This person merited comfort more than the others precisely because of her buried life and her religious faith: Clare. Francis, who did no forget her, ordered the friars to carry him to St. Damian. It was here that the crucifix had spoken to him for the first time. Now he was returning there crucified. It was here that a seed-bed of souls was growing, of little spiritual plants, as Lady Clare called them, which he himself had started. And he was to bring the grace received to it.

St. Francis had a hut built for himself near the small convent. He was very ill. Besides his general exhaustion and the five wounds, his eyes for almost sixty days now no longer could endure the light of day so that he could no longer see, not even the sun and fire which gave him so much joy. Moreover that hut was plagued by continuous incursions of mice which made it impossible for him to close his eyes at night, and by day they climbed on his table to steal the little food that he had.

"Devils, envious devils!" said the friars crossing themselves, and Clare, sorely afflicted by the sight, redoubled her prayers for her teacher and prepared swathings, ravelings and plasters of grass for his wounds and a pair of plushed, soft sandals for his nail-fierced feet. But the sufferings increased to the point where St. Francis, despite his great will to suffer, felt pity for himself and prayed, "Lord, help me to bear these infirmities patiently!"

An inner voice replied that those tribulations would earn him a treasure vastly superior to all the treasures of the earth: therefore he should bear them in peace, and be assured of paradise.

This promise gladdened him so much that he talked about it on the next morning to his companions. "If the emperor promised his kingdom to a vassal, should not that man be very glad? How can I thank my Lord Who has deigned to assure me, His unworthy servant, while I yet live in the flesh, the possession of His kingdom?" Gratitude, which had flowered perennially and exuberantly in his soul, suggested that he compose a new praise of the creatures of the Lord, and precisely of those who serve us every day and of whom we often make use, offending God, instead of thanking Him.

Seated on the grass, in the shade of olive trees, tortured in form and as serene in spirit, the saint pondered a while and then intoned this hymn, improvising as he went along:

> Most high, Omnipotent, good Lord,
> Thine are praise, glory, honor and all benedictions,
> To Thee alone, Most High, do they belong
> And no man is worthy to name Thee.
> Praise be to Thee, my Lord, with all Thy creatures,
>   Especially Brother Sun,
> Who is our day and lightens us therewith.
> Beautiful is he and radiant with great splendor,
>   Of Thee, Most High, he bears expression.
> Praise be to Thee, my Lord, for Sister Moon and for the stars,
> In the heaven which Thou hast formed bright, precious and
>   fair.
> Praise be to Thee, my Lord, for Brother Wind,
> And for the air and the cloud of fair and all weather
> Through which Thou givest sustenance to Thy creatures.
> Praise be, my Lord, for Sister Water
> Who is most useful, humble, precious and chaste,
> Praise be, my Lord, for Brother Fire
> By whom Thou lightest up the night,
> He is beautiful, merry, robust and strong.
> Praise be, my Lord, for our Sister, Mother Earth,
> Who sustains and governs us
> And brings forth diverse fruits with many-hued flowers and
>   grass.

The *laud* gushed forth like a spring because it had been

maturing for years in the heart of the saint. Friar Pacifico, the troubador who had been crowned King of Verses, liked it, and St. Francis himself taught it to his companions because he wanted them to sing it after sermons, like minstrels of God. And in compensation for the song they were to ask their listeners not for money, but for true penance.

St. Francis usually sang in Provençal: the language of the courts of love, his mother, and his past. For him that language enclosed the remembrance of all that which the man he once been had once admired. This man had not died but he was transforming himself just as he transformed the concepts and words taken from the troubadors.

Nothings recalls the past and the present, regret and dream, more than does music. Its spiritual indeterminacy permits the privilege of expressing what would be prohibited expression in any other way. One can say everything in music. Let him who has ears to hear, hear! Thus for Francis the Provençal song represented the last echo of the past.

At times he wrote and dictated in Latin, the language of the Church, of laws, of the universities, of the chancelleries, of documents, and of inscriptions. But at St. Damian, under Mount Subasio and before the Apennine range, neither Provençal nor Latin could any more suffice St. Francis. He had been completely renewed after the stigmata, the former man had died forever in the Crucified One, the new man felt a new lyrical impetus rise from the depths of the suffering, like the effervescence of a young wine, which breaks the old casks. He was near St. Damian, the church of his prayer and of his work, of his second coming and of his first mission, the church of Lady Poverty and of Sister Clare. The gentle mother who had given him the heart of a poet was gone forever. Nearby instead was the mighty virgin who, bowing her patrician head under the vail of poverty, had brought a redoubling of faith into his life; nearby were the daughters of his spirit who did not know Provençal, and only a little Latin. At St. Damian, near the convent of the Poor Ladies, one could sing only in the language of the Poor Ladies: the vulgar language. Such motives worked secretly in the heart of St. Francis and brought forth *The Canticle of Brother Sun*. He had something new to say and wanted to be understood by all because this something represented his conception of life, the epilogue of his life, the summary of a preaching which had remained in hearts but not on paper. Hearts are covetous, they transform words to suit their purposes whereas paper, which is more faithful, preserves them intact.

Therefore he wanted to "compose a new praise of the creatures of the Lord, in His praise, and for our consolation and for the edification of our neighbor." And he wanted "that his companions should recite it and sing it after their preaching in order to lift up the hearts of men and to lead them to a gladness of spirit." The language of the dead and the learned could not serve this purpose, nor could the vulgar language of a people on the other side of the mountain, the polished popular speech of the courtiers and of the troubadors. It was necessary to use the Italian spoken by the people. Latin, as Dante was to say later, would have given his benefit to few, whereas the vulgar tongue truly served many.

The language of the eaglets was necessary for the eaglets, for that people who, in the many centuries since the fall of the Roman Empire, had accomplished its feats without celebrating them in song, and had lived its love without recording it in the prose of romances. And even the vulgar tongue was new, like the man who had new things to express.

What was new in *The Canticle of Brother Sun* was the way to love God and creatures. The pagan world loved only creatures and with a love that was wholly rooted in the senses. The world of the Old Testament loved God, but with a servile love. The Christian world before St. Francis loved God with a love that was sufficiently filial, but it neglected creatures, fearing them like a temptation—it closed its eyes for fear of becoming enamored of them, for it had not yet read in the Gospel of the rehabilitation of nature through the loving look and blessing word of Lord Jesus. St. Francis was a born poet and therefore he saw the intrinsic beauty of things, even of the most humble, of those which fall within our range of vision at all moments and to which men, busy and non-poetic as they are, do not attend. But Francis became a saint, and therefore he sought for the Creator in the creatures. If he read the book of nature with evangelical eyes, as no one before or since has read it, it was because he saw the Author in its pages. And he stopped reading now and then to say to Him, "How good Thou art, my God!"

From the heights of divine love he descended to things with a more penetrating tenderness. He contemplated, admired, and kissed them with his eyes, and to the stars, fire, water, and grass he seemed to say, "You do not know that you are such beautiful creatures. Very well, I will tell you how beautiful you are! You merit admiration: I will admire you! I have the consciousness that you do not have, and for you I praise and thank Him Who has created you as He has created me, and in Whom you are my sisters."

Brothers and sisters! To give this new title to the lower creatures, it was necessary to discover the mystery of their life, to destroy the antitheses between nature and God, between matter and spirit, which the Cathars and the other heretical sects were setting forth and exaggerating. But this had to be done without falling into the error of the following centuries which identified the creatures with God. It was necessary to know how to put oneself in communion with things by means of that sense of human sympathy which is peculiar to poets together with that sense of divine sympathy, which is peculiar to saints and which, according to a great thinker, presupposes the human. But the latter is mightier than human, just as the infinite surpasses the finite.

This praise of life acquires greater value when we consider that it was composed in the saddest circumstances of his life, by a sick, wounded, almost blind, completely worn out man, living in a poverty that would have frightened a beggar. In comparison to this the *Book of Job,* who is so celebrated for his patience, seems almost like a lamentation. But Job did not know Jesus Christ, and he was still the man of the Old Testament.

Instead, *The Canticle of Brother Sun* was the first literary triumph of a language and of a people in the new ideal of a saint.

PRAISE OF MUSIC

Friar Elias used his authority as general of the Order to convince Francis to go to Rieti where at that time Honorius III had transferred his pontifical court. In agreement with Cardinal Ugolino he commanded St. Francis to try to cure his poor body, and especially his eyes. The cardinal, because of the great tenderness he felt for him, had written Francis to come to him at Rieti where there were good eye-doctors. Francis obeyed willingly. The richly verdant valley of Rieti with its rocky hermitages among the woods, Fonte Columbo, Poggio Bustone, Greccio reminded him of Mount La Verna and inspired him to the sweetness of prayer. St. Damian had finally given him a little relief. Clare, who did not preach and who did not write verses but inspired both sermons and poetry; Clare, who no longer left the cloister, made a pair of sandals so adapted to his tormented feet as to allow him to resume walking along the roads of the world.

But after receiving the cardinal's letter, St. Francis delayed his departure in order to give her and the other virgins his precious comfort. Before taking his leave from her he consoled her with holy words and then, mounted on his donkey, and accompanied by his faithful sentinels, he set forth on the road to Rieti. The abbess followed him with her eyes until he disappeared among the olive trees, then she knelt before the crucifix. Saint Francis walked along in silence. If he had talked the disciples would have preserved his words which already were being dutifully collected as angelic and prophetic statements. But that silent farewell to the fortress of Poverty must have been as painful as the farewell to Mount La Verna, if the most piercing pains are those that are not expressed.

Meanwhile the people of Rieti were awaiting him like the Messiah and they came to meet him in such numbers that St. Francis did not want to enter the city. He stopped at the Church of San Fabiano, two miles outside the city gate. But the people swarmed even there. The pastor of the church, after having received the saint in glory, began to think that the honor of playing host to him was too costly because the devotees, although they had flocked there to sanctify themselves, did not scruple to vintage, as it were, the grapes of his vineyard before time, plucking them and, still worse, crushing them underfoot.

St. Francis, who always divined the discomforts of others, said to him, "Dearest father, how many measures of wine does this vineyard yield a year when the yield is highest?"

"About twelve," replied the priest, blushing for fear of being understood too well. Then, with the air of a great lord, St. Francis promised, "I beseech you, father, suffer me patiently to sojourn here for a few days because I find much repose here, and for the love of God and of me, *Poverello,* let them all gather grapes from this vineyard, and I promise you in the name of Our Lord Jesus Christ that this year it will yield you twenty measures."

This happened. The virtue of faith was born in the soul of the miserly priest, and although he gathered few bunches at the vintage season, the yield, in the end, was twenty measures of wine of an excellent quality.

At Rieti St. Francis found not only an enthusiastic devotion in Cardinal Ugolino, in the curial prelates, in the physicians, and in the people. All this should have improved his condition. But it was of no use. He was sick and suffering from his liver, and from disorders of the spleen and stomach. His eyes burned and watered, the stigmata bled him white. As his eyes gradually lost the joy of seeing, a passion for music grew in him. And, just as since his youth he had expressed the dreams that words demean and imprison in song, so did he, now that he was almost trans-humanized in Christ, ask the expression of the ineffable from music.

One evening at Rieti he called Friar Pacifico, who was a musician and poet, and said to him,

"Friar, it is true that musical instruments which should praise God have become a worldly thing, and often an instrument of sin. Men no longer understand the divine mysteries. But if you would wish to please me, borrow a viol secretly and bring a little comfort to my Brother Body no part of which is without pain."

Friar Pacifico, become a knight of common sense, replied, "Father, what would people say if they hear me playing like a troubador! They will think me a very frivolous friar!"

"In that case let the matter rest," said Francis, always disposed to consider that others were right. "It is better to renounce many things than to give scandal."

In order to appear saintly Friar Pacifico had refused an act of charity, but he was punished by not understanding those which St. Francis had called "divine mysteries," that is to say, how the more a man lives in God the more he is man, enjoying all things in their original purity. On the other hand, St. Francis, who had renounced music out of a fineness born of charity, was consoled.

On the following night a sound of a viol broke into his insomnia. It was as though someone was coming and going under the window, playing notes so sweet as to drive all suffering from his mind. No one could be seen, but in the silent night the melody now seemed close, now far away, and it seemed to be the guarantee, at the level of the senses, of a higher world where everything that is loved and desired in dream here below becomes a reality.

Who was this mysterious cithern-player? An angel? A devotee of the saint? Or was it neither an angel nor a devotee, but the very soul of St. Francis become all music? Indeed the last months of his life were naught but music.

PRAISE OF BROTHER BODY

St. Francis spent the winter between the hermitage of Sant' Eleuterio and the hermitage of Fonte Colombo, denying himself every protection against the cold. In order not to wear the tunic, he consented to having patches sewed on his breast and on his shoulders, but only on the outside and well in view so that all might understand his weakness in respect to the Rule. Yet even the few concessions that he made to his sick body pricked his conscience.

"Does it not seem to you that you show too much indulgence to my body?" he asked Friar Leo, his confessor.

And Friar Leo, inspired by God, replied:

"Tell me, father, has not your body always been docile to your will?"

"Yes," acknowledged Francis, "I render it testimony that it has been obedient, that it has never avoided hardship, pains, sicknesses, in order to do my will. Indeed it has always come running precipitately, so to speak, at every command of mine, and we have always found ourselves in agreement, I and it, in serving Christ the Lord without any repugnance."

The reply was most noteworthy for a religious of the year 1226. The confessor, who was not his disciple for nothing, took advantage of this and now used the same arguments already used by the teacher in favor of the sick to defend his health. He said:

"You are not generous with your body. Is this the way to conduct oneself towards a loyal friend? It is not seemly to receive a benefice and requite it in evil when the benefactor is in need. How would you have been able to serve your Lord Jesus Christ without the help of your body?"

And St. Francis, grieved by these reasonings which he could make to everyone but himself, declared, "It is true, son, I acknowledge it!"

"It is not reasonable," continued Friar Leo, "to abandon so faithful a friend in time of need. This sin against the Lord, father, Who is the help and support of the afflicted, does not become you."

Humbly St. Francis thanked his companion for having calmed his scruples, and then he turned to his own body:

"Rejoice, Brother Body, and forgive me. Henceforth, here I am ready to satisfy your desires and to help you in your needs." Was there not a touch of irony in this concession which came too late? At any rate this useless dialogue in the interests of St. Francis' health is a thing of beauty in so far as it reveals that he did not consider the body as an enemy, not even when he treated it harshly. And he acknowledged its brotherly merits in the face of death.

PRAISE OF PARDON AND PENITENCE

Cardinal Ugolino and Friar Elias thought St. Francis should spend the winter in a town with a mild climate and they chose the nearest one, Siena.

But the saint found no improvement even in the beautiful city of the Blessed Virgin, which opens its big heart to visitors from the Camollia gate. In fact, here one night he had a violent hemorrhage which reduced him to the point of death. Then he made known his desire to return to Assisi. But travelling was no longer as simple as when he roamed through Italy and the Holy Land on foot and without a staff or wallet.

Now crowds waited for his arrival, they swarmed toward him, accompanied him, and fought over him. Now the people in every town in which he stopped piously hoped that he might die within their walls so that they could preserve his body as a precious relic. Now not only devotion but medieval superstition did violence to his sanctity. In order to spare him emotional excitement and dangers to his person, Friar Elias ordered the small escort to take a long way around along the less travelled roads, which were also the worst ones: Celle, Gubbio, Nocera. At Satriano, in the territory of Nocera, an escort of crossbowmen from the Commune of Assisi joined the friars to keep a guard around the man of God who was coming to die in their city. The bishop wanted him as his guest.

After twenty years Bishop Guido still preserved the proud impulsiveness of his florid maturity, when he had opened his mantle to the youth who had stripped himself bare for the love of God, and had fought in the courts against the Crucifers of the hospital of San Salvatore and against the Benedictines of Mount Subasio. Now Francis found him in an open state of war with the podestà of the city, Messer Berlingerio di Jacopo da Fiorenza, over one of those disagreements between the civil and religious authority which flared up so easily in the small circle of the commune. The bishop had had recourse to spiritual weapons, excommunicating the podestà; the podestà had had recourse to economic weapons, in an attempt to starve the bishop into submission, forbidding any citizen to sell him anything or buy anything from him, or make any contract with him. Today we would call it a boycott. The citizens of Assisi found themselves between two fires. If they dealt with the podestà they were excommunicated, and if they dealt with the bishop they incurred fines and reprisals.

This unhappy situation bore the seeds of an armed struggle between the parties, which would be disastrous for Assisi. Francis, who had preached peace all his life, urgently felt the need to save his native city. The way of bringing this peace about which he devised was indeed worthy of the man who sixteen years before had persuaded the doubting cardinals with a parable on love.

He said to his companions: "It is a great shame to us, servants of God, that the bishop and the podestà should hate each other so." Then he pondered a while. How beautiful would be a mutual pardon between the two parties. It would be more beautiful, more worthy of praise, more glorious for God than the beauty of natural creatures insofar as the will is higher than nature. And immediately, moved by inspiration, he had these verses added to *The Canticle of Brother Sun:*

Be Thou praised, my Lord,
By those who pardon for love of Thee,
And endure infirmities and tribulations.
Blessed are they who will endure it in peace,
For they will be crowned by
    Thee, Most High.

Afterwards he called one of his friars and said, "Go to the podestà and tell him in my name to go to the bishop's palace with the consuls, the magnates and all others he can take with him." Then he turned to his other companions who were the best singers and said, "Go before the bishop and the podestà and the others who will gather in the bishop's palace. Deliver no sermons, just sing *The Canticle of Brother Sun* as best you can. I trust that the song will move them and that they will be friends again as before."

The friars bowed their heads, their arms in the form of the

cross, and obeyed. But were it not for their great veneration of
the teacher, they would have thought Francis naive to think
that he could come between those two angry and stubborn
contenders with an idyllic song. But Messer Berlingerio, whose
conscience was disturbed because of the excommunication,
and who loved the blessed Francis, accepted the invitation.
Guido also agreed to meet the group, out of respect for his
great guest and because the podestà, by coming to his palace,
was taking the first step in the reconciliation. The podestà and
his men-at-arms and chancellors gathered in the cloister of the
bishopric where they were met by the bishop and his court
dressed in violet robes. At the door stood mace-bearers, valets
and clerics pushing back the people who, filled with curiosity,
had flocked around the bishop's palace. The bishop and the
podestà had that bearing which seemed to say, "I won't give
in. My dignity is at stake!" And their respective bloodhounds,
harsh, gruff and withdrawn, took each other's measure like
mastiffs. When the two friars appeared in the cloister, everybody thought, "Now we'll hear a sermon on death and Judgment Day." Instead, one of the friars said, "Blessed Francis
in his sickness composed praises of creatures in praise of the
Lord, and for the edification of his neighbor. Now we beseech
you to listen to them with great devotion."

Some of those present laughed as if to say, "A piece of buffoonery!" But these spirited men were deeply moved as the
song unfolded, with the sweep and sweetness of the horizon of
their native town, and in the humble colloquial speech of their
own mothers, with words and accent known to their hearts
since childhood, and then passed from the praise of the Most
High, Whom none is worthy to name, to the praise of indispensable and neglected beautiful creatures.

The podestà was the first to rise, clasping his hands together
and listening with rapt attention. The friars sang, and at that
enumeration of the free gifts of God the proud bishop was
forced to think of the graciousness of God who sends the sun
to shine on the just and the unjust. And the podestà had to
reflect upon the futility of hunger appeals in the face of
generosity of the earth and the Providence of God. Then, like

a flight of angels, the friars passed on to the verses of pardon which nobody knew, and then the verses of suffering which recalled the great man who was dying, and who in the name of God and his own asked only for peace. But he did more, he instilled peace in souls with music that placated without admonishing, with poetry without rhetoric, with goodness without moralizing. So all present were now disposed to reconciliation, and the podestà said, "In truth I tell you that I not only pardon the lord bishop, whom I wish to and must retain as my lord, but if someone had killed my brother, or my son, I would also pardon him." In confirmation of his words, he knelt before Guido, exclaiming,

"I am ready to make satisfaction for everything as it shall please you, for the love of Our Lord Jesus Christ and of his servant, the blessed Francis."

The bishop raised him with his own hands, confessing humbly, "I too am in need of your pardon, because by nature I am quick to anger, whereas my office bids me to be humble."

They embraced each other like old friends, while those present held this to be a miracle wrought by the blessed Francis. They were right.

Even at the brink of death the tamer of wolves accomplished his mission, by taming the eaglets of his Assisi with naught but song.

PRAISE OF DEATH

The dropsy, of which there had already been symptoms for about a month, became more serious, inflating Father Francis' stomach and legs. But this did not perturb him. One day, receiving a visit from Messer Bongiovanni (Good John), a worthy physician of Arezzo, he asked him, "What do you think of this, my infirmity of dropsy."

Messer Benivegnate understood that illusions do not become the brave, so he made a most exact prognosis.

"Manifestly, Father Francis, according to our science, your infirmity is incurable. And I believe that you will die either at the end of September or on the fourth day of October."

Sitting upright in bed, the saint smiled. Then, raising his eyes and hands toward heaven, he also found an expression of love for the skeletal visitor, and uttered in a voice of perfect joy, "Welcome, my Sister Death!"

After the doctor's death sentence, a zealous friar delivered a beautiful little sermon to him on the tribulations of life, on the paradisiacal consolations that death unlocks and on the necessity of making a good death. With this in view he politely admonished him that just as in all his life he had been a mirror of holiness, so now he must take heed to maintain the bearing of a saint even *in extremis* for the edification of present and future generations.

St. Francis did not need such admonitions, but he accepted them with joy, as a confirmation of the physician's forecast. And he could not find a better preparation for death than song. Therefore he said to his counsellor, "If it pleases the Lord that I must quickly die, call Friar Angelo and Friar Leo so that they may sing to me of Sister Death."

The courteous knight and the little lamb of God, in whom the saint found the closest affinity of spirit, came running at his call. Weeping, they began to sing the *Canticle of Brother Sun*. When they came to the last verse, St. Francis continued:

> Be Thou praised, My Lord,
> For our Sister Bodily Death,
> From whom no living man can flee.
> Woe to those who die in mortal sin.
> Blessed are they who shall be found in Thy most Holy will,
> To them, the second death will bring no ill.
> Praise and bless my Lord,
> And thank and serve him with great humility.

The praise of creatures was now truly completed with these verses. For the first nine verses, composed at St. Damian, sang only the beauty of nature in which the candid poet did not see suffering and death. But in the tenth, added for the reconciliation of the bishop and the podestà, he rose to the contemplation of the greatest moral beauty: pardon for the love of God, resignation before infirmity and misfortune. And in the last verse he faced the darkest enigma of all, from which no man can flee: death. And he did not see her as a horrid apparition with her cavernous skull but as a sister, which is the sweetest and the most chaste of women's attributes. And behind death he did not see a fierce judge but, after a "Woe to those who die in mortal sin," he glimpsed the beatitude of him whose days are finished in the will of God.

Ever mindful not to afflict, or inconvenience others, and above all mindful to keep others in a state of gaiety because constant gaiety is half-holiness, St. Francis often had his companions sing the praises. And not only by day, but also by night, not only for their own comfort and his, but for the consolation of the halleberdiers whom the commune had sent as a guard around the bishop's palace so that no one might hazard to steal off with the dying or dead saint. He knew what music could do to men of labor and men of war.

But the knights of common sense felt that this somehow bordered on buffoonery. Friar Elias who always viewed things in terms of their effects, desired an esthetic death for the teacher, in the old style, in accordance with the schemes of common sanctity. Therefore this frequent singing appeared as incongruous and inconvenient. He, who would have broadened the Rule to include scattered houses and lands, was scandalized by that agony so unwonted that it would shame a minstrel. Death is a serious, sad affair, the prelude to Judgment, the portal to eternity. Could one really await her, singing?

And if the people should think that Francis, *Il Poverello,* had gone out of his mind in the last days of his life, where would his glory end and what would be the future of the Order? Therefore he screwed up his courage and observed to the sick man, "Dearest father, your joy much consoles and edifies me. But since the men of this city venerate you as a saint and know of the gravity of your infirmity, by hearing all this singing night and day they might ask: 'How could he show such gladness, when he should be thinking of death?'"

St. Francis replied, "It is so long now that by the grace of God I have been thinking upon my end day and night! But from the time when you had that vision at Foligno and said to me that someone had told you that only two more years of life remained to me, I have never ceased to meditate upon my death."

As for the opinion of people, this time St. Francis did not surrender as he had done with Friar Pacifico. Fervently, he said, "Let me rejoice in the Lord, in His praises, and in my infirmities! By the grace of the Holy Ghost I am so united and wedded to my Lord that I can well be merry in the Most High!"

But common sense did not understand the new heroism of dying in gladness.

PRAISE OF PAST AND FUTURE

While the friars sang, St. Francis remembered, prayed, and pondered. Afterward he would repeat his remembrances and counsels to his companions, and Friar Leo would write them down faithfully. Just as all the lights of the day fuse in the sky at twilight, so do remembrances at the moment of agony. And the agony of St. Francis had the long luminosity of October twilights on the Umbrian hills.

He did not recall the confusion of his youth. For him the rememberable past began from the moment the Lord called him to penance. Now in his mind's eye he again saw the leper whom he had embraced and who in the embrace had turned into sweetness all that which formerly had seemed bitter to him. Now he saw himself again as the mason of St. Damian and Porziuncola, enkindled with faith for the churches since he found the living Jesus Christ in them, and enkindled with veneration for Catholic priests as the dispensers of the divine word and of the Sacraments, converting bread and wine into the Body and Blood of Christ.

The hours of the sick go by slowly, and Francis remembered the first friars whom the Lord sent him, the first months of the Round Table, the uncertainty with regard to the norms to follow, the code of the new knights found so easily in the Gospel, that Rule consisting of only a few clear words, confirmed by Pope Innocent III.

The hours of his sickness went by slowly also in the bishop's palace, which was guarded like a prison. For one who wanted to sleep on the ground the bed was painful, and for one who had lived on summits and in the forests the room was narrow and confining. And Francis remembered the knights of the first hour, the twelve who had given all their belongings to the poor, and who were content with a single patched tunic, the rope girdle, and their breeches. They wanted nothing else. He remembered the times when they said the Divine Office in the churches because they did not have their own oratory, and when they swept and dusted them, and when they willingly spent the night in abandoned chapels, and the times when they were ignorant and subservient to all.

The hours dragged along in the bishop's palace and Francis would have liked to work still, with his hands, as he had worked at Rivo Torto at Porziuncola, at Carceri, and as his companions worked, not for gain but to set a good example and keep idleness at a distance.

This is what the blessed Francis remembered during the immobility imposed on him by his infirmity. And the remembrance was a praise of gratitude to the Most High who had granted him the grace to live according to His way and not according to the way of the world. But now the past seemed to be more beautiful to him than it was and this led him to consider the present: the Round Table no longer round, Lady Poverty was forgotten, and the knights of God had become the knights of common sense. Then he turned to his friars with the authority of one on the verge of death, as to his legitimate heirs, commending his dearest woman to them, and commanding that they love her faithfully, that they take heed not to possess houses, churches, lands, and not live in habitations save as pilgrims and strangers, not to accept honors, and not to solicit prebends and privileges. Further, he commanded that they obey their superiors, observe the Rule, subject themselves to the Church, that they do not change his words. He commanded . . .

But what good is a command? Is there not something that constrains more than an imposition? So he repeated the words already dictated to Friar Benedict of Prato when he was on the verge of death in Siena:

"Write how I do bless all my friars who are and who will be in the Order until the end of days. And since on account of my weakness and the pain of my infirmity I cannot speak, I briefly make known my will to all brethren, future and present, in these three words: Namely that in token of my memory and blessing and last will, they love one another as I have loved them and do still love them; that they forever love and observe our Lady Poverty; and that they always be loyal and subject to the prelates and clerics of Holy Mother Church."

The sick man no longer looked backward, he looked ahead. And according to the promises of Christ he saw men and women from all over the world coming into his Order; rich and poor, ignorant and learned, sovereigns and subjects. Every century was to bring a new wave of souls, every generation was a Spring season renewing the leaves and flowers of the great tree. The saint saw these children who were to love him on earth without seeing him, who were to follow him without hearing his voice, and who were to elect his ideal without succeeding in living it completely, and he blessed them all.

"Whosoever shall observe my Rule let him be filled in heaven with the blessing of the Most High Father, and on earth with the blessing His beloved Son, together with the Most Holy Spirit, the Paraclete, and all the virtues of heaven and all the saints."

Then suddenly his great humility took hold of him again in the face of such a boundless future, and he concluded,

"I, Friar Francis, the least among you and your servant, insofar as I can, confirm unto you within and without this most holy blessing."

PRAISE OF HIS NATIVE COUNTRY

Since the singing continued Friar Elias observed that it was not seemly for the friars to be among lay-folk and he advised that they all go to St. Mary of the Angels.

"I consent and the counsel pleases me, but find a way to carry me because walk I cannot."

The friars placed him in a litter and left the bishop's palace surrounded by the soldiers of the commune, and followed by a great throng of people who wanted to accompany the saint.

Upon arriving at the leper-hospital, where he had begun to serve God in the misery of his neighbor, Francis bade the bearers, "Set the litter down and turn me toward the city." He could hardly see now and the others had to point out Assisi to him.

He raised himself a little on his bed and with his face turned toward the city, which stood out tiny and proud with its towers, its campanile, and its walls studded with battlements against the background of Mount Subasio. He blessed the city with many benedictions as if Assisi had given him naught but joy.

Perhaps in a confused sweetness he remembered his mother, the house of his parents, his friends, his first companions, Clare of Coccorano, his preachings, his humiliations, his triumphs. Without seeing it, he again felt the beauty of that horizon which had spoken to him of God, of that valley of Spoleto from which he never wanted to uproot himself, where he had found his vocation and the gift of Pardon.

Certainly if at that moment he had had to leave his native country, as he had left Mount La Verna, the suffering would have been terrible. Nonetheless the melancholy of the imminent separation and the sweetness of remembrance flowed together with the blessings he showed upon Assisi.

"Lord, if in the past this city was a place of pagans, now because of Thy mercy Thou hast shown forth to favor her singularly by electing her to be the dwelling of those who should acknowledge Thee in truth and give glory to Thy Holy Name, and offer to all Christian people an example of holy life, of most true doctrine, and of evangelical perfection. I beseech Thee, Lord Jesus, Father of mercies, that Thou consider not our ingratitude but be mindful only of Thine own tenderness which Thou hast shown toward Assisi, that she may ever be the dwelling of those who acknowledge Thee truly. And may they glorify Thy blessed and most glorious name for ever and ever.

"And may thou be blessed by God, holy city, since through thee many souls will be saved, and many servants of God will dwell in thee, and many of thy inhabitants will be elected to the realm of eternal life."

The friars wept, the citizens wept, and the sky and the hills and the valley, the olive-trees, and the solitary cypresses seemed to borrow a physiognomy from his countenance, an expression from his voice, and an enchantment of beauty from that figure they were never again to lose. Everything which his native land had given to its poet and saint was now being restored to it a hundred-fold. Everything of an unmistakably unique character which Assisi has about it today comes from his life and benediction.

PRAISE OF FRIENDSHIP

Friar Elias had truly divined the desire of Francis by bringing him back to Porziuncola, which was his favorite place, most warmly commended to the friars as the native center blessed by the Virgin. The sick man was placed in the best cell, the infirmary, assisted by his friars who watched over him, although he wasted away from day to day. The paternal tenderness of St. Francis became more refined in its solicitude as death approached. In the bishop's palace at Assisi he had already blessed his near and distant sons beginning with Friar Elias who, as vicar, represented them all. All dissonance of ideas vanished for the saint in the face of eternity. He sensed that Friar Elias loved him without understanding him and he was grateful to him for this love. He also sensed that his passion, his work, and his ideal would be interpreted in various ways because men and times vary, but that every interpretation could lead to good provided it were sincere and devout. Just as he had faithfully copied Jesus Christ, so his work was to have a reflection of the universality of the Church which permits diverse currents in her bosom, yet remains one in spirit. Therefore on the day when he placed his right hand on the head of a friar kneeling beside his bed, he asked, "Upon whose head is my right hand?" and was answered, "On Friar Elias," Francis said, "That is as I wish." And he added:

"I bless you, my son, in all things and through all things. And as the Most High has multiplied my brothers and sons under your guidance, so upon you and in you I do bless them all."

In the words of St. Francis there was a delicate recognition of the uncommon value of Friar Elias as the organizer and director of the Order. He continued with an intensity of affection and humility:

"I bless you as far as I can and more than I can. May He who can do all things do in you what I cannot do. May God remember your work and your labor, and may your fate be preserved in the retribution of the just."

It seemed that with these words Francis was noting the merits of Elias before God's tribunal for Elias would have need of them later when he left the Order and, following his enterprising and impetuous nature, he sided with the excommunicated Frederick II. But Francis had other friends to whom to give the blessing of his heart. And he thought of Bernard of Quintavalle, the first knight of the Round Table who was most faithful to him and who progressed constantly in holiness so much so that, having made an agreement with him that wherever they met he should harshly correct and rebuke him for his defects, St. Francis avoided seeing him in order not to be lacking in respect to him.

He thought about his "first-born" son, and one day having received a small fine dish for the relief of Brother Body, he remembered that Bernard was fond of this dish and he said, "This food is good for Friar Bernard. Call him."

Bernard came, and deeply moved and encouraged by that attention from the dying teacher, he asked him for something much more precious than the sweetmeat.

"Father, I beseech you to bless me and to show forth your love, for if you will demonstrate your paternal affection for me, I believe that God Himself and all the friars will love me more."

Even Bernard, like Leo, like the majority of his faithful.

desired a sign of predilection: The ego is so greedy! But one never asked for love from St. Francis in vain. He had some for all, and it was not the same for all but special to each one. At the request of his friend, he extended his hand to bless him, but being almost blind, he placed his hand upon the head of Friar Giles. He noticed this. "This is not the head of my Friar Bernard."

Then Friar Bernard drew closer to him.

"May the Eternal Father bless you," said St. Francis placing his hand on Friar Bernard's head, "since you are the first-born, elected in this holy Order to set the evangelical example by following Christ in poverty. Not only did you distribute your belongings entirely and freely to the poor for the love of Christ, but you offered yourself in a sacrifice of sweetness. May you be blessed therefore with eternal blessings by our Lord Jesus Christ and by me his poor little servant; blessed going, standing, waking and sleeping, living and dying. And I wish that whosoever will be general to minister honor to Bernard as myself."

Friar Bernard was never again to forget this precious benediction of his teacher, and in his future temptations he was to make use of it like a shield. Meanwhile Francis, approaching death, thought of the absent ones, and two figures of women came to his heart in those hours that sanctify all affections, the only two women on whom his chaste eyes had ever fixed themselves. Lady Jacqueline of Settesoli, in her marble palace on the Asquiline hill, perhaps did not know of the seriousness of the teacher's infirmity. Francis saw her in the pupils of his half-blind eyes as he had always known her: strong and delicate, active and prudent, masculine and maternal. He again heard her sustaining words, and remembered her attentions, her solicitude, the times that she had spun and weaved with her own hands, and the sweet almond-cakes, the *mostaccioli*, that she herself had baked for him. It was necessary to give a final blessing to this woman friend and disciple, who had given him the flower of Christian courtesy, and who could be considered the ideal mother of his Third Order. Therefore he said to Friar Leo: "Lady Jacqueline of Settesoli, so dear to us and so devoted to our Order, would be saddened to know of my death and not to have been present. Go, then, and bring me ink, paper and write down what I shall say to you."

The secretary ran to obey and St. Francis dictated: "To Lady Jacqueline, servant of God, Friar Francis the little poor one of God, augurs salvation in the Lord.

"Know, dearest Lady, that the blessed Christ through His grace has revealed the end of my life which will be soon. Hence if you would see me alive, upon seeing this letter, come to St. Mary of the Angels. If you come later than Saturday, you will not find me alive. And bring with you a garment of hair-cloth in which to wrap my body, and candles for the burial. I beseech you to bring me those things to eat that you used to give me when I was sick in Rome."

At this point Francis interrupted his dictation, asking Friar Leo to preserve the letter without sending it because it was no longer necessary. And while the friars asked why, they heard a knock at the door of the enclosure. A friar entered, flushed with joy.

"Father, Lady Jacqueline is here with her two sons and a great retinue of horsemen. Shall we let her in? Shall we let her come into your cell?" asked a bashful friar because, according to the Rule, no women were allowed. But St. Francis, who never enclosed himself in formalism, exclaimed, "The Rule concerning women is not for Friar Jacqueline who has made such a long journey for me."

Lady Jacqueline entered and went directly to the infirmary, happy to find the teacher still alive. She had everything with her: the garment of gray-cloth, a shroud, the candles and even the almond-cakes, because the Lord had alerted her in a dream of the wishes of the dying Francis. And she had something else of great value which she did not tell about in order not to contradict Lady Poverty. St. Francis was somewhat comforted upon seeing her, he tasted the almond-cakes, smiled and blessed her. The noblewoman knelt at his feet, uncovered the stigmata and kissed the wounds, weeping with so great a devotion that the friars thought of Magdalene at the feet of the Crucified.

But another woman was present in the heart of blessed Francis: Clare. Clare, herself stricken with sickness, had asked him to stop at St. Damian on the way from Assisi to Porziuncola. She had also asked for permission to come and see him herself, despite her sickness, but neither the one nor the other had been possible. While Friar Jacqueline enjoyed the dolorous sweetness of bringing the teacher the comfort of her womanly tenderness, the virgin cloistered in St. Damian agonized with him, for while St. Francis sang the praises of Sister Death, Clare wept, thinking that she would no longer be able to see her consoler and teacher, her only friend after God. The saint, who divined everything, sent her his blessing in writing, and absolution for whatever violation she might have committed against the Rule. In addition he bade a friar take a message to her: "Go and ask Sister Clare to put aside all sorrow and sadness at not being able to see me. But let her know in truth that before her death, she and her sisters will see me, and will be much consoled."

Clare resigned herself and perhaps understood that this was a proof of the teacher's affection. For all women do not have the same mission. There are those who sow and those who reap, those who inspire and administer, those who counsel and serve, those who play the role of Magdalene and those who play the role of Martha. Clare, having chosen the best role, had to stay away. To her was assigned the most noble place and the loftiest suffering, the predilection of the teacher and distance from him.

PRAISE OF LADY POVERTY

In the two years following the stigmata, that is from September 1224 to September 1226, the blessed Francis had celebrated with praises and blessings all that which he had loved in life as a gift of God. It remained for him to celebrate in a special way that which he loved above all and called not his sister, but his bride. He had remained faithful to Lady Poverty, even in the relative comforts which his sickness obliged him to have. He accepted all medical treatment in holy obedience and as alms, choosing always the least and the worst. He dressed in sack-cloth even in the bishop's palace, covering his head with a cap made of coarse cloth which irritated the skin instead of protecting it. But all this concerned his ordinary relations with Lady Poverty, whereas in the face of death a celebration worthy of love was needful.

When he learned that he had only a few days to live, St. Francis wanted to renew the nuptial ceremony of twenty years before. Just as he had cut himself off naked from his father, so did he want to cut himself off naked from life. He bade his friars remove his tunic and lay him upon the bare ground. Then turning his face up to heaven and placing his left hand on his right side, to hide the glory of the lance-wound, he said to his friars weeping inconsolably and yet transported by his heroic furor:

"Brothers, I have done my part; may Christ teach you to do yours."

The warden, divining the desire of the saint, brought Francis his tunic, breeches and sack-cloth cap and said to him, "I lent you this tunic, breeches, and sack-cloth cap in holy obedience, and I forbid you to give them to others now because they are not your property."

St. Francis let himself be dressed, pleased and exalting the Lord. Then he comforted the friars with sweet words, still commending his bride to them, and beseeching them that after his death they again lay him naked upon the ground and leave him thus for as long as it would conveniently take to walk a mile.

At dawn on the second of October, a Friday, after having spent a night wracked by spasms, he sat up on his straw-mattress and ordered loaves of bread brought to him. He blessed the bread and commanded them to break it into as many portions as there were friars present. Then, with his wounded hands, he distributed a portion to each one, in memory of the Last Supper of Jesus and to signify that he too, like the Master, loved his children unto death, and that he would be ready to die for them and wished to transmit something of himself to them in a physical sense. Now everything was truly consummated. He grew worse on Saturday, and toward evening, feeling himself dying, he intoned the Psalm which begins, *Voce nea ad Dominum clamavi,* "I cried to the Lord with my voice," and he continued singing it until Sister Death extinguished his voice.

THE WOMEN FRIENDS

It was night and the halleberdiers on their tour of guard duty at Porziuncola were taking cat-naps on the sawed off trunks and on the rocks near the cell of the saint, when one of them observed,

"Listen to the chirping of the birds, it looks like morning."

"They are larks," said another.

"Larks at this hour. They sing in the sun and fly high in midday. Larks are not owls or night-hawks."

Nonetheless a flock of larks was flying over and around the saint's cell, whether for joy or sadness nobody knew. The little winged and singing friends, which Francis always beheld with joy as heralds of good tidings, were celebrating his blessed passage to eternity and they were the first to praise it in song.

Meanwhile, Friar Jacqueline, weeping bitterly, claimed the right to dress the blessed body herself, since she had been miraculously called by God. The vicar, out of pity for her sorrow, placed him between her arms and he looked like a dead Christ. The noblewoman kissed him, wailing loudly, and uncovered his sides to see the wounds. The stigmata could now be seen in all their reality, with their twisted and riveted dark nails, so enormous in the hands and feet that a hole like a ring had formed between the nail and the flesh. Still weeping, and not only out of sorrow, the Roman noblewoman dressed the sacred body in the hair-shirt that Francis had ordered from her. But since now the trial was over and the glorification was beginning she put a magnificent red pillow embroidered in gold with figures of eagles and lions under the head of the teacher and then she advised the friars to open the doors so that the people might see the saint and the miraculous stigmata. The candles which she had brought were burning, illuminating the cell even from afar and summoning peasants and citizens to the saint's bedside like a signal. The whole night was spent in psalm-singing, in praising, and in praying, while above the roof flew the larks, weaving arabesques of song, and the stars shone as if there were a great festivity in heaven.

The cry "The saint is dead!" echoed in the valley, and it rose to the hills and mountains. The people streamed towards Porziuncola like a flood, against an obbligato of tolling bells.

The cry immediately reached St. Damian and the sorrow of the sisters was great. "We will never see him again!" wailed the virgins, with a sense of loss and pain that strained to resign itself, so cruel did it seem to them that his daughters should be denied the last paternal comfort. But St. Francis was to keep his promise from heaven. In the morning the funeral cortege moving out of St. Mary of the Angels did not climb directly up to the city, but cut across the valley and went around by St. Damian. This was not a funeral procession, it was an apotheosis.

All Assisi participated in it: clergy, consuls, podestà magnates, archers, halleberdiers, and men-at-arms on horseback who surrounded the bier as though it were a great treasure. And there was also an immense crowd of friars and of people who walked in procession intoning psalms amid the blasts of the trumpeteers of the commune and the loud ringing of the church bells. All carried lighted candles and olive branches.

The Poor Ladies did not go outside. The immense cortege came to a halt on the small church grounds and the pallbearers deposited the bier in the little church where the crucifix that had spoken to Francis still opened its black eyes in the shadows. They removed the grate from which the virgins received Communion, and introduced the holy body inside so that the sisters, flocking like larks near the little window, could see him and kiss him. But the abbess had them approach the bier one by one, in a disciplined manner. And amid the lamentations, recalling the irreplaceable father whom they would no longer see or talk with, who would never return and who was going far away, she approached that countenance which smiled on the princely pillow prepared by Lady Jacqueline, that body wrapped in yellow oriental silk embroidered with parrots, flowers and fantastic animals, the beautiful silks brought by Lady Jacqueline.

Poor Lady Clare of Coccorano did not weep. She did not weep, because her heart had petrified. But with a lucid and daring will, she uncovered the stigmata of the teacher on the side under the splendid silks, and while repeating a gesture made so often, she pressed her lips upon it and tried to wrest the supernatural nail away with her teeth. But that nail was a muscle of iron in the flesh and resisted every violence of the disciple. Clare resigned herself and dipped two handkerchiefs in the sacred wounds and hid them on her to preserve them.

Clare did not weep, but her face of alabaster stiffened with one of those resolutions that are taken only over the dead who are beloved and that have the value of an oath. "My teacher, my father, my all after God," she told him, regarding the pale face to which death had given an infinite sweetness, "my teacher whom they have brought up to Assisi amid such pomp of brocades of gold, I know all of your ideal; I will defend it unto death, against all, I will be you in your bride Lady Poverty."

The bier was removed, the grate was closed, and the cortege resumed its way up the hill singing, amid the clangor of trumpets and churchbells. And while the virgins continued to moan, Clare, alone and on her knees, spoke with God and her teacher.

II

PRAISE OF ST. CLARE

WHEN ST. FRANCIS died, Clare was a little past thirty. How many more seasons were still in the offing for the little plant without a gardener! But the little plant was now hardy, and the direction of the stalk determined forever. Death santified all the more that ideal of poverty with which Clare had identified herself with the teacher. The way she knew how to live it and to defend it demonstrated how well the faithful virgin had expressed and loved it.

In 1228, Pope Gregory IX, when he was in Assisi for the canonization of St. Francis, often visited Clare. He felt again the spirit of his great friend in the virgin, and he always found something of that supernatural vision of life, that serenity of spirit and that knowing simplicity which one finds only in saints. The Pontiff asked questions in order to listen, and he hid his admiration so as not to offend the humility of this woman whom he considered a great teacher of the spirit.

One day, while the Pope was discoursing with her about divine matters, Clare, who never forgot what might be useful to her sisters, had the table prepared with all that which the property of the convent offered, dry bread. And on her knees she beseeched the Pope to sanctify it with his blessing. But the Holy Father replied, "Most faithful Sister Clare, I would that you do bless this bread, and that you make it the sign of the Cross of Christ to which you have given yourself entirely." In her humility Clare attempted to resist.

"Most Holy Father, forgive me, for I would be worthy of too great a reprehension were I, who am but a vile little woman, should presume to make such a blessing before the Vicar of Christ."

The Pope replied, "In order that this may not be reputed to presumption, but to the merit of obedience, I command you by holy obedience that you make the mark of the Cross on these loaves, and bless them in the name of God." Clare, a daughter of obedience, made no reply and traced the sign of the Cross, pronouncing the words of the rite. But what did the saint think and feel as she performed this proud gesture?

Her ardor must have communicated itself to things, because on every roll there appeared the visible incision of a Cross, in confirmation of her blessing. Gregory IX and the prelates present each took a loaf with them in remembrance of the prodigy and the sanctity of Clare. The miracle of the bread marked with a Cross sensibly signified a common verity. We leave the imprint of our passion in everything that we do, and since the Passion of Jesus Christ was the passion of Clare, her every word and gesture had the virtue of imprinting the Cross on things done and in the souls she met.

GO FORTH IN PEACE

Twenty-seven years had passed since the death of St. Francis. For twenty-seven years Clare alone directed herself and the sisters in a strict poverty, in the face of Popes, in the face of liberalizing minister generals, in the face of other monasteries of the Second Order less faithful than St. Damian. She persevered in loyalty to the ideal despite the weakness of her body which was slowly wearing itself out. For twenty-five years she languished in illness because of her penances, the voluntary chores, the desire for God. The interior flame was about to consume the alabaster.

Innocent IV went to visit her at St. Damian in April or May, 1253. The sick woman, profoundly humble before the great honor that the Pontiff was paying her, asked to kiss his feet and not only his hand which he had proferred to her. Innocent

IV, with a simplicity worthy of the place and of the on-looking Farnciscan nuns, mounted a small bench at the same height as the pillow so that Clare might perform her reverent act. Then with an angelic face she asked for the remission of all her sins. Deeply moved the Pope replied, "Would to heaven that I myself had so little need!"

Days went by and Clare's condition grew worse. So, like father Francis, she dictated her testament in which gratitude, which is the flower of humility and the purest seed of love, animated every word: gratitude for the Lord, then immediately, an immense gratitude for St. Francis. Clare had begun to live the day on which she came to know him; for her the years before this encounter did not exist, they almost belonged to unconsciousness.

"Since the Most High Heavenly Father through His grace has deigned to illuminate my heart, so that by following the example and the doctrine of the most blessed father St. Francis, I should do penance. Shortly after his conversion, together with my sisters, I promised him voluntary obedience. The saintly father, our Francis, was our pillar, the only consolation, and the only force after God . . . Moved by pity for us, he obligated himself, personally or through his Order, ever to have diligent care and particular solicitude for us as for his friars."

With a spontaneity that doubles the value of the modesty and the offering, St. Clare hid her work as a foundress. Seemingly she had no other will save that of Francis, and she strove not to present any other example, Rule, or words except his, almost fearing as if her own might be a diminution or an obstacle. From this overflowing gratitude gushed forth the faithful love for that which was the passion of the teacher, poverty. It was the legacy of the saint to her daughters.

Days went by. Clare was dying, and there was a constant coming and going of visitors in the rustic dormitory. The few surviving companions of St. Francis gathered around her pallet: Juniper, Leo, Angelo Tancredi. From Monticelli came her sister Agnes, whose direction of a new monastery had for years kept her far away from her Clare, from St. Damian. Priests, prelates, cardinals came. The sisters wept. Agnes was unable to control her sorrow; Friar Leo, the most faithful friend of Francis and afterwards of Clare, the affectionate soul of the first minors, "the little lamb of God," wept, kissing the bed of the sick woman. And Clare, stronger than all, comforted all.

"Be not saddened. Soon, through the will of the Lord, you will be consoled. And you, my dearest Agnes, weep not. I am leaving this world because it pleases the Most High. Soon you, too, as you desire, will follow me and come to the Lord."

The consoler had no need of comforting words from human beings, but she was suffering. When Friar Reginald, her confessor, exhorted her to patience in her infirmity, she replied boldly,

"Ever since, by means of His servant Francis, I have known the grace of my Lord Jesus Christ, I have never in my whole life found any pain or sickness that could afflict me."

The secret of Clare's sanctity lies in these words.

For her living was Jesus Christ through St. Francis, and on the bed of agony she still repeated her gratitude for the human teacher who had guided her to the divine. But these were also the last words addressed to the memory of the venerated man, beloved above all. In the last days even he disappeared from the mind of the woman in agony, to leave it to be ruled by God alone. The little plant sought for the sun and found it, without the help of a gardener. Strange words poured from her bloodless lips:

"Go forth in peace, for you have followed the good road, for He that created you has sanctified you, since before creating you he infused the Holy Ghost in you and has protected you like a mother protects her little child."

Sister Anastasia, leaned over her and asked, "To whom are you speaking, lady?"

"I am speaking to my blessed soul."

In the last moments of her life, when a person's whole past unfolds, at the hour of remorse and of terrors, she could say to her soul, with that humility which is awareness, "Go forth in peace!" But not through her merits; but through the infinite goodness of God to which the saint abandoned herself joyfully, like a child to its mother. Her agony is the most joyful in the history of martyrology.

"Blessed be Thou for having created me."

This was really an awaiting of death, singing. At that moment Clare was not aware of it because she was all absorbed in the Lord. But the one who was telling her, "Go forth in peace," who was guaranteeing her "a good road," and who was reassuring her blessed soul, was not herself. It was the spirit of St. Francis speaking in her.

Yet something was lacking to the happiness of her departure: the pontifical confirmation of the Rule of austere poverty which she herself had composed at St. Damian: *the privilege of poverty,* re-affirmed by her daughters against the temperaments of other monasteries less faithful.

Oh, to be sure that her will would be passed on to the daughters of her soul, in the form of apostolic authority! Oh, to obtain it before dying! "If only one day I could take it to my lips and kiss it, and then to die on the next day . . ."

It came to pass, as she wished. On the ninth of August, Innocent IV confirmed it with a letter, *Solet annuere Sedes Apostolica* . . . , the Rule of poverty. On the 10th of August a friar brought it to St. Damian, and Clare could kiss it as she had desired. On the 11th of August the saint expired serenely in the name of Jesus amid the weeping of the sisters and of Friar Leo, Friar Juniper, and Friar Angelo, the ancient knight. On the twelfth of August her remains were borne in a triumphant cortege from St. Damian to the Church of St. George in Assisi where she was buried in the rock with that blessed Rule on her heart, like a warrior in his flag, the Rule that represented the ideal of St. Francis.

HER LETTERS

The life of St. Clare, although confined to the Commune of Assisi, about forty-two years of which were lived at St. Damian, had aroused great admiration in Italy and beyond the Alps. Other women, seized by the Franciscan ideal, had imitated her, and other monasteries had risen modelled on that of St. Damian. The foundresses had always directly or indirectly turned to her like a mother and teacher.

One of the most fervent was Agnes of Prague, daughter of the King of Bohemia. She had been betrothed against her will to Boleslaus of Silesia, then to Henry of Sweden, and then to Frederick II. Destined to a throne, although attracted by the religious life, one by one Agnes escaped from her unwanted betrothals through the help of God and of the Pope. Free at last in her monastery of Prague, she wrote to Clare asking for spiritual counsel. Clare replied in four letters which still survive. The first, dated 1234, began ceremoniously, as if the daughter of the Counts of Coccorano felt inhibited before "Lady Agnes, daughter of the most excellent and unconquered king of Bohemia." But the honor of birth was put into relief only in order to stress the even greater honor of being the bride of Christ and therefore as poor as Him. St. Clare exalted virginity and poverty, so that Agnes might appreciate their infinite value, and terminated the letter supplicating her to persevere in the divine service, to progress without pause, to go from virtue to virtue. The second letter, written between 1234 and 1235, repeated the same theme of perseverance and progress with a magnificent fervor of spirit: "Keep good custody of the results at which you have arrived; whatever you do, do it well. Never stop, indeed make haste, with the agile step of those who seem to fear that even the dust of the streets might retard their progress. And go forward confidently and gladly along the road which you have chosen, without falling and without consenting to anyone who might want to lead you away from your design and put obstacles in your course."

The third, dated 1238, invited her to a more intimate union with God and meditated upon the nobility of the soul that welcomes and keeps custody in itself of the Lord. The fourth letter repeated the invitation to meditate upon the life and Passion of Jesus Christ, in a language adorned with biblical reminiscenses, and permeated with a lofty esteem of virginal dignity, enlivened by an intrinsic vivacity and by a maternal ardor palpitating in a mystic surge toward the Infinite.

From the first to the fourth letter there is a notable increase in tenderness toward Agnes, as if Clare's soul opened itself little by little to the warm and affectionate admiration of the distant princess, become the daughter of St. Francis. "Farewell, dearest sister . . ." Thus ended the second letter.

"To the virgin that I honor in Jesus Christ, more than every other and whom in my love I place above all other human creatures, to my sister Agnes . . ." Thus began the third letter.

"To her who is the goal of my love, the special sanctuary of divine love, Agnes most serene queen, my most beloved mother and my daughter, dear among all the others . . . O my mother and my daughter, bride of the King of all the centuries, I pray you not to anguish if I do not write you as frequently as my soul and yours would desire; persuade yourself that the ardent love which I bear you has never been spent not even a little. Think that I love you just as your very own mother . . . Remember your mother and think that your sweet remembrance is engraved in the deepest recesses of my heart, since you are dear to me among all."

These expressions are to be found in the fourth letter, and these and the others reveal how St. Clare knew how to love: bearing in mind Agnes's royal birth, but, much more than the birth, respecting in her the regalness of the bride of Christ, and loving her soul with a supernatural loftiness together with a human spontaneity and tenderness. These four letters—the first on virginity and poverty, the second on progressive action, the third on divine love, and the fourth on contemplation—give us the character of the great abbess in her passion for poverty, in her active and contemplative life, in her fervid and swift love which, more than with others, surmounted very grave obstacles in order to run behind her teacher.

THE WOMAN AND THE SAINT

The life of St. Clare, from Palm Sunday of 1211 to the eleventh of August 1253, developed so straight-forwardly that it could be defined with a single word—faithfulness. In the virgin were both the little child and the woman. St. Clare was pure, humble, poor and most grateful because she was humble, and she was happy because she was pure and poor. Her interior life had the gladdening timbre of the little grooved bell with which she invited the sisters to "sing morning songs to the Bridegroom." But St. Clare was also a woman who, as soon as she came to know the perfection of the Gospel, desired it for herself, pursuing it throughout her life without doubt or hesitation. She was the woman who, without ever stepping beyond the vow of obedience, never surrendered to her superiors in her defense of poverty. She never surrendered to infirmity. Nor did she surrender to death itself until Rome had guaranteed the ideal of St. Francis to her daughters. She did not surrender to the fear of Judgment, and died serenely sure of herself and of God.

On one side, her life is the proof of the influence that a teacher can exercise on a feminine soul; on the other, it is proof of how a feminine soul knew how to incarnate, defend and transmit the ideal of the teacher himself, almost absorbing his virility and in exchange transfusing her own sweetness in him. The daughter of the Offreducci already knew Jesus Christ, and, in her purity, she would always have followed Him. But if she had not met *Il Poverello*, the way of her sanctification would have been different. St. Francis never made known what St. Clare had been for him; he has left the interpretation of this to his biographers. But from the first, St. Clare repeated what St. Francis had been for her, and by defining herself as "his little plant" she perfectly defined the need she had for him, her attitude toward him, her whole womanly soul, which requires a support of some kind. But in a certain way she shared in the merit of finding this support and of forming it in a manner worthy of herself. St. Clare desired that her life, like her testament, be in all a hymn of gratitude to the saint who revealed Jesus Christ to her, in all an effort to conceal herself so as to leave the work of the teacher in a full light, all its own.

Despite this desire for self-annihilation, St. Clare has an image that is peculiarly hers, which was given to her by her very devotion to St. Francis.

She was the foundress of a new Order, different from the

Benedictine because of its passion for poverty; different from the Carmelite because of its love and obligation to work; different from the congregations that were to rise later because it united action and contemplative life in strict enclosure and poverty.

For St. Francis and his friars poverty signified freedom. When one throws away one's wallet, staff and shoes wings sprout. For no one else do the stars shine so resplendently as for him who has no money to count; for no one else is water so pleasant, the berries of the bush so sweet, the stones of the road so white and smooth as for him who no longer knows the comforts of well-set tables. Poverty is freedom. The whole world belonged to these divine vagabonds who were always at home wherever they went, and they went from one end of the earth to the other with the insouciant airiness of birds. Poverty is freedom. Any trade whatsoever was good enough to earn a crust of bread: repairing crockery, mending shoes, chopping wood, being a water-carrier, sacristan, sweeper, grave-digger; all trades were indifferently good to them. And when work was not enough, when bread could not be bartered for with the sweat of one's brow, they went begging without blushing because begging for the love of God is not inferior to labor, the humility of asking being on a par with the generosity of giving. But Clare did not hope for freedom from poverty. She and her sisters were not permitted to beg. The vast world was not for their enjoyment, nor the summits of mountains and forests, nor the endless seas for their contemplation. They could not come and go through cities. For them, anchored to the slopes of Mount Subasio, was reserved only the help of brotherly charity, when and how it might please Providence to send it.

But the external poverty was nothing but a reflection of a most intimate poverty, that poverty of heart, whence derives the humility that obeys, the purity that loves, in short, sanctity, so that in the preference of St. Francis for his ideal bride there was the profound intuition of the man who perceived gathered in Clare all the virtues of the other monastic vows. Poverty of heart includes suffering the desire for liberty, love, glory, sensible felicity, as one suffers hunger, thirst, cold, discomforts, since the soul awakens each morning with exigencies that are more voracious and less gratifiable than those of the body.

Prayer and work, poverty and claustral silence formed a character peculiar to the Franciscan Second Order. The light was not hidden under a bushel. Little St. Damian had an extraordinary power of radiation. "Clare concealed her life but she was known to all; Clare was silent, but her fame cried out; she was locked in her cell, yet she preached through the city," said Alexander IV in his bull of canonization.

Dante, with an intuition worthy of Clare herself, dedicated a canto to St. Francis and only three lines to St. Clare, almost as if he were respecting the modest humility of the "little plant." But that *terzina* says very much: "Life perfect and high merit enheavens a lady more aloft . . . by whose rule in your world below there are those who clothe and veil themselves."

The perfect life of Clare diffused an ineffable pure sweetness from the horizon of Mount Subasio to the valley of Spoleto.

Her name was sounded in the bells of Assisi, clearer than silver, and the bells pealed it on from the "Carceri" to the "Angeli," festively admonishing that the woman who is lacking in dedication and the silence of a "Poor Clare" cannot be a true Franciscan, and that the man who does not understand the value of womanliness cannot be a true Franciscan.

The great abbess sleeps in the rock of the basilica which has been named after her, under an illuminated arch of candles and little electric votive lamps.

But the roots of the "little plant" remain clingingly imbedded there where her gardener transplanted them. The heart of St. Clare lies at St. Damian which was reconstructed for her and her sisters by St. Francis. It lies in the poor convent where she conquered the pride and ardor of her Umbrian nature with the stones of poverty; in the little choir where she prayed and listened to her teacher; in the dark refectory where she marked and multiplied the bread; in the little garden where she heard and repeated *The Canticle of Brother Sun;* in the dormitory, bare as a granary, facing the small, rough-hewn and flower-strewn cloister which Mount Subasio watches over and dominates from on high. On the threshold of St. Damian, the virgin Clare still appears as she appeared to the Saracens, holding the greatest good against her heart—the Blessed Sacrament. And where Clare is, there also is the most beloved ideal of St. Francis—poverty.

St. Damian today is not only a thaumaturgic sanctuary, where vows are hung for healings received, dangers escaped, human goods conferred; it is the blessed place where those mutilated in their hearts find themselves again, where the blind in spirit again behold the sun.

CONCLUSION

ONE DAY FRIAR MASSEO, who considered himself a handsome man, went toward the blessed Francis who was emerging from the bristly wood of Porziuncola, and suddenly asked him,

"Why after you? Why after you? Why after you?"

"What do you mean to say?" answered St. Francis.

"I mean why does all the world follow you, and why does every man desire to see you and to hear you and to obey you? You are not beautiful to look upon, you are not a man of great knowledge, you are not of noble birth. Why, then, does all the world follow you?"

St. Francis, beaming with joy over this triple unpleasing compliment, raised his face to heaven and for a time remained rapt, absorbed in God. Then he knelt down and gave praise and thanks to God, and finally he turned toward Friar Masseo and said:

"Would you know why they follow after me? Because the eyes of the Most High God have not seen anywhere among the sinners anyone more vile, or more imperfect, or a greater sinner than I. And in order to accomplish the marvelous work which He intends He has elected me to confound the nobility, the majesty, the right, the beauty, and the wisdom of the world, in order to make it known that every virtue and every good thing comes from Him and not from the creature."

In this famous dialogue Friar Masseo, because of mental grossness, did not understand the gifts of St. Francis, and St. Francis because of his humility did not recognize his correspondence to the gifts of God. First of all, the Most High made him a poet in the ancient sense of the Greeks, when poetry meant action; so much so that St. Francis did not like poetry that is read, only that which is thought, felt, suffered, that which is gathered in a flash in the fugitiveness of creatures, poetry which is lived, by working, sacrificing oneself, fighting, dying. Therefore instead of singing and writing the praises of poverty, he preferred to strip himself bare and to live as the poor. Instead of singing charity in verses, he preferred to nurse the lepers, and to give his tunic to a beggar. Instead of exalting flowers and birds, woods and mountains, he preferred to live with them and to become like one of them. Yet even in making a poem of his own life, a certain dissatisfaction remained; for the truest poetry is that which is never exhausted, and which, not finding an outlet in action, refines and sublimates itself by seeking satisfaction in a higher sphere.

St. Francis had this very poetry in his being. But in order that he might not fall into the defect of terrestrial poets who, by virtue of their divine disquietude claim the infinite from creatures and therefore leave the heart hanging on all the thorns in shreds and pieces, the Lord endowed him with another incalculable gift: he had Francis become enamored of Himself. The love of God made him return to the poverty of the Gospel, according to the spirit of the Roman Church, and it made him carry out a perfect imitation of Christ as perhaps had not been seen since the apostles.

After his nuptials with Lady Poverty, he never used "mine," the greedy word of desire, the proud word of possession, the vehement word of selfish love. Nor did he ever utter the word "yours," which is the word of unrestrained dedication, of himself, for anybody, in an absolute way.

Such a detachment could have led St. Francis to that dualism between spirit and matter which marked the heretics of his time, but his poet's nature made him still turn to earthly beauty and his adoration for the Creator reminded him of his obligation to admire it as a work of God. It is not religious to devalue this life in order to make renunciation easier, but it is not easy to know how to love life without remaining possessed by it. And it is desire that is the chain of our servitude. St. Francis broke the chain by binding himself to poverty, and he succeeded in loving creatures with the perfect joy of the esthete as well as with the beatitude of a believer, because that which disturbs the contemplation of beauty is the covetousness of possession. Thus while we debate the problem of love and of loves, of the one and the many, St. Francis teaches us to resolve it with the poverty of love, that is to say with love without the selfishness of desire. His love of God communicated this intuition to the souls who approached him, to the men called to the apostolate, to the virgins consecrated to God, to all the faithful, and to the infidels by creating three Orders, each of which is most singular in itself: the First Order because it transplanted the monastic tents into the busy world and brought the virtues of the cloister to all the people, nobles and plebians, merchants and savants, soldiers and peasants, with example, preaching, and spiritual friendship; the Second Order because it established mendicant poverty also for virgins, and participation in social life even within the cloister, by means of atoning prayer; the Third Order because it makes of all Christians a disciplined army with the same virtues of the religious, with that perfection of poverty, chastity, obedience which the duties of one's social status can arrive at, and with a precise version of justice, peace, and of charity in the social organism.

In the torpor and terror of the piety of his time, St. Francis brought back the immediate intuition of the Gospel; the crib of Greccio to soften hearts frozen by the fear of the Antichrist; the stigmata to re-awaken the devotion to the passion of the Lord; and the re-awakening of the cult of the Virgin who intercedes for the Great Pardon.

But St. Francis also brought his genius as a poet, renewing preaching by the introduction of themes and arguments which adhered more closely to life, expressed in a language taken from the people; the praises in the vulgar language which launched a new wave of gladness in the ancient faith; the contempt for self, the renunciation, the mortification, the penance—virtues which the world finds most repugnant, which reappeared in their heroic beauty through the brilliant colors so dear to the world of love and chivalry.

The love of God, perfectly lived, made St. Francis see goodness in all creatures and a virile and serene friend in women not united to him in the bonds of kinship, so that he could sing *The Canticle of Brother Sun* and at the same time educate those two womanly masterpieces, St. Clare and Lady Jacqueline of Settesoli. From his new blessed conception of nature and of woman the new literature was to develop along different lines; the popular way of the praises, the aristocratic style of the *dolce stil nuovo*. From it was also to develop the new art which studied (as St. Francis saw) the Crucified Jesus in the dying, the Infant Jesus in infants, the Madonna in young women and mothers, the saints in friars and devout persons, the country of the Gospel in the landscape of the reality nearest at hand, paradise in the gardens of May.

The love of God made him find gladness everywhere, but especially in perfect suffering, and hence the conclusion that life is good, and all the more good the more it entails suffering. It made him embrace death as a sister. Thus if poets often had understood that love is death, St. Francis declared that death is love. Dante was to understand this and it will be understood by all those who do not find love in life and who, on the word of the saint, firmly await it in their moment of agony.

After seven centuries this great legacy of St. Francis, precisely because it was born of the love of God, is more alive than before. Still alive are his three Orders which, without any fanfare, indeed as true *minores* as their progenitor wanted them to be, nourish a current of compassion that flows within the social structure, with simplicity and poverty. Still alive are the missions, whereas the Crusades have long since passed. His conception of life which reconciles dedication to one's neighbor and spiritual fraternity with respect for property, authority, hierarchy, by distinguishing the duties of man consecrated to the apostolate from those of men destined to a familial and civil mission, has the perennial actuality of ideas born of the Gospel, as Rome understands it. His conception of knowledge—as an instrument and not as an end—acquires the significance of a revelation after the moral and political consequences of the Renaissance demonstrated that scholarship and the arts are not enough to form the character of a people, that is to save nations.

The Renaissance demonstrated the truth of St. Francis' thesis that it is better to be Roland or Oliver than to write about their feats, and that a man who has only studied, and never loved and worked and suffered for others, will find himself empty in the hour of tribulation.

His conception of suffering and of death, which are resolved in love, is still the most consoling conception for moderns as for the ancients. No philosophy has been able to find a better one. Even today, whoever truly understands the Franciscan ideal can say along with St. Clare that, after having known Jesus Christ through St. Francis, no suffering, no trial, no sacrifice seems heavy.

The love of God gave St. Francis that consoling power which after seven centuries made the whole world follow after him, as Friar Masseo very rightly said. If, in his time, he penetrated everywhere, into castles and hovels, into bishopries and tiny parishes, and went through the public squares as through the countryside bringing all to the Lord with his art of loving, today even more are attracted to him either for the one or the other aspect of his sanctity. He who does not love him for his penance, loves him for his poetry, and he who does not understand him as a saint admires him as a reformer of customs and a benefactor of mankind. And he who does not share his conception of life, would still like to share his perfect joy.

Thus the legacy of St. Francis, of which the Church alone is the custodian as a whole, endures and spreads in the world.

LORD, make me an instrument of Thy peace.
Where there is hatred let me sow love;
Where there is injury, pardon;
Where there is doubt, faith;
Where there is despair, hope;
Where there is darkness, light;
Where there is sadness, joy.

O DIVINE MASTER, grant that I may not so much seek
To be consoled as to console;
To be understood as to understand;
To be loved as to love:
For it is in giving that we receive;
It is in pardoning that we are pardoned;
It is in dying that we are born to eternal life.

—ST. FRANCIS OF ASSISI

THE AUTHOR AND HER BOOK

MARIA STICCO was born in Perugia, in St. Francis' own province of Umbria, a descendant on her mother's side of Baldo degli Ubaldi, a fourteenth century jurist, whom Miss Sticco calls in her book "the glory of Perugian scholarship." Miss Sticco studied at Firenze and at Rome and later became a teacher of the history of Italian literature in the Faculty of Teaching of the Università Cattolica del Sacro Cuore in Milan. There she worked with the famed Franciscan scholar, Agostino Gemelli, O.F.M., who wrote the introduction to this book, which has gone through seventeen printings in Italy. She is also the author of a number of other books on Italian literature and of biographies of Catholic saints, including Pensiero e poesia di S. Bernardino da Siena, La poesia religiosa del Risorgimento, Arte e sincerità, Il romanzo Italiano contemporaneo, Jacopone da Todi, S. Caterina da Siena, S. Bernardino da Siena, *and a number of short stories.*

THE PEACE OF ST. FRANCIS was manufactured in the United States. The text type is Baskerville, a transitional face based on designs made by the English typographer John Baskerville in 1760, and was set by Pyramid Composition Co., Inc., of New York. The foundry type is Solemnis, hand set by Philmac Typographers, Inc., of New York. The printing and binding were done by Van Rees Press. Nancy Dale drew the calligraphy for the endpapers. The color illustrations were printed by Barton-Cotton, Inc., of Baltimore.

the canticle

Most high, omnipotent,
  good Lord,
Thine are all praise, glory, honor and
  all benedictions.
To Thee alone, Most High, do they belong
And no man is worthy to name Thee.

Praise be to Thee, my Lord, with all
  Thy creatures,
Especially Brother Sun,
Who is our day and lightens us
  therewith.
Beautiful is he and radiant with great
  splendor;
Of Thee, Most High, he bears expression.

Praise be to Thee, my Lord, for Sister
  Moon, and for the stars
In the heavens which Thou has formed
  bright, precious and fair.